A THEORY OF PRODUCTION

A THEORY OF PRODUCTION

Tasks, Processes, and
Technical Practices

ROBERTO SCAZZIERI

CLARENDON PRESS · OXFORD
1993

Oxford University Press, Walton Street, Oxford OX2 6DP

Oxford   New York   Toronto
Delhi   Bombay   Calcutta   Madras   Karachi
Kuala Lumpur   Singapore   Hong Kong   Tokyo
Nairobi   Dar es Salaam   Cape Town
Melbourne   Auckland   Madrid
and associated companies in
Berlin   Ibadan

Oxford is a trade mark of Oxford University Press

Published in the United States
by Oxford University Press Inc., New York

British Library Cataloguing in Publication Data
Data available

Library of Congress Cataloging in Publication Data
Scazzieri, Roberto.
A theory of production: tasks, processes, and technical practices
/ Roberto Scazzieri.
Includes bibliographical references and index.
1. Production (Economic theory)   I. Title.
HB241.S2873 1993 338.5—dc20 92-32577
ISBN 0-19-828373-3

Phototypeset by Alliance Phototypesetters, Pondicherry
Printed in Great Britain
on acid-free paper by
Bookcraft (Bath) Ltd., Midsomer Norton, Avon

To
Cristina and Luigi

Preface

This study presents a new theoretical framework for the investigation of the production process and applies it to the analysis of the concept of productive scale, which is found to perform a critical role in production theory. This inquiry was originally stimulated by the realization that the concept of scale of production may be associated with a number of distinct analytical treatments, and that the way in which productive scale is described is rooted in the fundamental logical structure of the corresponding theoretical framework (see Scazzieri, 1979; 1981; 1982).

In subsequent years I began to realize that a comprehensive treatment of the scale phenomena relevant in the economic theory of production requires a description of the production process in terms of tasks, capabilities, and material transformations, that is features that are not exhaustively considered in standard economic theory. As a result, a new theoretical framework began to emerge, which owes its inspiration to the theories of the classical economists (to Smith's theory of division of labour in particular) and takes up a number of contributions to be found in subsequent literature, from Gioja–Babbage's law of multiples to Marshall's analysis of the industrial district and Georgescu-Roegen's model of fund and flow-input utilization. The unifying framework for the above theories is provided by the concept of 'technical interrelatedness', which may be defined as the interdependence among operations performed within a particular production process, or within a network of interrelated processes, quite independently of explicit transactions among productive units (see also Scazzieri, 1987*a* for a first outline of this approach).

The present study formulates an economic theory of tasks and processes that may be associated with the above general framework. In particular, the implications of three interconnected ideas will be explored: (i) the production process is described as a network of primitive operations (or 'tasks'), rather than as a combination of input and output quantities; (ii) the structure of each production process is associated with the particular way in which the tasks required to obtain a given type of output are performed by the productive agents capable of executing them; (iii) the scale of each production process is identified with the number of simultaneous tasks that are performed within it, rather than with the level of output delivered at any given time.

The three lines of research mentioned above have been integrated in the present volume, in which a general formulation of what may be called the 'task-process' approach to the analysis of production and scale is attempted (the detailed structure of this study is presented in section 1.4).

My research has received invaluable help from many different scholars, with whom I had the opportunity to discuss both the general conceptual framework of my own work and the detailed analytical treatment of a number of specific issues. Of all these, I would particularly like to mention Alberto Quadrio-Curzio, who prompted my interest in the theory of production during my form-ative years at Bologna through his firm belief in the complexity and relative autonomy of production phenomena, and who has constantly encouraged my work in that field ever since; Michael Bacharach, who gave stimulation and advice when supervising my M.Litt. and D.Phil. theses at Oxford, and provided me with the challenging experience of intellectual curiosity matched with rigour and with a broadminded attitude towards new lines of inquiry; the late Sir John Hicks, who exerted a profound influence on my overall approach to economic issues, especially by prompting my interest in the analyt-ical implications of the relationship between economic theory and economic history; Nicholas Georgescu-Roegen, who encouraged my attempt to formulate a theoretical framework that owes a great deal to his own reformulation of the Smithian approach to produc-tion analysis; Luigi Pasinetti, who, in the course of long and stimulating conversations, drew my attention to the relationships between the theory of the production process and the analysis of structural economic dynamics, and also induced me to reformulate a number of specific points of the present theoretical framework. During my years of research, my work has also been stimulated in a most critical way by discussion with friends. In particular, Michael Landesmann and Mauro Baranzini have discussed with me the conceptual framework of this study, as well as a number of detailed points, providing me with the encouragement deriving from the experience that a personal research project is part of a common endeavour. An anonymous referee has provided detailed comments and criticisms that have been especially helpful in the preparation of the final manuscript.

I have also benefited from conversation and advice from many other scholars, of whom I would particularly like to mention the late Lady Ursula Hicks, J. A. C. Brown, and Sukhamoy Chakravarty; Heinrich Bortis, John Enos, Polly Hill, Timothy McDermott, Ferdinando Meacci, Alessandro Romagnoli, Amartya Sen, Nick von Tunzelmann.

Finally, I would like to express my gratitude to the University of Bologna, where I received my first education as an economist, and to the University of Oxford (in particular to Linacre College), where I carried out a long and most important part of this research project, which originally took shape as M.Litt. and D.Phil. theses submitted to that University. I am also grateful to the academic institutions in which I have subsequently taught: to the University of Bologna (in particular the Faculties of Political Sciences and of Economics and Commerce) and the University of Padua (in particular the Faculty of Statistics); and to the other institutions that have provided a stimulating intellectual environment and research facilities at various stages in the preparation of this study, in particular the Economics Departments of the Universities of Bologna and Padua, the Centre for Research in Economic Analysis (CRANEC) of the Catholic University of Milan, the Research Institute on the Dynamics of Economic Systems (CNR, Milan), and the University of Cambridge (Department of Applied Economics). The splendid academic environment of Clare Hall, Cambridge, provided a unique setting for the final revision of this work, carried out while I was a Visiting Fellow there.

Indexing and bibliographical preparation has been provided by my wife, Maria Cristina Bacchi, senior assistant librarian at Bologna University Library. The references are either to the original editions or to English translations and modern critical editions. In the case of the last two, we give in brackets the date of the edition in which the passage in question first appeared.

R.S.

University of Bologna
and Clare Hall, Cambridge
June 1992

Contents

1

Introduction

1.1. SCOPE OF THE VOLUME AND HISTORICAL PERSPECTIVES

The aim of this study is to consider the structure of productive processes within a general description of human, technical, and environmental capabilities and their utilization in 'supporting' networks of productive tasks. As a result of this investigation, the view will emerge of the overall economic system as a set of interdependent funds (such as workers, machinery, natural resources) executing, according to a co-ordinated pattern, a certain transformation or set of transformations. Such patterns will affect the physical characteristics of the material environment and/or the capabilities of the funds involved in productive activity.

1.1.1. *The pre-classical heritage*

In order to provide a historical perspective, we explore the way in which the above research programme may be traced back to certain themes of pre-classical and classical economic theory. In particular, the association between power and wealth (see e.g. Hobbes, 1651: I. x) had already, in the course of the seventeenth century, drawn attention to the function of certain items of wealth (the productive funds) in ensuring the maintenance of *relative* wealth over time. (The relative wealth of two economic systems is likely to remain constant under static conditions, but not if either economy undertakes an expansion of its wealth by means of productive activity; in the latter case, the pattern of utilization of productive funds is a critical factor in determining the relative position of economic units at any given point of time.)

In mercantilist literature, national wealth is often associated with the *availability* of productive funds (land, productive establishments, ships, skilled workers) rather than with the *effectiveness* with which such funds are being used. As Sir Josiah Child put it, '[w]hatever does advance the value of land in purchase, improve the rent of farms, [i]ncrease the bulk of foreign trade, multiply domestick artificers,

[i]ncline the nation to thriftiness, employ the poor, [i]ncrease the stock of people, must be a procuring cause of riches' (Child, 1693: 46; quoted in Suviranta, 1923: 155 n.). More particularly, for the case of labour, Child wrote: '[T]hat most nations, in the civilized parts of the world, are more or less rich or poor, proportionable to the paucity or plenty of their people. The whole world is witness to the truth of it' (p. 195; quoted in Suviranta, 1923: 129). The idea that productive funds may be associated with different organizational patterns, and that an economically relevant measure of national (or social) wealth should reflect the effectiveness of funds in delivering goods, emerged only gradually from a combination of the following distinct intellectual developments:

(i) The discovery that 'natural' wealth (associated with land and agriculture) is distinct from 'artificial' wealth (associated with human capital and manufactures), essentially because the former is 'ready and certain' (Mun, 1664: 81–2), whereas the latter is exposed to the uncertainty inherent in trade relationships, and for this reason requires 'vigilancy, literature, arts and policy' (ibid. 82);

(ii) The emphasis on the greater efficiency of funds involved in the production of 'artificial' wealth (manufactures), as a result of task specialization and division of labour (see e.g. Serra, 1613; Petty, 1899 [1683]);

(iii) The explicit recognition that national (or social) wealth, as distinguished from individual wealth, cannot be increased unless existing funds are used to generate an increasing flow of the 'necessaries and conveniences of life' which are annually consumed within any given economic system (see Smith, 1976 [1776]: 10).

The relationship between the productive utilization of funds and the formation of social wealth is already clearly put forward in Boisguillebert's analysis of the division of labour, in which attention is called upon the role of mutual exchange as a mechanism by which the maintenance of funds can be ensured.[1]

The relationship between division of labour and effective utilization of funds is also related to the discovery that a measure of

---

[1] 'Nobody will buy the product of his neighbour, nor the fruit of his labour, except on a condition . . . which is seldom explicit, namely that the seller will behave like the buyer, either immediately, which is what happens on certain occasions, or by means of the circulation of different intermediaries . . . and, in the absence of this, land will be destroyed under his feet, and he will bring his personal bankruptcy about' (Boisguillebert, 1707: 384; quoted in Horn, 1867: 340; my translation).

social wealth may be provided by the amount of produce over and above what is necessary to maintaining the funds' productive power intact. Hume's essay *Of Commerce* (Hume, 1752) emphasizes this particular point by arguing that the more labour is 'stored' in the production of surplus goods (that are identified with manufactured products), the more effective will the economic system be in facing uncertainty, and thus in diverting resources from one pattern of utilization to another: 'manufactures increase the power of the state only as they store up so much labour, and that of a kind to which the public may lay claim without depriving any one of the necessaries of life. The more labour, therefore, is employed beyond mere necessaries, the more powerful is any state; since persons engaged in that labour may easily be converted to the public service' (Hume, 1987 [1752]: 262).

1.1.2. *The classical contribution and its forerunners*

An explicit linkage between the formation of a surplus and the production of necessaries over and above what is required to maintain the productive power of funds may also be found in the physiocratic doctrine that 'the artisan destroys in the form of subsistence as much as he produces by his labour' (Quesnay, 1962*a* [1757]: 73), whereas '[t]he profit or revenue which the proprietors draw from their landed property . . . constitutes the true wealth of the nation' (Quesnay, 1962*b* [MS 1757]: 104).

Quesnay's viewpoint may be explained as an attempt to identify social wealth with a net addition to the reinvestment needed for the maintenance of productive funds (essentially, land and labour). But the physiocratic emphasis upon the productiveness of agriculture and the 'sterility' of manufactures is rooted in a concentration of attention upon the 'circular flow' of wealth production and reproduction, whereas features such as the degree of utilization of *existing* productive funds are relegated to the background. The different implications of an approach that emphasizes the pattern of utilization of existing funds, rather than the 'circular' reproduction of social wealth, may be seen when considering the contribution of Sir James Steuart, in particular his definitions of 'industry' and 'trade'. The former is defined as 'the application to ingenious labour in a free man, in order to procure, *by the means of trade*, an equivalent, fit for the supplying every want' (Steuart, 1966 [1767]: 146;

my italics). The latter is defined as 'an operation, by which the wealth, or work, either of individuals, or of societies, may, by a set of men called merchants, be exchanged, for an equivalent, proper for supplying every want, *without any interruption to industry, or any check upon consumption*' (ibid.; my italics). Steuart's analysis draws attention to the *saving of time* that the interaction between industry and trade makes possible, by allowing for longer utilization periods of workers and tools and by making it unnecessary for producers to maintain stocks of finished commodities for long periods. The contribution to social wealth made possible by a more effective utilization of existing funds is well described by Steuart in the following passage:

I walk out of the gates of a city in a morning, and meet with five hundred persons, men and women, every one bringing to market a small parcel of herbs, chickens, eggs, fruits, etc. It occurs to me immediately that these people must have little to do at home, since they come to market for so small a value. Some years afterwards, I find nothing but horses, carts, and waggons, carrying the same provisions. I must then conclude, that either those I used to meet before are no more in the country, but purged off, as being found useless, after a method has been found of collecting all their burdens into a few carts; or that they have found out a more profitable employment than carrying eggs and greens to market . . . The consequence is, that a great deal of labour is saved; that is to say, the cart gives time to twenty people to labour, if they are disposed to it; and when wants increase, they will be ready to supply them.   (Steuart, 1966 [1767]: 150–1.)

The contribution of Adam Smith is noteworthy for his concentration on the 'microeconomic' advantages of division of labour in terms of shorter idle periods of workers and tools, greater effectiveness in task execution, and faster learning processes (see Smith, 1976 [1776]: vol. i, ch. 1; see also section 3.2.2 below). But Smith's analysis is also remarkable for his consideration of the 'macroeconomic' features of division of labour, that is, essentially, the capital-accumulation requirements that need to be satisfied if division of labour is to be introduced. As a matter of fact, Smith pointed out that no individual can devote himself (or herself) to a single-minded activity unless '[a] stock of goods of different kinds [is] stored up somewhere sufficient to maintain him, and to supply him with the materials and tools of his work' (ibid.: i. 276), thus allowing him (or her) sufficient time until the product is finished and sold.

Smith's appraisal of the relationship between capital accumulation and division of labour makes it clear that higher efficiency of specialized productive funds cannot be achieved unless these funds are part of a network that must be 'supported' by an adequate stock of circulating capital goods.[2]

Among the contributions of post-Smithian classical literature, it is important to note the emphasis on the role of immaterial activities (such as education) within the network of division of labour of a 'civilized' society (see, in particular, Storch, 1823), and the consideration of forms of rigidity that may be associated with an extended division of labour, if the latter requires the utilization of production techniques with a high proportion of fixed to circulating capital (see, in particular, the chapter 'On Sudden Changes in the Channels of Trade' in Ricardo's *Principles* (Ricardo, 1951 [1817]: ch. 19).

1.1.3. *Post-classical development*

The post-classical period is characterized by the slow withering away of the interest in a detailed investigation of the production process, at the level both of the individual productive unit and of the economic system as a whole. In this connection, Mill's reformulation of the Smithian theory of the advantages of division of labour is worth mentioning (see Mill, 1848). For Mill adopted a formulation that blends the Smithian theory with Babbage's emphasis on the advantages of large factories, but at the same time neglected to consider in detail the implications of Babbage's 'law of multiples', which stresses the discontinuous character of the relationship between scale and productive efficiency (see Chapter 3 below). The theory of large-scale economies that emerged as a result of this reformulation drew attention away from the internal structure of the production processes, which was at the centre of Smith's analysis.

The post-classical theory of production is characterized by a

---

[2] Circulating capital, according to Smith, 'is continually going from [the producer or merchant] in one shape and returning to him in another, and it is only by means of such circulation, or successive exchanges, that it can yield him any profit' (p. 279). The need to support the operation of productive funds by means of a network of 'circulating capital' flows is stressed by Smith as follows: '[n]o fixed capital can yield any revenue but by means of a circulating capital. The most useful machines and instruments of trade will produce nothing without the circulating capital which affords the materials they are employed upon, and the maintenance of the workmen who employ them. Land, however improved, will yield no revenue without a circulating capital, which maintains the labourers who cultivate and collect its produce' (ibid. 283).

simplified representation of the production processes and by the formulation of an analytical framework covering both the micro-economic and the macroeconomic features of production activity. This result is achieved by describing the single production process as a combination of productive factors, and by considering the influence of production technique upon macroeconomic phenomena, such as income distribution, in terms of a direct linkage between classes of income-receivers (workers, capitalists, *rentiers*) and broad aggregates of productive factors (such as labour, capital, land). In this way, it could be argued that a change in income distribution (say, a rise in the rate of interest) may unambiguously be associated with a change in the optimal proportion between productive factors at the microeconomic level. The simple device of introducing a symmetrical representation of the production process at the micro and macro levels made it possible to build a bridge between technical choice within individual production units and broad social phenomena such as changes in income distribution.

In this connection, the early attempts by Johann-Heinrich von Thünen (1826) and Mountifort Longfield (1834) to formulate a marginal-productivity theory of income distribution based upon the symmetry between micro and macro production processes, and the principle of technical substitution between productive factors, were followed by the contributions by Eugen von Böhm-Bawerk (1889), Friedrich von Wieser (1889), Philip Henry Wicksteed (1894), and John Bates Clark (1899). The more mature formulations of marginal productivity theory highlight a number of related features, which are all connected with the representation of production activity:

(1) Production techniques are described in terms of the pattern of utilization of certain critical inputs, such as land and labour. Some contributions emphasize that the life of a process may be split into phases associated with a more or less intensive utilization of the input under consideration (see in particular Böhm-Bawerk, 1889; see also Hicks, 1973). Another important feature of production technique emerging from the consideration of the time-structure of production is the distinction between fixed and circulating capital. Such a distinction, which is related to the classical roots of post-classical production theories, is here connected with the subjective notion of 'time preference', as developed in particular by Irving Fisher (see Fisher, 1906).

(2) The symmetry between micro and macro representations of production technology introduces a direct connection between the determination of the prices of productive inputs at the level of the overall economic system and the choice of the optimal input combination at the micro level (see Wieser, 1889; Wicksteed, 1894).

(3) The specific features of individual inputs (say, spades versus lathes) may be associated with a limited number of *economic functions*. The above reduction makes it possible to identify broad productive factors, such as capital, and allows for the analysis of technical change in terms of a reshuffling that takes place within such broad factors (see Clark, 1899).

Later developments in production theory have followed a dual course. On the one hand, the extension of the analytical core of Walrasian general equilibrium from exchange to production, already attempted by Walras himself (see, on this issue, Jaffé, 1983: 227–35), led a number of economists to outline a complete reduction of production theory to exchange theory.

This means that production processes came to be considered as transactions of a particular type, and that no feature of production activity was associated with conceptual issues different from those dealt with in exchange theory. This approach is explicit in Vilfredo Pareto's analysis of production activity in terms of the 'transformation curve', a locus whose construction implies the possibility of 'trading' one productive factor for another once a certain output goal is set (see Pareto, 1906: 273–325; see also Hennings, 1986: 223–6).

Later contributions have considered two different relationships between production and time within the exchange framework. On the one hand, the transition over time from less to more efficient techniques has been investigated in terms of the realization of allocative surpluses (see Allais, 1981; 1986). On the other hand, the time-structure of production has been modelled, within an activity-analysis framework, by overlooking the 'objective' complementarities over time due to the process of materials transformation and emphasizing instead the 'subjective' trade-off between using an input now and obtaining a product tomorrow (see e.g. Debreu, 1959; de Montbrial, 1974).

A distinct theoretical development stems from the early formulations of activity analysis (Koopmans, 1951), leading on the one hand to the detailed investigation of classes of production functions and the associated laws of return (Shephard, 1953; 1970; K. Menger, 1954; Färe; 1988), and on the other hand to the analysis of the production process as a network of operations or fabrication stages executed according to a specific organizational pattern (see Georgescu-Roegen, 1969, 1986, 1990; Shephard, Al-Ayat, and Leachman, 1977; Scazzieri, 1983; Tani, 1988; Hackman and Leachman, 1989). Important anticipations of the latter line of research may be found in Leontief's and Chenery's work on the conditions permitting the representation of a network of material flows by a set of production functions (see Leontief, 1947; Chenery, 1949).

1.2. TECHNICAL CAPABILITIES AND PRODUCTIVE FUNDS: AN APPRAISAL OF RECENT CONTRIBUTIONS

The aim of this section is to discuss a number of recent contributions and to assess in which way such contributions, considered as a whole, suggest an important change of perspective in the economic theory of the production process.

We first examine research in the field of human capabilities and entitlements (see in particular Sen, 1985). One important result in this direction is the discovery that the definition of human skills is related in a fundamental way to individuals' rights recognized as a consequence of the actual practice of those skills. As a result, human capabilities in general, and even capabilities related to production activity, are distinct from *technical capabilities* narrowly identified. The reason is that the latter come to depend upon a precise identification of producers' rights within a particular institutional and technological set-up, whereas production capabilities in general are independent of such a set-up and may sometimes be considerably broader than technical capabilities. In other words, technological and economic institutions, by relating the practice of a capability to some legitimate claim or right (generally, the claim to a certain share of the existing stock and/or product), often end up by restricting considerably the range of production capabilities that may be used in the economic system.

The above conceptual framework suggests that the historical and institutional identification of technical capabilities reflects a particular distribution of entitlements to produce, so that the latter may in turn be linked with the existing structure of technology.

In particular, the need to use a complex productive apparatus or an organizational network requiring long hierarchies is often associated with an unequal distribution of 'production entitlements', which may be concentrated in a limited number of individuals. This situation is often associated with a wide dispersion of technical capabilities among individuals involved in production activity. In other words, a centralized control of production entitlements is often associated with detailed specialization of tasks assigned to different individuals. As a result, technical capabilities, as reflected in the technical structure, may be considerably narrower than the virtual production capabilities of human beings.

The above considerations point to the fundamental importance of property rights in determining technology in use and its dynamics over time. In this connection, contributions by Alchian and Demsetz (1972) and other scholars (see in particular Marglin, 1974) have drawn attention to the specific features of production organizations, in which an unequal distribution of 'withdrawal capacities' among participants has to be consistent with the formation of a technical structure based upon the co-operation of distinct and specialized technical capabilities. More recently, Axel Leijonhufvud (1986) has noted the relationship between division of labour and the time-structure of the production process, and has emphasized in particular the linkage between the organizational arrangement of the productive unit and the continuous or semi-continuous utilization of production facilities.

Another important line of research underlying the present study is the analysis of production activity as the interaction of productive factors that are permanently available but not necessarily in use within the productive unit (*fund factors*). The seminal contribution by Nicholas Georgescu-Roegen (1969; 1970; 1971; 1986; 1990) has shown in which way different forms of productive organization may ultimately be reduced to different patterns according to which the operations of fund factors are arranged over time. In particular, Georgescu-Roegen has emphasized that fundamental differences in the pattern of fund-factor utilization may be due to a difference in the 'dominant' fund factor (respectively, land in agriculture and machinery in modern industry). Other contributions to this line of research have considered the 'capability space' that may be associated with any given fund, and have examined how different forms of productive organization may also be described by different patterns (rigid or flexible) by which the capabilities of each fund are related with one another and with those of other funds (see Landesmann, 1986; Landesmann and Scazzieri, 1991*a* and 1991*b*).

The time-structure of productive activity is also reflected in the time-profile of the process by which raw materials are transformed into finished goods. As a matter of fact, stocks of intermediate products may pile up at certain fabrication stages and be depleted at other stages, depending on the relative speed of the elementary transformation processes carried out at each stage. (A fabrication stage requiring transformation processes whose durations are very different from one another is likely to generate stocks of partial products, which may then be depleted in the course of a subsequent, more 'balanced', stage.) Recent literature has considered analytical issues related to the time structure of the materials transformation process by following two distinct approaches (see also Baranzini and Scazzieri, 1990: 227–333). On the one hand, a number of contributions have considered production processes as vertically integrated sectors, in which each productive activity is split into a number of successive fabrication stages, which include both the transformation of raw materials into finished products and the fabrication of tools and machinery (see in particular Hicks, 1973; 1977; Amendola and Gaffard, 1988). On the other hand, other contributions have examined the 'horizontal' relationship among simultaneously operated processes, by emphasizing the possibility of treating the time structure of production in terms of 'intermediate' production periods (Morishima, 1989: 249–51; Baldone, 1989; 1992) and considering the role of commodity stocks in carrying over from one period to another disequilibria and bottle-necks arising from within the network of horizontal interdependencies. In particular, Adolph Löwe (1976) has analysed the consequences of bottle-necks in influencing the speed of transitional paths (or traverses); while Alberto Quadrio-Curzio (1986; 1990; see also Quadrio-Curzio, Manara, and Faliva, 1992; and Quadrio-Curzio and Pellizzari, 1991) has expounded the nature of the residuals generated by discontinuities of the technical structure and their capacity to generate non-proportional dynamics.

The richness and variety of interdependencies underlying the network of production activities suggest the introduction of a simplifying framework in order to reduce the dynamics of production systems to a limited number of fundamental relationships. In particular, the interaction between social and technological factors, which is a characteristic feature in the transformation of production activities, has drawn the attention of economists and technologists to the distinction between social and technical division of labour. In this connection, George Stigler's analysis of the variety of forms of production organization made possible by a given set of technological principles (Stigler, 1951) has been followed by a number of studies of the internal dynamics of technical division of labour in terms of learning processes (Kilbridge and Wester, 1966) and of objective constraints upon task-specialization due to the physical characteristics of the material in process (Rushing, 1968; Cohendet, Ledoux, and Zuskovitch, 1988). On the other hand, *social* division of labour is the main focus of contributions that consider the cost of transactions among firms delivering different fractions of the same product (see e.g. Ippolito, 1977; Sabel and Zeitlin, 1985; Becattini, 1987).

The distinction between 'production systems' and 'structures of production' (see Barbiroli, 1991) provides a conceptual framework within which to consider the relative weight of technological and social factors in describing any given set of technical practices.

Finally, Luigi Pasinetti, in a number of recent contributions (1981; 1986; 1988; 1993), has stressed the possibility of reducing the number of characteristics relevant in technology description by considering the analytical simplification of a 'pure labour economy'. This is a type of economic system in which all final consumer goods are produced by means of labour only, so that the division of total employment among workers (or workers' groups) specialized in producing particular products, or fractions of a product (social division of labour), coincides with the splitting of a complex job among its constituent tasks (technical division of labour). It is worth stressing that the above coincidence depends upon the simplified description of production technology in terms of (direct) labour coefficients.

On the other hand, a production system in which tasks are performed by workers *and* tools (or machines) is one in which social and technical division of labour would not necessarily coincide. (For example, the splitting of total employment among different partial products would not be identical with the splitting of the corresponding complete job into constituent tasks, since a considerable number of tasks may be performed by machines rather than by workers.) In this case, the technical 'division' of a job to be executed requires the participation of different types of productive factors, whereas the associated social division of labour implies that total employment is split into shares that may correspond either to 'vertical' sectors (labour necessary to make a finished consumer good and its means of production) or to 'horizontal' sectors (labour directly used in making a finished consumer *or* instrumental good).

The one-to-one mapping of productive tasks on to employment shares within a stylized labour economy is replaced by a more complex relationship in which, first, tasks are associated with productive factors and, second, the employment shares corresponding to the formation of (produced) productive factors and the employment shares corresponding to the direct formation of finished goods are added up.

A distinction emerges between the technological assignment of tasks to productive factors and the splitting of total labour among relatively independent branches of production. In particular, a given assignment of tasks to factors may be compatible with more than one pattern of subdivision of total employment among productive branches. For example, a given technological system may often be implemented either by the internal production of tools and machines within each sector producing a final consumer good (a vertically integrated sector) or by the independent production of consumer goods and capital goods.

The analytical device of a pure labour economy may be applied to an 'advanced' technological set-up on condition that (i) a clear distinction is introduced between technical division of jobs and social division of labour, and (ii) the 'horizontal' splitting of overall employment into interdependent industries is replaced by its subdivision into a number of vertically integrated sectors. In this way, the representation of the production system as a set of labour coefficients may be considered as a simple device by which the technical structure is described in terms of a particular division of overall employment among productive branches. The above simplification, however, does not conceal the fact that production jobs may be of a complex type, and that each production process may require the co-operation of different categories of 'direct' agents. It could also be maintained that, in the case of a technologically advanced economy, the network of interrelated labour capabilities comes to the fore, and that such a network appears to be more fundamental than the relationships among material agents or commodity flows (see also Scazzieri, 1992*b*).

1.3. TASKS, PROCESSES, AND THE THEORY
OF PRODUCTION

The contributions briefly considered in the previous section, taken as a whole, suggest a new perspective in the analysis of production. We intend to examine here, from a general point of view, the most important features of this new perspective, which is at the basis of the present theoretical investigation.

The distinction between technical subdivision of a job and social division of labour (see above) suggests the possibility of considering the production process as a network of operations performed in a sequence to be determined (tasks), quite independently of the agents (workers or machines) who are performing such operations, and also independently of the flows of materials in process and finished products.

A concentration of attention upon tasks and jobs implies the consideration of production as a particular type of purpose-oriented activity (see Espinas, 1897; Kotarbiński, 1960; see also Durbin, 1990). The identification of tasks is impossible unless one is also considering the way in which a specific action or operation is connected with the achievement of a certain productive transformation. As a result, the analysis of production as a network of tasks implies that production is considered as a particular application of the 'logic of change' (von Wright, 1963). In other words, the identification of tasks logically implies the description of production as a *process*, i.e. as a sequence of fabrication stages.

A theory of production based upon the consideration of tasks and processes presupposes the identification of a set of feasible operations (Ω) and of a set of feasible transformations (T). The former is the subset of all operations conceivable within a given technology that may be carried out on the basis of *existing capabilities* (i.e. on the basis of existing skills, as they are embodied in workers, machinery, and other equipment). The latter (T) is the subset of all *conceivable transformations* that may be achieved with given materials. A feasible operation may be associated with a non-empty or empty set of feasible transformations, depending on whether existing capabilities are matched by appropriate materials or not. Symmetrically, a feasible transformation may or may not be associated with a non-empty set of feasible operations, depending on whether or not given materials' characteristics are matched by suitable capabilities of workers and productive equipment.

This framework enables us to consider the production process as a set of realized opportunities within a wider space of virtual transformations. A visual representation of this feature is presented in the Venn diagrams in Fig. 1.1. (C and M are, respectively, the set of 'theoretical' capabilities and of 'theoretical' transformations, i.e. the capabilities and materials set that may be conceived within existing scientific knowledge; V and T are, respectively, the set of capabilities and of transformations realized within available technology.) A number of different cases are considered in Fig. 1.1. Mapping $c_1 \rightarrow t_1$ describes a purely theoretical production process, which could only be achieved with advances in equipment and materials technology. Mapping $c_2 \rightarrow t_2$ describes a partially realized opportunity: the corresponding process is feasible with existing capabilities on condition that a suitable new material is found. Mapping $c_3 \rightarrow T' = \{t_3\}$ shows a feasible process, such that capability c_3 is associated with the set of transformations $\{t_3\}$. Finally, mapping $c_4 \rightarrow t_4$ describes another partially realized opportunity: the corresponding process is compatible with available materials but requires a capability yet to be attained.

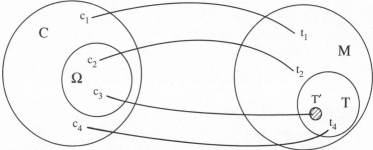

Fig. 1.1. *Capabilities and productive transformations*

In this way, emphasis is laid upon the relationship between the *abstract* production possibilities characterizing existing technology (technical knowledge) and the *real* processes that may be obtained when available capabilities and materials are considered. In this connection, a theory of production may be formulated starting with the abstract identification of tasks, and with the analysis of task arrangements, independently of the capabilities of workers and machines and of the characteristics of materials. Hence, the first stage of production theory will consider the purely operational set-up of a production process, that is, the pattern according to which elementary operations are combined into productive tasks, and these into more complex jobs that ultimately compose a complete production process. Tasks and processes are thus the fundamental components of an analytical framework in which real production processes may be considered as realized arrangements of operations, selected from within a wider space of (virtual) operational opportunities on the basis of the available capabilities and materials.

A theoretical framework built upon this basis would thus conform to a conception of scientific investigation that has recently been described by René Thom (1989: 40; see also Casti and Karlqvist, 1989) as follows:

if a science is *more* than just naïve description, this is due to the fact that it has constructed a set of 'virtual' (i.e. imaginary) processes among which it is capable of selecting the real, observable ones. Hence the criterion for true scientificity lies not in the veracity of observation or in its accuracy, nor in the use of instruments to help increase the set of observable facts, but in the building of a virtuality of phenomena from which the real ones can be selected by a well defined logical or mathematical procedure.

An early recognition of the importance of virtual phenomena in constructing the theoretical frameworks of empirical science may be found in the work of Federigo Enriques, according to whom 'the scientific fact takes on the form of a *simplified fact, a type of a series of possible facts*' (Enriques, 1914: 81). This particular view of the relationship between theory and description was also held by William Whewell, who maintained that a scientific discovery is generally such that 'a *new* conception [is] applied in order to bind together observed facts. And though the conjunction of the observed facts [is] in each case an example of logical *Induction*, it [is] not the induction process merely, but the *novelty* of the result in each case which [gives] its peculiar character to [the history of inductive sciences]' (Whewell, 1860: p. v).

The concentration of attention upon tasks and processes leads to the isolation of the purely operational features of production activity with respect to features associated with agents and materials. However, production processes derive from agents and materials a number of features that are also essential when considering the 'pure' task–process structure of production activity. In particular, the relationship between agents and tasks calls attention upon the purposive character of production, and emphasizes the fact that the task–process structure of production may reflect the (hierarchical) structure of human choice. As a result, tasks belonging to the same process may be co-ordinated in different ways depending on whether certain critical decisions are anticipated or delayed (the possibility of delaying irreversible decisions is often a characteristic feature of modern flexible technology). On the other hand, the relationship between materials and tasks brings to the fore the physical causality embedded in production activity. Any given task–process structure reflects the fact that the transformation of materials in process has to go through a precise sequence of fabrication stages if a certain finished product is to be obtained. For instance, if fabrication stages a, b, c have to be operated in this sequence, it would normally follow that the partial sequence a, d precludes fabrication stage c from taking place.

Each production process is thus characterized by a dual sequential structure: the *subjective* structure connected with the role of initial and intermediate decisions in arranging tasks over time, and the *objective* structure reflecting the physical linkages between fabrication stages. Complementarities over time are a distinctive feature of production activity, and they have separate roots depending on whether we consider the structure of 'nested' decisions (each decision is part of a 'tree' such that what is being decided at t precludes or makes possible a given alternative at $t + 1$), or the structure of 'nested' transformations of the materials in process (here each transformation stage would be part of a 'tree' such that the stage carried out at t makes it feasible or not to undertake another particular stage at $t + 1$) (see also Scazzieri, 1992c).

Decisions or transformations relative to *different* processes may be made in an 'interlocking' way, so that what appears to be a decision (or a transformation) blocking a certain process could actually be a decision (or a transformation) permitting a different process to proceed further (this situation is fairly common in traditional artisan production or in modern forms of job-shop manufacturing). (See also Landesmann and Scazzieri, 1991a; 1991b.)

The task–process framework adopts a representation of production activity that emphasizes the network of operations as the primitive basis of production. In this way, it implies a concentration of attention upon the organizational features of the production process, independently of the particular agents involved or materials being processed. Here, the production process appears, first of all, as an *abstract network*, that is, as a network of tasks and processes that can, at least in principle, be implemented in a variety of ways (on the distinction between abstract and implemented networks, see Marschak and Radner, 1972: 268). By adopting a task–process framework, we may thus be capable of distinguishing between the features of the production process that are independent of active factors and materials and the features that critically depend upon the capabilities of agents and the structure of the work-in-process.

A theory of production primarily based upon consideration of the abstract network of tasks and processes suggests a separate formulation for (i) the analysis of such an abstract network, (ii) the examination of its implementation in terms of active factors and their capabilities, and (iii) the analysis of network implementation in terms of fabrication stages of the work-in-process.

The distinction between the abstract task–process network and the active factors executing tasks leads one to distinguish between the organizational pattern associated with a given technology and the institutional arrangement reflecting available workers and productive apparatus. In particular, a given technological set-up is often compatible with a variety of productive structures, so that, for example, a certain commodity could be produced either within a single large establishment or by operating different establishments of various sizes. In this case, institutional variety shows that tasks and processes may be executed in different ways, and that the organizational scheme underlying productive operations may be implemented by using different types of agent (and also, presumably, different types of capability). In a similar way, the distinction between the task–process network and the precise characteristics of work-in-process materials makes it possible to consider how 'new' materials could implement a given abstract network more effectively than the materials currently in use. This could happen if the co-ordination pattern among tasks within a process were realized only imperfectly with available materials, and if the introduction of improved materials permitted a better implementation of a technological programme.

1.4. PLAN OF THE VOLUME

This volume presents a general formulation of the task–process approach to production analysis, and investigates in detail the relationship linking the technical structure of the production process, the scale of that process, and the size of the productive unit in which it is carried out.

Part I introduces the origins of this study, and discusses the conceptual framework of the following analysis. In particular, Chapter 2 presents a preliminary discussion of the relationship between descriptive and theoretical frameworks in production analysis, identifies the specific object of this research, and outlines the general plan of the following chapters. In this chapter, the case is made for a theory of the production process based upon the distinction between the network of interdependent operations identifying the 'logical form' of that process and the pool of productive inputs whose operation (or transformation) makes productive activity possible.

In this connection, the relationship between the structure of productive activity (*technical practice*) and the corresponding level of operation (*scale*) emerges as a critical feature of the production process, especially because different representations of productive activity lead to alternative specifications of scale and technical practice, and also to the consideration of distinct patterns of relationship between them. Chapter 3 presents a historical reconstruction of different analytical treatments of the relationship between the technical practice and scale (in the general sense considered above). There, it will be argued that the Smithian 'task–process' standpoint leads to the consideration of scale as a feature of productive activity that is logically independent of the size or capacity of the productive unit. By contrast, a different analytical tradition may be identified, in which any given technical practice is described as a specific combination of productive factors, and in which scale measures input and output levels, regardless of the number of tasks and of their arrangement. The latter approach has exerted a pervasive influence upon economic theory, from Turgot's original formulation of the law of variable proportions to the modern set-theoretical descriptions of the producer's production possibility set. This chapter presents a comparative assessment of the two approaches, and outlines the most general features of a conceptual framework in which consideration of the operational structure of technical practice may be integrated with that of 'productive funds' (i.e. of the active elements of production available within the productive unit) and of work-in-process materials (i.e. of the raw materials and semi-finished products transformed by productive activity).

The detailed theoretical framework of the present research is set out in Part II. In particular, Chapter 4 presents a framework of analysis in which the production process is described as a network of interrelated elementary operations or *tasks*. Precedence relations between tasks determine the characteristics of *elementary processes*, i.e. of time-arrangements of tasks leading to one unit of finished product.

The *production process* is a time-arrangement of elementary processes, whose structure may be identified by having recourse to either of the two following models of organization (or to a combination of them): the *straight-line pattern* or the *job-shop pattern*. In the former case, the production process consists of a time-arrangement of tasks that follow one another according to a predetermined time schedule (note that this involves the a priori determination of each task's length). In the latter case, the production process consists of a time-arrangement of tasks connected with one another in a 'functional', rather than operational, way (an important consequence is that it would generally be possible to vary the sequential order of tasks and task durations).

In production processes of the straight-line type, the elementary processes may be arranged with respect to time according to any one of three fundamental patterns: (i) *arrangement in series* (the elementary processes follow one another in time, so that different elementary processes never overlap); (ii) *arrangement in parallel* (two or more elementary processes are simultaneously started and are then repeated at regular intervals); (iii) *arrangement in line* (the elementary processes are started at regular intervals, which are obtained by dividing the duration of the elementary process into equal intervals, so that the elementary processes overlap in time).

We shall define as the *scale* of a production process the number of elementary processes simultaneously operated in a productive unit. A special case would be that of a process consisting of a single elementary process at any given time. This concept of scale allows us to distinguish between two phenomena that often give rise to misunderstanding in the economic literature: the scale of the production process and the level of output. In particular, we shall find that a productive establishment may increase or decrease the output level of certain commodities without necessarily changing the scale of production. On the other hand, a change of scale is possible even if not all commodity outputs are varied. Such a property of the present theoretical framework draws attention to the fundamental reason for changes in the set of feasible practices as process scale is varied: the change in the pattern of utilization of the 'task-performing' capabilities that exist in a productive unit at any given time.

A distinctive feature of the task–process view of productive activity is the 'open' character of the structural specification associated with it. For any given production process would simply be identified by a particular arrangement of tasks and elementary processes, and would be independent of specific productive agents and particular types of product. As a result, the analytical features that one may identify by means of task–process analysis generally have a considerable generality, and often apply to a large variety of institutional set-ups and historical cases. On the other hand, the detailed analysis of such cases generally requires the consideration of other features of productive activity as well. In particular, investigation into the purely operational characteristics of scale must be supplemented by the identification of the particular resources and product specifications associated with the productive unit under consideration. It is in this connection that the *size* of the productive unit may be considered an essential feature of the production process.

The above theoretical approach is further developed in Chapters 5 and 6, by considering a problem that has received little attention in the economic literature so far—the fact that decisions about the scale of production are closely linked with the adoption of a technical practice by a given producer (technical adoption), as a result of technical constraints.

One important reason for economists' lack of interest in this issue is that economists are generally concerned with the immediate influence of a change in the level of output on some variable relevant to the technical-adoption decision (such as input productivity or unit cost of production). The situation generally considered in economic literature blurs the distinction between the feasibility problem (i.e. which practices are feasible for any given scale) and the technical-adoption problem (given the practices feasible for a given scale, which one of such practices is actually adopted at that scale). Standard approaches in terms of production functions or production possibility sets make the above distinction difficult by considering *efficient* combinations of inputs, i.e. input combinations such that the assigned level of output is obtained with minimum use of productive resources. In this way, changes in the amount of any given input are immediately associated with the maximum level of output (and changes in the level of output are associated with the corresponding changes in the set of efficient input combinations). As a result, changes in the *feasible* technical set are overlooked, and scale variations are directly associated with a different pattern of technical choice. It is worth noting that the above conceptual framework, by emphasizing what is best for any given scale, makes it difficult to consider how the switch to a different scale could free an existing productive potential and lead to a 'superior' set of efficient technical practices. (This could be a special case of the general situation examined in Allais, 1981; 1986.)

Our feasibility analysis explicitly considers the possibility that a change in the scale of production may determine a change in feasible practices before the technical adoption problem is dealt with. A remarkable outcome is the discovery that both technology expansion and technology contraction are possible in either of the two following situations: (i) the process scale is changed but the output mix is constant, so that the output level of each commodity is also changed; (ii) both the process scale and the output mix are changed, so that not all output levels need to change. Case (ii) shows that the production of certain commodities may be affected by a change in the set of feasible practices independently of a change in the corresponding output levels, provided such commodities are delivered by a production process whose scale is varied. This case also shows that a change of process scale may determine technology expansion or contraction by bringing about a change in the degree of utilization of the productive resources which exist in a productive unit at any given scale, independently of the output level of any commodity.

The above discovery emerges from the three following features of our analysis: (i) a definition of scale that is process-based, rather than output-based; (ii) the distinction between the feasibility problem and the technical-adoption problem (so that the set of feasible practices is determined independently of the output mix); (iii) the consideration of production processes that may deliver more than a single type of commodity at any given time.

Different patterns of technology expansion and contraction are possible, depending on the following factors: (i) the intensity and frequency of resource utilization by any given practice (i.e. how much input capacity is used by any elementary process at any given time, and how often such an input is required in each elementary process); (ii) the quantity of productive resources available at any given time and the frequency of resource renewals in the production process under consideration.

Chapters 5 and 6 examine the ways in which the above factors, by interacting with each other, determine the set of technical practices feasible for any given scale. Here, we anticipate a few general results: (i) given the resource endowment, a more *intensive* utilization of productive capacity makes technology contraction more likely; (ii) given the resource endowment and the intensity of capacity utilization, a more *frequent* use of the existing capacity brings about technology expansion; (iii) given a constant, positive rate of resource expansion, the *full* utilization of productive capacity may not be compatible with the *continuous* utilization of the same capacity through time.

Technology expansion and contraction may or may not be associated with an actual change of technical practice, depending on how the producer deals with the underlying technical-adoption problem. This topic is considered in Chapter 7, where we compare two different criteria for the selection of a technical practice: (i) sequential search, according to which the producer considers the technical alternatives one by one, following a strategy of scrutiny determined by parametric characteristics of the environment (such as the previous history of the productive establishment and/or its size, in the sense discussed above); (ii) instantaneous search, according to which the producer, in any given state of nature, ranks all the practices known to be feasible for the assigned scale, and then adopts the practice having the 'top' position in that ranking.

To my knowledge, the economic literature has examined in detail criterion (ii) only. Interest in criterion (i) arose recently as a result of research into the historical patterns of technical change (see Rosenberg, 1976; 1982) and into problems of bounded rationality (see Simon, 1955; 1979; 1983).

The present study shows that the sequential scrutiny of practices known to be feasible for any assigned scale may be incompatible with any regular association between the scale of production and productive efficiency, if the latter is defined as the position of the actual practice in the producer's ranking of practices. A necessary condition for the existence of any such association (i.e. for the existence of a *scale–efficiency relation*) is that, for any process scale, technical adoption should be the consequence of global ranking and instantaneous scrutiny of all feasible practices. In this case a change of practice reflects a change in the 'top' feasible practice, and the expansion or contraction in the set of feasible practices determines the actual practice in a precise way.

Chapter 8 argues that economic literature relates scale to efficiency in a way that is sometimes consistent and sometimes inconsistent with the above condition. Such a discovery permits the distinction between what may be called 'true' and 'spurious' scale–efficiency relations: the former based upon *ex ante* ranking and choice, the latter deriving from special assumptions about the change of feasible practices and the structure of the *ex post* preferences of the producer over the practices feasible for the different scales.

The analysis of Part II is mainly of an abstract kind, even though actual examples are sometimes considered to illustrate the theoretical argument. In particular, Part II presents a theoretical framework built upon the task–process view of productive activity. As a result, its main conclusions are independent of those features of the production process that are not explicitly considered when attention is focused upon the purely operational aspects of productive transformation. Part III makes an attempt to consider how the general conclusions of Part II are modified when specific productive units are examined. (Productive units are characterized not only by the operation of a particular task–process network but also by a given stock of productive resources—including agents with given capabilities—and by a particular set of flows of work-in-process materials.) The concept of 'size' is a critical element in distinguishing the general propositions of task–process theory from the analysis of concrete cases, for the size of a productive unit cannot be identified unless agents and materials are clearly described.

Chapter 9 shows that the distinction between scale and size is essential in the analysis of historical relations between scale and technical practice, since the particular shape of such relations critically depends upon the way in which productive units are defined and the corresponding size is determined. In particular, this chapter considers the distinction between 'large-scale' production and 'large-capacity' production (the former referring to the production process, the latter to the productive unit), and shows that the sufficient conditions for the effective operation of the former may be different from the conditions ensuring the effective operation of the latter. In this connection, alternative patterns of division of the production process are examined, and their relation to different forms of production organization is analysed.

Chapter 10 attempts a general assessment of the theoretical framework of the present study and of its implications for the analysis of real economic systems. In this connection, it is emphasized that the distinction between process scale and size of the productive unit is essential in order to ensure the analytical generality of task–process theory and its descriptive relevance in a variety of historical and institutional circumstances. The specific features of the task–process approach are then compared with other approaches to the analysis of scale and size, such as the 'capital-circulation' approach proposed by a number of classical economists and recently taken up by Hicks, the cost-transactional approach, the asset-specificity approach of Baumol and his school, and the time-structure view of production processes and productive institutions in the Austrian and Swedish traditions. This chapter is concluded by an epilogue in which a number of general implications of task–process theory are considered, and possible lines of further research are outlined and evaluated. In particular, an attempt is made to assess the possible utilization of the present framework in considering different institutional arrangements, in setting up a conceptual background for the 'analytical history' of different forms of production organization, and in identifying explanatory hypotheses for the actual course of changes in economic structure.

PART I

Theoretical Perspectives on Process and Scale

2

The Analytical Representation of Productive Activity

2.1. THE DESCRIPTIVE PATTERNS OF PRODUCTIVE ACTIVITY

Any given type of productive activity may lead to a number of distinct patterns of description. First, it may be considered as a combination of goal-oriented operations by means of which material objects take a particular shape according to given specifications, or immaterial services are supplied. Second, productive activity may be described as a combination of 'transformation stages' (usually a sequence), which leads material objects or human capabilities from a state of nature that is conventionally considered as original to a different state of nature that is conventionally considered as final. Last, productive activity may be identified with those human and non-human factors that must be available within each productive unit if some process of 'technical transformation, or production' (Hicks, 1939: 78) has to take place.

Economic theorists have generally adopted one or another of the above standpoints in considering the productive process and its relationship with other features of economic activity. For example, the 'praxeological' aspects of productive organization (those aspects that may be understood in terms of a general theory of human action) have been especially examined by Smith (1976 [1776]) and writers in the Smithian tradition, such as Rae (1834), Ferrara (1860), and Marshall (1961 [1890]; 1920). On the other hand, the 'sequential' description of the productive process as a combination of transformation stages that follow one another in time is at the root of the Austrian and Neo-Austrian theories of a production economy (see e.g. Böhm-Bawerk, 1889; Hayek, 1941; Hicks, 1973). Finally, the description of productive activity as the combination of the productive factors in use at any given time is a common feature of the marginalist production function (see e.g. Wicksteed, 1894), of its modern set-theoretical reformulations (see Debreu, 1959; Frank, 1969), and also of so-called 'linear' production theories (see von Neumann, 1937; Leontief, 1941; Sraffa, 1960).

The analytical starting-point of the present investigation is the realization that a comprehensive study of productive activity requires a thorough appraisal of the descriptive basis of production theory, and that recognition of the multi-dimensional character of the productive process has to be reflected in a suitable descriptive framework if theoretical research is to permit analysis of the relationship among the different features of productive activity.

In the following study, by integrating the three above-mentioned approaches, each productive process will be considered as a specific arrangement of human actions and non-human operations within which a number of tasks have to be completed to effect a certain technical transformation, while productive funds, such as labour, land, or capital, are being used for a variety of purposes.

2.2. ANALYTICAL FEATURES OF TECHNOLOGICAL INTERRELATEDNESS

This study will attempt the formulation of a comprehensive theoretical framework, with the aim of investigating the analytical implications of the general descriptive pattern set out above. Such a theoretical framework is based upon the concept of 'technological interrelatedness', i.e. upon the consideration of interdependencies among operations performed within any given network of primitive operations (or *tasks*) and of elementary processes leading to different batches of finished product.

A remarkable outcome of this approach is that consideration of time emerges as an essential feature in the description of the productive process. The reason for this is that no productive process may adequately be described in terms of its constituent tasks unless the precedence pattern of tasks is also identified. As a matter of fact, a productive process consisting of tasks *a*, *b*, and *c* cannot be completely identified unless it is also known which tasks must be performed before the others, and which tasks must or can be executed at the same time. A precedence relationship among tasks expresses a relationship of 'material implication'. In particular, this type of implication is always associated with a precedence relationship of the technological type whenever an *effective* productive process is considered: task *a* implies task *b* if we consider a productive process in which *a* must precede *b* in order to bring a specific technical transformation about.

If the above general framework is adopted, the structure of the productive process (i.e. the specific form taken by any given technical practice) may be associated with the arrangement of the operations performed by workers and machines, and with the sequence of fabrication stages that are thus brought about. Each technical practice describes a particular way in which the tasks required to obtain a specific product are associated with the productive agents able to execute them. Such productive agents would generally be 'fund inputs', i.e. inputs that, after performing a particular task within a given process, maintain the ability to perform other tasks within the same or within different types of process (see Georgescu-Roegen, 1969).

There is, in general, no unique way of associating tasks with fund inputs, for any given task may often be performed by alternative combinations of fund inputs, while any given fund-input combination generally permits more than a single pattern of task co-ordination. As a result, the producer's decision to acquire a certain fund-input combination often has a loose relationship with the determination of the technical practice, except in the narrow sense that certain technical practices may be feasible with certain input combinations only.

This view of technical practice suggests that the 'adoption' of any particular practice is a two-dimensional process, since (i) a certain combination of inputs must be assembled, and (ii) a certain procedure must be followed in performing the required tasks. This dual character of technical adoption is often associated with a sequential process, in which the producer's decision concerning (i) precedes that concerning (ii), or vice versa. A remarkable implication of the latter feature of technical adoption is that bottle-necks within the technical transformation process, and technological disequilibria among different fund-input categories, are a common feature of actual technical practices.

The above concept of technical structure draws attention to the number of simultaneous operations performed within any given process, i.e. upon a specific *scale dimension* of productive activity. (The pattern of interrelatedness among fund-inputs, and among the elementary processes within which such fund-inputs are used, often critically depends upon the number of operations to be performed at any given time within the productive unit under consideration.) Here, the scale of the productive process will be considered as a special feature of the technological interrelatedness among tasks, and will be distinguished from the quantity of each specific product that is delivered at any given time; it will also be distinguished from the capacity of any given productive unit.

A remarkable feature of the above approach is that the concept of process scale (as defined above) may be used to investigate important features of the technical practice that are independent of fund input capacities and of the arrangement of flow inputs and work-in-process materials. Such features would simply reflect the pattern of task co-ordination over time. In particular, a comprehensive interpretation may be attempted of phenomena such as the economies of large-scale production and the economies of specialization, for both types of relationship may be explained in terms of the same general principles of task co-ordination and fund-input utilization.

The process-based concept of scale that will be considered in this study allows us to distinguish two types of relationship between scale and technical practice: one type of relationship derives from the possibility of operating different patterns of task co-ordination at different scales; the other is associated with the existence of tasks that may only be performed with indivisible inputs. The latter case gives rise to the familiar situation of decreasing unit cost as process scale is increased and size of plant is unchanged. By contrast, the former case is independent of fund-input natural units and of the overall capacity of the productive unit in which fund inputs are used. Here, the relevant issue is whether or not any given fund input is continuously used to perform the same type of task, or tasks of different types, during the working day, whereas the number of tasks performed at any given time by a particular fund input is not directly considered.

2.3. SCALE AND SIZE

The above considerations call attention to the abstract theory of tasks and processes: in other words, essential features of technological interrelatedness may be examined without directly considering active factors and materials. There is, in fact, a feature of productive activity (perhaps its most general characteristic) that is independent of specific institutional set-ups, and also of the physical properties and time-profile of the flows of work-in-process. For technical knowledge is first expressed in terms of purpose-oriented operations forming an abstract network, whereas the implementation of that network may be left to a subsequent stage of investigation.[1]

In other words, it is generally possible to decompose the problem of how to achieve a certain production goal into three distinct organizational issues: (i) how to identify suitable operations and arrangements of operations (jobs and processes); (ii) how to set up, or call upon, a suitable productive apparatus, i.e. a body of capabilities by which the above operations can be performed; (iii) how to arrange the suitable flows of work-in-process materials and finished products that have to be supplied by one 'working station' to another. In practice, these three problems have to be dealt with at the same time whenever a production activity is being undertaken. However, it is often possible to identify a hierarchy of issues, which may also suggest a hierarchical planning system (see Dempster *et al.*, 1981). From a theoretical point of view, the arrangement of operations into jobs and processes logically precedes their allocation to specific agents and the organization of a network of consistent material flows. In a sense, jobs and processes express in the most general way the praxeological features of production activity, i.e. its connection with the organization of human actions. On the other hand, there may be more than one way of implementing a given (abstract) production programme, by introducing alternative productive apparatuses or alternative networks of material flows.

The analysis of the task–process network highlights a fundamental layer of the production process. At this level, the technological and organizational logic finds an expression that reflects technical knowledge and general management principles (for example, assembly-line or just-in-time production). However, the task–process network may still be compatible with a variety of capabilities and material flows. We may discover alternative ways of implementing the given network by shifting existing capabilities from one production programme to another, or by changing the materials-in-process, and possibly moving to a different product specification.

As pointed out above, the consideration of tasks and processes may be connected with a concept of scale defined purely in operational terms, disregarding both the *capacities* of active factors (an important feature of their *capabilities*) and the scale dimensions

---

[1] This feature of production activity had been recognized by Gottl-Ottlilienfeld (1923) (see also Di Nunzio, 1988: vol. i).

of flow inputs and work-in-process materials. In this case, scale directly describes the organizational logic, and is independent of the 'material' features of the productive process.

However, any given task–process network is implemented by using a certain set of productive facilities and establishing a certain pattern of flows of work-in-process materials, which are transferred from one activity, or elementary transformation process, to another. A particular network of tasks and processes may be identified in a variety of ways, depending on which activities we decide to include. After such a selection is made, we may identify a particular *production process*, which is a distinct task–process network conventionally separated from other tasks and processes.[2] The boundaries of any real production process (of a 'material' type) permit the identification of a particular set of productive agents and of a particular network of work-in-process materials. This also permits us to associate a particular *size* with the *productive unit* thus considered. In a more formal way, we may say that, for each productive unit, size may be identified with the vector of scale dimensions measuring the capacities of the productive installation and the flows of materials-in-process within it (see also Gold, 1981; Buzacott, 1982).

Any implemented task–process network with definite boundaries is thus associated with a productive unit of given size. In principle, size is a multi-dimensional variable (see above). For practical purposes, however, it may be useful to measure *observed size* by the number of material transformation processes carried out within the productive unit, and to compare this value with the number of potential transformation processes that could be executed within the existing installation. (It is, of course, only in the case of full-capacity utilization that the two values will coincide.)

In general, a particular production process, defined as a task–process network, may be compatible with a variety of productive installations and material flows. It follows that a given *scale* of the process may also be compatible with a number of different arrangements concerning *size*. For example, as will be shown below (see section 5.5.4), the same condition for the continuous utilization of fund inputs may be satisfied by operating a large factory or by splitting the production process into sub-processes carried out by semi-independent establishments within an industrial district. The

---

[2] The conventional character of boundaries between production processes is stressed by Georgescu-Roegen (1970; 1971).

size of a productive unit is determined, within the present frame-work, by the active factors (generally, the fund inputs) available in a productive installation and by the material flows carried out within that installation, *after* a particular production process is specified.[3] It follows that it is possible to say whether a given productive unit is large or small in size, not in general, but only in relation to the production programme of that particular unit. For example, it may well be that the size (in our sense) of the process carried out in a large installation is smaller than that of an artisan's workshop if the former is only capable of delivering a single batch of produce per unit of time, while the latter may serve a number of different cus-tomers at the same time.

[3] The identification of a productive unit, and of its size, is thus partly conventional because of the conventional character of the analytical boundaries between different processes (see above). An early discussion of the conventional aspect of productive units may be found in the debates of the 1920s on the laws of return at the industrial level (see Sraffa, 1926). A discussion of the analytical implications of the concept of 'industry' within the above perspective may be found in Becattini (1962).

3

Scale and Technical Practice:
A Rational Reconstruction

3.1. THE PROBLEM OF SCALE IN PRODUCTION THEORY

3.1.1. *Scale and the description of the production process*

Economists describe a production process either (i) as an arrangement of productive operations (or *tasks*) or (ii) as a mapping of input quantities into output quantities. The former approach was used by a number of classical economists (Smith and Marx in particular) and, more recently, by Nicholas Georgescu-Roegen.[1] The latter approach is common to 'neoclassical' production theory, activity analysis, and input–output models.

Both approaches require the measurement of certain scale variables. In the former case, this is shown by the fact that any task implies an action or a change of state. It follows that, in order to describe a task completely, we need to consider the object on which the action is performed, or the object undergoing the change. Now, each such object has a given size. As a result, the specification of each task is 'scaled', depending on the size of the object entering the task's description. (A task described as 'cutting a piece of wood of length ℓ into two rods of equal length' is different from a task described as 'cutting a piece of wood of length ℓ' into two rods of equal length', unless, for the productive need under consideration, the length of the piece of wood which is being cut is immaterial.) However, a task such as 'cutting a piece of wood of length ℓ into two rods of equal length' may sometimes be reckoned to be performed on a piece of wood of length $\ell' \geqslant \ell$. In this case two possibilities arise. If ℓ' is not an integer multiple of ℓ, it is possible to execute the task a number of times and leave a piece of wood over. On the other hand, if ℓ' is an integer multiple of ℓ, the task will be performed a certain number of times and there will be no residual. In both cases,

---

[1] See section 4.5.

there is no change of task (in particular, there is no change in the size of the object entering the task's description).

A different approach to scale can be found when the production process is described as an input–output combination. In this case, any change in input or output scale leads to a different process description. As a result, the identity of each production process is not scale-independent, unless we introduce special assumptions ensuring that different input–output combinations describe the same production process (a simple example is the linear homogeneity assumption in activity analysis).

Each way of describing the production process is associated with a particular concept of *process scale*. If the production process is considered as an arrangement of tasks, there is no presumption that process scale should measure the material objects processed in a particular productive unit during a conventional time period. (In the wood-cutting example above, a greater size of wood is not necessarily associated with a greater number of tasks of the given type.) As a result, process scale would generally measure the number of tasks that are simultaneously performed in a given productive unit, regardless of input and output levels. On the other hand, if the production process is considered as an input–output combination, process scale measures input and output levels, regardless of the number of tasks that are simultaneously performed in the productive unit.

3.1.2. *Scale and technical practice*

Economists' interest in the scale of production processes derives from the belief that changes in technical practice may be induced by changes in scale, and that such an association conforms to the following pattern: (i) changes in scale induce changes in technical practice because of upper and lower bounds on the scale at which certain practices are feasible; (ii) a scale-induced change in technical practice is associated with the introduction of a 'better' or 'worse' practice. (Here 'better' and 'worse' simply refer to the relative position of the new practice in a producer's ranking of feasible practices, and do not necessarily refer to objective superiority or inferiority. This matter will be discussed in section 7.3.)

A non-trivial relationship between scale and technical practice presupposes that any change in technical practice can be *described* independently of changes in scale. For scale cannot 'determine' technical practice in an interesting sense if the change in scale cannot be distinguished from the change in practice. Such 'scale-independence' of the technical-practice description can be achieved in a number of different ways, depending on whether the production process is considered as an input–output combination or as an arrangement of tasks. In the former case, we need a specification of the class of input–output transformations that leave the technical practice unchanged. In the latter case, we need task descriptions independent of changes in process scale (in particular, the size of each object entering a task's description should remain constant, if process scale is varied).

There is no natural experiment in which the technical practice varies with scale and time is unchanged, for any change in scale takes time. However, the relationship between scale and technical practice considered in the economic literature derives from feasibility constraints that are independent of time. (The way technical practice is related to scale results from technical indivisibilities and resource constraints: in both cases the relationship between practice and scale is independent of technical progress and of intertemporal changes in the amount of available resources.)

This chapter outlines the historical evolution of the pure theory of scale–practice relationships. It will focus on the contributions in which scale is related to practice regardless of the institutional framework and of changes in technical knowledge.

3.2. SCALE AND DIVISION OF LABOUR: FROM SERRA TO MILL

3.2.1. *Productive specialization and extent of the market before Adam Smith*

The idea that certain important characteristics of a production process may change as a result of a change in productive scale has been widespread since early economic literature. Antonio Serra, whose work was published in 1613, pointed out that in manufactures 'products may be multiplied, so that they may be doubled not only once but one hundred times. And all this may be obtained with a less than proportional increase in expense' (Serra, 1803 [1613]: 24; my translation). The reasons for this tendency towards decreasing unit cost in manufacturing are examined by Serra in another passage, in which he mentions, as an important cause of the prosperity of Venice,

the number of manufactures in that city, which gives a great number of people occasion to go to that place; and the number of manufactures is not the only cause . . . since both the number of manufactures and the extent of commerce work to the same effect, and one cause strengthens the other. The number of people going to Venice for the sake of commerce and thanks to her position is made larger by the number of her manufactures, and the number of manufactures is made larger by the great extent of commercial activity.   (p. 32; my translation)

Serra's argument, as presented above, anticipates a number of points that were expanded upon by later economists. In particular, he stresses the relationship between scale and cost of production in the case of manufacturing. He also identifies an association between the number of specialized production processes and the extent of the market.

In the course of the seventeenth and eighteenth centuries, the division of labour—that is, the co-operation of individuals performing different productive tasks which are co-ordinated with one another either directly or through the market—slowly emerged as the fundamental reason for the tendency towards decreasing unit cost in manufacturing (see Groenewegen, 1987). Sir William Petty argued that, in a large city, 'manufactures will beget one another, and each manufacture will be divided into as many parts as possible, whereby the work of each artisan will be simple and easy; as, for example, in the making of a watch, if one man shall make the wheels, another the spring, another shall engrave the dial-plate and another shall make the cases, then the watch will be better and cheaper than if the whole work be put upon any one man' (Petty, 1899 [1683]: 473).

In particular, division of labour within a single productive establishment emerged as a distinct phenomenon from division of labour in society among the different professions. Division of labour of the former type was clearly described in the article 'Art' of the French *Encyclopédie*:

As to the rapidity with which the work can be executed and the goodness of the article, these depend entirely on the number of workmen brought together. When a manufacture is conducted by a large number of persons, each operation is performed by a different man. One workman throughout his life has done and will do only one single thing; the result of which is that each thing is well and quickly done and moreover, that the best-made article is the cheapest.   (*Encyclopédie*, i (1751), 717; translation in Cannan, 1929: 95)

A notable aspect of the above passage is the explicit connection between the degree of division of labour in a particular productive establishment and the scale of the production process (division of labour depends on 'the number of workmen brought together', and 'each operation is performed by a different man' on condition that 'a large number of persons' work in the same productive establishment).

3.2.2. *Size of productive establishment and symmetrical division of labour: the contribution of Adam Smith*

Adam Smith's account of the division of labour combines an interest in the division between trades or professions with an interest in the division between workers operating in a single productive establishment. In particular, the analysis carried out in chapter 1 of *Wealth of Nations* suggests that the two phenomena have important results in common, so that '[t]he effects of the division of labour, in the general business of society, will be more easily understood by considering in what manner it operates in some particular manufactures' (Smith, 1976 [1776]: 14).

It is worth quoting Smith's opinion in full:

[Division of labour] is commonly supposed to be carried furthest in some very trifling [manufactures]; not perhaps that it really is carried further in them than in others of more importance: but in those trifling manufactures which are destined to supply the small wants of but a small number of people, the whole number of workmen must necessarily be small; and those employed in every different branch of the work can often be collected into the same workhouse, and placed at once under the view of the spectator. In those great manufactures, on the contrary, which are destined to supply the great wants of the great body of the people, every different branch of the work employs so great a number of workmen that it is impossible to collect them all into the same workhouse. We can seldom see more, at one time, than those employed in one single branch. Though in them, therefore, the work may really be divided into a much greater number of parts than in those of a more trifling nature, the division is not near so obvious, and has accordingly been much less observed.   (p. 14)

This argument presupposes that division of labour is regulated by the same general principles, independently of the size of the productive unit under consideration. This approach seems to be at variance with the treatment of division of labour in the *Encyclopédie* article on one basic issue: the importance of production scale in determining the degree of division of labour in any given productive establishment. For, in the *Encyclopédie*, large-scale production (in the sense of a production process that physically brings together 'a large number of persons') is considered a necessary condition for having complete division of labour (i.e. a situation in which 'each operation is performed by a different man'). By contrast, Smith maintains that the theory of division of labour can be derived by considering productive establishments in which 'the whole number of workmen is small'.

In fact, the *Encyclopédie* 'model' is a special case of Smith's theory. This can be seen by considering that, in general, the scale of production which limits the scope for division of labour depends on the technical characteristics of the production process in question. In particular, for each production process there is a minimum scale (and hence a minimum 'number of workmen brought together') at which complete division of labour is feasible. This complete division of labour does not require in every case the employment of a large number of workers in one productive establishment. Smith's theory offers a general conceptual framework which may be applied to a variety of technological situations, and which explains the advantages of division of labour in different kinds of productive organization (such as specialized processes performed in small workshops or large-scale production carried out in big factories). But Smith's belief that division of labour can be best illustrated by considering small workshops, such as the pin-making manufacture described in *Wealth of Nations*, book i, chapter 1 (Smith, 1976 [1776]: 14–15), leads him to examine phenomena that are especially important in the small workshop case:

This great increase of the quantity of work, which, in consequence of the division of labour, the same number of people are capable of performing, is owing to three different circumstances; first, . . . the increase of dexterity in every particular workman; secondly, . . . the saving of the time which is commonly lost in passing from one species of work to another; and lastly, . . . the invention of a great number of machines which facilitate and abridge labour, and enable one man to do the work of many.   (p. 17)

All the advantages mentioned by Smith are independent of the number of tasks of a given type that are performed simultaneously in the productive establishment. Smith's advantages may thus be fully operative even in the case of small-scale production.

The assumptions behind Smith's analysis of pin-making may be examined by considering a characteristic of production processes in which the final output results from a time-sequence of operations (this is the type of process considered by Smith). As pointed out by Kilbridge and Wester, in such processes there is generally an upper limit to the division of the total work needed to complete each output unit. This limit is due to the existence of irreducible 'work elements'. Each 'work element' is a productive task (or set of tasks) 'which for technical reasons cannot be subdivided . . . That is, it cannot be split between two operators' (Kilbridge and Wester, 1966: B259). Irreducible work elements determine the feasible *cycle times* (i.e. the minimum and maximum periods in which a certain product may be processed by any given worker or set of workers). In particular, '[t]he largest such work element . . . will be assumed to set the lower limit of feasible cycle times. The upper limit is the total . . . work done as a one-man operation. Between these limits, and typically quite close to the lower one, industry chooses its cycle time' (p. B259).

In production processes of the sequential type, the total work needed to complete one output unit may be divided between *work stations* (or groups of operators and tools co-operating with one another in the same task or in the same undivided set of tasks). Division of total work may be *symmetrical* or not (note that a symmetrical division of work implies that the product spends an equal part of the complete time for each cycle at each work station). A symmetrical division of work between work stations is not necessarily associated with a symmetrical division of work between individual operators (any work station may consist of a different number of individuals). On the other hand, a symmetrical division of work between individuals is generally associated with a symmetrical division of work between work stations (any work station would normally consist of the same number of individuals). If the production process requires operators and tools of different skill, speed, and so forth, a symmetrical division of work between individual operators is normally impossible. This would make it impossible to achieve the full and continuous utilization of all operators and tools simply by assigning any given task to a different individual and tool. In this case, continuous utilization may be obtained by lumping together a number of different tasks and having them performed by the same individual. But this would often mean that certain individuals are partially employed in tasks below their skill, speed, and so forth. This type of waste can be avoided by introducing an alternative arrangement of the production process in which each task is performed by a specialized work station (note that such stations may have a different number of individuals performing a given task at the same time).

Smith's theory of the division of labour is based on the assumption that a symmetrical division of work between individuals is possible. (His description of the production process overlooks the fact that different task durations make a symmetrical division of work impossible if every work station has the same number of operators.) This assumption allows Smith to consider the advantages of division of labour regardless of whether the productive establishment is large or small (indeed, Smith believes that the advantages to be found in small workshops are also available in 'great manufactures').[2] The case in which it is impossible for there to be a symmetrical division of work between work stations all having the same number of individuals emphasizes a further advantage of the division of labour as well as an important link between division of labour and the scale of production. We shall consider this case in the following section.

3.2.3. *Non-symmetrical division of labour and large-scale production: the contributions of Gioja, Babbage, Hermann, and Rae*

The study of production processes in which a symmetrical division of work between individuals is impossible was associated with

---

[2] Smith's pin-making example contains a reference to the fact that the degree of the division of labour may vary, depending on the size of the individual workshop: 'the important business of making a pin is, in this manner, divided into about eighteen distinct operations, which, in some manufactories, *are all performed by distinct hands*, though in others the same man will sometimes perform *two or three of them*. I have seen a small manufactory of this kind where ten men only were employed, and where some of them consequently performed two or three distinct operations' (Smith, 1976 [1776]: 15; my italics). Smith makes no explicit reference to the fact that a complete division of work between individuals (in which each individual performs a single task) requires a minimum scale, if tasks requiring different degrees of speed, strength, etc. make symmetrical division of work between individuals impossible. In this connection, Negishi has noted the coexistence in Smith of two distinct 'models' of division of labour: 'One is concerned with an interfirm division of labour or the specialization of firms in the same industry, the extent of which is limited by the industrial demand, while the other is concerned with the subdivision of different operations to produce a given product, the extent of which is limited by the demand for the output of the plant' (Negishi, 1985: 17).

important changes in the attitude of economists to the relationship between the division of labour and the scale of production (see also Pagano, 1985: 41–5). The fact that a complete division of work between *groups of individuals* may be possible, even if a symmetrical division of work between individuals is impossible, was first recognized by Melchiorre Gioja. Gioja stressed that, in this case, division of labour makes it possible to avoid waste of skill, strength, etc.:

If we consider that different types of work may require different degrees of strength, and that workers themselves may be different with regard to their strength, we understand that the workers of least strength ought to content themselves with the types of work which were left free by workers of higher strength. For weakness would not succeed where strength was necessary, and it would not be advantageous to employ strength in those types of work for which weakness was sufficient. The same argument applies to dexterity since, on the assumption of equal strengths, the least able workers cannot succeed in such works which may be easily performed by the skilled ones.   (Gioja, 1815–17: i. 100; my translation)

But a necessary condition for this sort of arrangement is large-scale production, which makes it possible to have several individuals performing the same task simultaneously:

The division of labour is always possible in large workshops, not in small ones. For instance, a hat-maker who is employing six workmen may use one of them in forming the laps, another in twisting the wool, two in fulling the wool, the fifth in dyeing, the sixth and himself in performing the final tasks. On the other hand, if we had seven hat-makers instead of one, all the above operations would be performed by each of them, and this would bring about an immense loss of time. Moreover, division of labour makes it easier to measure the different types of work, and to pay the workers not by the day but according to the actual amount of work they perform, thus bringing about higher speed.   (ii. 117; my translation)

Charles Babbage stressed the same advantage:

the master manufacturer, by dividing the work to be executed into different processes, each requiring different degrees of skill or of force, can purchase exactly that precise quantity of both which is necessary for each process; whereas, if the whole work were executed by one workman, that person must possess sufficient skill to perform the most difficult, and sufficient strength to execute the most laborious, of the operations into which the art is divided.   (Babbage, 1835: 175–6)[3]

[3] In a footnote to this passage, Babbage writes: 'I have already stated that this principle presented itself to me after a personal examination of a number of

Babbage too saw a connection between the scope for division of labour and the size of a productive establishment:

When the number of processes into which it is most advantageous to divide [production], and the number of individuals to be employed in it, are ascertained, then all factories which do not employ a direct multiple of this latter number, will produce the article at a greater cost. This principle ought always to be kept in view in great establishments, although it is quite impossible, even with the best division of labour, to attend to it rigidly in practice. The proportional number of the persons who possess the greatest skill, is of course to be first attended to. That exact ratio which is most profitable for a factory employing a hundred workmen, may not be quite the best where there are five hundred; and the arrangements of both may probably admit of variations, without materially increasing the cost of their produce. But it is quite certain that no individual, nor in the case of pin-making could any five individuals, ever hope to compete with an extensive establishment. Hence arises one cause of the great size of manufacturing establishments, which has increased with the progress of civilization.   (pp. 212–13)

Here Babbage stresses that, when a symmetrical division of work between individuals is impossible, the pattern of division of total work between groups of individuals (the 'number of processes into which it is most advantageous to divide' the production of a given commodity) has to be determined at the same time as the scale of

manufactories and workshops devoted to different purposes; but I have since found that it had been distinctly pointed out, in the work of Gioja, *Nuovo prospetto delle Scienze Economiche*, 1815, tom. I, cap. IV' (Babbage, 1835: 176). Here Babbage refers to the first passage by Gioja quoted above. The same advantage from division of labour was also noted by Friedrich von Hermann: 'If a production process is made of different successive tasks, and such tasks require different degrees of strength and different skills, then one man performing all such tasks one after the other, must possess the skill and strength required for each task. As a result, he must possess the greatest strength and the utmost dexterity. Under such conditions, the strength of that man would be only partially utilized by the remaining tasks, even if he were to ask for the salary which he deserved as a worker of great ability and strength . . . If the tasks are subdivided among the individual workers, then it is possible to utilize exactly that strength for which any worker is paid: the weakest and least able among men, women and children may find a job and a salary adequate to their capacity. As a result, it is possible to utilize labour capacities that are limited from the physical or mental point of view, thus increasing employment. At the same time, it is possible to avoid the non-economic utilization of the strongest workers in tasks for which a lower labour capacity is sufficient' (Hermann, 1870 [1832]: 196; my translation). The Gioja–Babbage principle may also be related to an important prerequisite of engineering structures: the 'least-work principle' identified by Castigliano (1879–80). (See also Charlton, 1982; Addis, 1983.)

productive activity ('the number of individuals to be employed' in such an activity). This property results from the fact that, if tasks require 'different degrees of skill or of force', a necessary condition for the full and continuous utilization of 'task specific' workers is that a few workers of the strong or quick type be combined with more workers of the weak or slow type. (In a production process consisting of tasks *a* and *b*, such that *a* takes twice the time of *b*, the number of workers specialized in *a* would normally be twice the number of workers specialized in *b*.) This requirement (rather than division of labour *per se*) is then considered to be 'one cause of the great size of manufacturing establishments'.[4]

For similar reasons, a number of authors associated division of labour with greater utilization of tools and machines (both per unit of time and over time).

This latter phenomenon had been noted by Gioja, who mentioned, among the causes of division of labour, the fact that certain production processes require factors, such as tools and machines, which do not continuously perform, in the production of each unit of final output, the task(s) for which they are needed:

Let us assume that Pietro, Paolo, Martino . . . instead of limiting themselves to their respective activities A, B, C . . . be employed in all of them: on this assumption everybody will need the corresponding machines; if, for instance, everybody wants to get as much olive oil as he needs for his individual

---

[4] Our interpretation is supported by a particular example considered by Babbage (Mr Mordan's factory of the 'ever-pointed pencils'): 'one room is devoted to some of the processes by which steel pens are manufactured. Six fly-presses are here constantly at work: in the first a sheet of thin steel is brought by *the workman* under the die which at each blow cuts out a flat piece of the metal, having the form intended for the pen. *Two other workmen* are employed in placing these flat pieces under two other presses, in which a steel chisel cuts the slit. *Three other workmen* occupy other presses, in which the pieces so prepared receive their semi-cylindrical form. The longer time required for adjusting the small pieces in the two latter operations renders them less rapid in execution than the first; so that *two workmen* are fully occupied in slitting, and *three* in bending the flat pieces, which *one man* can punch out of the sheet of steel. If, therefore, it were necessary to enlarge this factory, it is clear that twelve or eighteen presses would be worked out with more economy than any number not a multiple of six' (Babbage, 1835: 211–12). The technical practice described by Babbage is only feasible above a certain minimum scale. For the differences in the degrees of 'skill or of force' required by the various tasks make it impossible to keep 3 different categories of specialized workers (i.e. workers respectively specialized in 'punching out', 'slitting', and 'bending the flat pieces') continuously active throughout each working day, unless the scale of the production process permits the simultaneous employment of at least 6 workers specialized in 3 different tasks.

consumption, society would need as many presses as it has members, presses which would work for a couple of hours, and then remain idle for the rest of the year; the same applies to all the other machines and tools required in the various arts and manufactures. On the other hand, when the productive activities are subdivided, one press is sufficient for the needs of 4,000 people, one mangle for the needs of 5,000, one oven for the needs of 6,000. (Gioja, 1815–17: i. 101; my translation)

One important reason for the division of labour is thus that 'the practice of mixing all activities would require the introduction and useless waste of enormous capital' and that '[t]his waste is avoided by the division of labour' (ibid.).

John Rae considered this problem further:

As the knowledge which mankind possess of the course of nature advances, and they discover a greater number of means to provide for their future wants, the instruments they employ for this purpose become very various. The exercise of the arts of the weaver, the blacksmith, the carpenter, the farmer, implies the existence of a very great variety of tools with which they may be carried on. But, as a man can only do one thing at once, if any man had all the tools which these several occupations require, at least three fourths of them would constantly lie idle and useless. It were clearly then better, were any society to exist where each man had all these tools, and alternately carried on each of these occupations, that the members of it should if possible divide them amongst them, each restricting himself to some particular employment. There would then be no superfluous implement, each set of tools would form an instrument much more speedily exhausted . . . The advantages of the change to the whole community, and therefore to every individual in it, are great. In the first place, the various implements being in constant employment yield a better return for what has been laid out in procuring them . . . In consequence, their owners can afford to have them of better quality and more complete construction . . . The result of both events is, that a larger provision is made for the future wants of the whole society. (Rae, 1834: 164–5)

Division of labour, by 'dividing the work to be executed into different processes, each requiring different degrees of skill or of force' (Babbage, 1835: 175), also makes it possible to avoid the kind of waste associated with the use of unspecialized tools. This latter advantage was clearly noted by Marx:

Tools of the same kind, such as knives, drills, gimlets, hammers, etc., may be employed in different processes; and the same tool may serve various purposes in a single process. But so soon as the different operations of a labour-process are disconnected the one from the other, and each fractional operation acquires in the hands of the detail labourer a suitable and peculiar form, alterations become necessary in the implements that previously served more than one purpose. The direction taken by this change is determined by the difficulties experienced in consequence of the unchanged form of the implement. Manufacture is characterized by the differentiation of the instruments of labour—a differentiation whereby implements of a given sort acquire fixed shapes, adapted to each particular application, and by the specialisation of those instruments, giving to each special implement its full play only in the hands of a specific detail labourer. (Marx, 1983 [1867]: 322–3)

Babbage's law of multiples determines which process scales allow the full utilization of task specific workers and tools, thus avoiding the waste associated with the use of workers and tools that 'possess sufficient skill to perform the most difficult, and sufficient strength to execute the most laborious, of the operations into which [any given art] is divided' (Babbage, 1835: 175).

3.2.4. *Association of works, machinery, and large-scale production: from Gioja to Mill*

The advantage of combining the actions of different individuals (or the operations of different machines) in performing identical tasks was recognized at an early stage by various economists. Gioja, in particular, stressed that the 'association of works' is an important factor in increasing labour productivity

when the resistance of external objects defeats the powers of isolated individuals, even if these latter make use of machinery . . . when the duration of work in isolation might worsen the product . . . when work in isolation uses time which is needed for more useful tasks, thus making it impossible to employ the same individuals at later periods . . . when the lack or scarcity of capital is made good by the abundance of human forces . . . when similar or different actions are required in different places at the same time or one after the other . . . when the business requires large capital. (Gioja, 1815–17: i. 94–7)

Machinery was sometimes considered an important inducement to the co-operation of different individuals doing identical tasks (particularly in the case of tasks that can use the same mechanical power at the same time). Gioja himself extended the concept of 'association of works' to the co-operation of different productive establishments using the same source of power: 'the steam engine is not economical in a small factory, since its operation cannot be continuous . . . But if a considerable number of small factories combine with one another, the same machine that was too expensive for the individual factory becomes economical for their association' (Gioja, 1819: 138).

The importance of the association of individuals performing identical tasks was also stressed by Edward Gibbon Wakefield in his own notes to Smith's *Wealth of Nations* (Wakefield, 1835–43: i. 26). There Wakefield introduces the distinction between *simple co-operation* ('such co-operation as takes place when several persons help each other in the same employment') and *complex co-operation* ('such co-operation as takes place when several persons help each other in different employments').

The advantages of simple co-operation are described by Wakefield as follows:

In a vast number of simple operations performed by human exertion, it is quite obvious that two men working together will do more than four, or four times four men, each of whom should work alone. In the lifting of heavy weights, for example in the felling of trees, in the sawing of timber, in the gathering of much hay or corn during a short period of fine weather, in draining a large extent of land during the short season when such a work may be properly conducted, in the pulling of ropes on board ships, in the rowing of large boats, in some mining operations, in the erection of a scaffolding for building, and in the breaking of stones for the repair of a road, so that the whole of the road shall always be kept in good order; in all these simple operations, and thousands more, it is absolutely necessary that many persons should work together, at the same time, in the same place, and in the same way. (ibid.)

Writing a few years later, on 'the circumstances which promote the productiveness of labour', John Stuart Mill noted that 'Mr Wakefield was . . . the first to point out, that a part of the subject had, with injurious effect, been mistaken for the whole; that a more fundamental principle lies beneath that of the division of labour, and comprehends it' (Mill, 1965 [1848]: i. 116). 'Combination of labour' is considered by Mill to be the general principle behind simple and complex co-operation (chs. 8–9). This belief led him to a substantial reformulation of the classical theory of the relationship between division of labour and large-scale production:

From the importance of combination of labour, it is an obvious conclusion, that there are many cases in which production is made much more effective by being conducted on a large scale. Whenever it is essential to the greatest efficiency of labour that many labourers should combine even though only in the way of simple co-operation, the scale of the enterprise must be such as to bring labourers together and the capital must be large enough to maintain them. Still more needful is this when the nature of employment allows, and the extent of the possible market encourages, a considerable division of labour. The larger the enterprise, the farther the division of labour may be carried. This is one of the principal causes of large manufactures. Even when no additional subdivision of the work would follow an enlargement of the operations, there will be good economy in enlarging them to the point at which every person to whom it is convenient to assign a special occupation, will have full employment in that occupation.   (ibid. 131)

The interest of Mill's argument comes from the fact that he takes large-scale production (in the sense of many operations performed at the same time in the same physical workplace) to be a sufficient condition for greater efficiency independently of the division of labour (the first part of Mill's passage describes a situation in which productive efficiency is increased by having several persons performing identical operations at the same time). Furthermore, he describes the relationship between scale and division of labour in a way that is suggestive of a continuous function, since no mention of discrete increments is made ('[t]he larger the enterprise, the farther the division of labour may be carried'). This latter view contrasts with Babbage's opinion: 'When the number of processes into which it is most advantageous to divide it [a productive activity], and the number of individuals to be employed in it, are ascertained, then all factories which do not employ a direct multiple of this latter number, will produce the article at a greater cost' (Babbage, 1835: 212).

Mill's neglect of process indivisibilities led him to overlook Babbage's law of multiples, and to formulate the principle of the advantages of increasing size of the enterprise in a way unknown to earlier classical economists: '*Every* increase of business would enable the whole to be carried on with a proportionally smaller amount of labour. As a general rule, the expenses of a business do not increase by any means proportionally to the quantity of business' (Mill, 1965 [1848]: i. 132; my italics).

The literature on scale and division of labour which has been considered so far shows the need to distinguish between two meanings of 'production scale' which are often confused in the economic treatments: (i) the quantity of any particular commodity (or commodity basket) which is produced in any given establishment during a conventional time-interval (say, the working day); (ii) the number of productive operations using the same fixed resources (machinery, land, and so forth) at the same time. The classical theory of the division of labour shows that, in some cases, output per unit of time may be increased without increasing at the same time the number of productive operations simultaneously performed in a productive establishment (this may be obtained by employing specialized labour in specialized tasks and thus carrying out the productive operations in a shorter time). On the other hand, a higher number of simultaneous and identical operations is generally associated with greater output per unit of time. The former case is considered by Smith. The latter case, which was initially examined by Gioja and Babbage, became the basis of the modern theory of the economies of large-scale production. This led many economists to think that a necessary condition for large output is a large number of simultaneous operations performed in the same productive establishment, and that an increasing size of the establishment is a necessary and sufficient condition for higher productive efficiency (see Mill's passages above).

3.3. SCALE AND 'LIMITS TO PRODUCTION'

3.3.1. *Two alternative approaches*

A similar evolution may be found in the literature about the relationship between inputs that cannot be augmented (at establishment, industry, or economy level) and the adoption of technical practices. In this case, two stages may be identified in the evolution of theory.

At an early stage, the main focus was on the existence of a *fixed* upper bound on agricultural output. (This bound is a result of the fact that the quantity of output obtainable from a given plot of land per unit of time was considered to be fixed.) An extreme formulation of this view is to be found in Serra's statement that 'in manufacturing, the multiplication of production is possible, thereby multiplying the revenue, whereas this is impossible in the production of primary produce, which cannot be multiplied. For example, nobody can sow 150 *tomola* of corn on a territory in which only 100 can be sown' (Serra, 1803 [1613]: 32; my translation). Smith shares the substance of this view, while admitting the possibility of some improvements in agricultural practices:

The nature of agriculture . . . does not admit of so many divisions of labour, nor of so complete a separation of one business from another, as manufactures. It is impossible to separate so entirely the business of the grazier from that of the corn-farmer as the trade of the carpenter is commonly separated from that of the smith. The spinner is almost always a distinct person from the weaver; but the ploughman, the harrower, the sower of the seed, and the reaper of the corn, are often the same. The occasions for those different sorts of labour returning with the different seasons of the year, it is impossible that one man should be constantly employed in any one of them. The impossibility of making so complete and entire a separation of all the different branches of labour employed in agriculture is perhaps the reason why the improvement of the productive powers of labour in this art does not always keep pace with their improvement in manufactures.   (Smith, 1976 [1776]: 16)

Other economists drew attention to the relationship between the different inputs needed in agricultural processes, and saw the cause of the technical inferiority of agriculture in the limited availability of fertile land. Sir James Steuart and Anne-Robert-Jacques Turgot were among the first to note the special relationship between land availability and agricultural efficiency. The former wrote that it is generally possible to increase the number of people living on a given territory, but only by 'introducing a more operose species of agriculture, the produce of which may be *absolutely* greater, though *relatively* less' (Steuart, 1966 [1767]: i. 129). Turgot wrote:

Seed thrown on a soil naturally fertile but totally unprepared would be an advance almost entirely lost. If it were once tilled the produce will be greater; tilling it a second, a third time, might not merely double and triple, but quadruple or decuple the produce, which will thus augment in a much larger proportion than the advances increase, and that up to a certain point, at which the produce will be as great as possible compared with the advances. Past this point, if the advances be still increased, the produce will still increase but less, and always less and less until the fecundity of the earth being exhausted, and art unable to add anything further, an addition to the advances will add nothing whatever to the produce.   (Turgot, 1808: 317; translation in Cannan, 1929: 75)

Both Steuart and Turgot focused on the relationship between labour and land, and concluded that, if land is fixed, an increase in the quantity of labour is, after a certain point, associated with a less than proportional increase in the quantity of output. This claim is at variance with Serra's statement that there is an absolute upper bound on the quantity of agricultural output that can be obtained from any given territory. The reason for the disagreement is that Serra is considering a case in which technical practice is given.

An important feature which Smith and Serra have in common is the consideration of technical practices as arrangements of productive *operations* (or *tasks*). Steuart and Turgot, on the other hand, divert attention from such characteristics of production processes by considering each technical practice as a combination of original inputs (land, labour, and seed) rather than as a network of tasks. In the following sections we shall examine the implications of both approaches.

3.3.2. *The standard classical model and its transformations*

Classical economists such as Malthus, Ricardo, and West returned to a more detailed consideration of agricultural practices, partly as a result of the importance they attached to the existence of different land qualities. A general formulation of their approach is given in Malthus's pamphlet on the *Nature and Progress of Rent*:

The machines which produce corn and raw materials . . . are the gifts of nature, not the works of men; and we find, by experience, that these gifts have very different qualities and powers. The most fertile lands of a country, those which, like the best machinery in manufactures, yield the greatest products with the least labour and capital, are never found sufficient to supply the effective demand of an increasing population. The price of raw produce, therefore, naturally rises till it becomes sufficiently high to pay the cost of raising it with inferior machines and by a more expensive process; and as there cannot be two prices for corn of the same quality, all the other machines, the working of which requires less capital compared with the produce, must yield rents in proportion of their goodness. Every extensive country may thus be considered as possessing a gradation of machines for the production of corn and raw materials, including in this gradation not only all the various qualities of poor land, of which every large territory has generally abundance, but the inferior machinery which may be said to be employed when good land is further and further forced for additional produce. As the price of raw produce continues to rise, these inferior machines are successively called into action; and as the price of raw produce continues to fall, they are successively thrown out of action.   (Malthus, 1815*b*: 38–9)

An important characteristic of Malthus's approach (and that of West and Ricardo as well) is that it does not consider different technical practices simply as different combinations of the same inputs (for different practices might require different inputs). This characteristic highlights a fundamental difference between this approach and that of Turgot, and is worth considering in some detail.

First of all, Turgot's study of production is based on different assumptions from those underlying the theories of Malthus, West, and Ricardo. These latter economists consider a set of exogenously given practices known to the producer. Each such practice is associated with a particular vector of input–output coefficients. Any change in the input–output coefficients for the production of a given commodity is described as a change in the technical practice used to produce this commodity. Turgot's theory, on the other hand, starts with the consideration of a set of alternative input–output vectors (i.e. *quantities* of labour, land, seed, and output). Different technical practices are generated by variations in the quantity of labour, on the assumption that the amounts of seed and land are fixed. The consequences of the above distinction are far-reaching:

(i) In the classical model, the producer knows a certain set of technical practices independently of land availability, whereas in Turgot's model the technical practices come to be known only as input availability does.

(ii) In the classical model, the producer's adoption of a technical practice is not necessarily subject to constraints on input quantities (there is no constraint on input availability in the case of processes in which only producible inputs are needed). In Turgot's model, however, the generation mechanism of technical practices is such that the adoption of a particular practice is necessarily associated with the assumption that at least one essential input is fixed.[5]

(iii) In the classical model, production 'scale' is thought of as determined by the number of simultaneous and independent operations carried out on the same pool of non-producible resources (a high 'scale' consists of the simultaneous execution of many sequences

[5] In a sense, Turgot's model assumes away the problem of what determines the adoption of a technical practice by a given producer (*technical adoption*), if technical adoption is regarded as a process of deliberate choice based on the comparison of alternative options. For, given the quantity of fixed inputs, there is a single quantity of the variable input which permits a producer to obtain the assigned output level. (On Turgot's production model, and its relation to the classical model, see also Scazzieri, 1979; 1982).

of such operations); in Turgot's model, the 'production process' is in fact a vector of input–output coefficients multiplied by a scalar, and 'scale' is, effectively, this scalar (high 'scale' cannot even be *described* unless the inputs and outputs are used, or produced, in large quantities).

An important consequence of (iii) is that, in the classical approach, scale variations are compatible with changes in the composition of output. (In fact, the classical approach allows the consideration of *heterogeneous* 'processes', all using the same land endowment.) Turgot's description of the 'production process', on the other hand, implies that any scale variation brings changes in the output levels of the produced commodities which leave the *composition* of output unchanged. (If 'scale of production' is a single scalar, it is impossible to distinguish between alternative compositions of the output-mix.)

The difference between Turgot's approach (later taken up by certain post-classical economists) and that of the classical economists may be illustrated by Wicksteed's distinction between 'functional curves' and 'descriptive curves'. The ranking among different methods of production considered by the classical economists may be represented by *descriptive curves*. In this case, 'a diagram may easily be constructed in which different qualities of land are represented along the axis of X and their supposed relative fertilities to a fixed application of labour and capital along the axis of Y. The "marginal" land will occupy the extreme place to the right. *This is not a functional curve*; for the height of y does not depend upon the length of x, the units being expressly so placed on OX as to produce a declining y' (Wicksteed, 1933: 790; originally published as Wicksteed, 1914; my italics). Functional curves, on the other hand, are introduced as follows:

the same figure has been used as a functional curve in connection with the theory of rent. Take a given fixed area of land of a certain quality and consider what would be its yield if it were 'dosed' with a certain quantity of labour and capital represented by a unit on the axis of X. Increase the doses till a further increment of labour and capital would not produce as large an increment in the yield of this land as it would if applied to some other piece of land of the same or different quality, or if turned to some non-agricultural business. The last increment actually applied is the 'marginal' increment, and it measures the distributive share of a unit 'dose' in the product . . . it is essential to point out that the descriptive and the functional curves just described both present the same appearance, both represent 'rent' by a curvilinear surface, both use the term 'margin', though in entirely different senses, as determining rent, and are both just as applicable to anything else as to land.   (Wicksteed, 1933: 790)

(Conceptions of economic law relevant to the analysis of Wicksteed's distinction are considered in Zamagni, 1980; 1987.)

The relationship between land utilization and 'scale of production' is a matter on which there is an important difference between classical and post-classical economic theories. This difference is already apparent in Mill's *Principles*:

After a certain, and not very advanced, stage in the progress of agriculture, it is the law of production from the land, that in any given state of agricultural skill and knowledge, by increasing the labour, the produce is not increased in an equal degree; doubling the labour does not double the produce; or, to express the same thing in other words, every increase of produce is obtained by a more than proportional increase in the application of labour to the land.   (Mill, 1965 [1865]: i. 174)

The above passage gives a formulation of the theory of decreasing agricultural efficiency similar to that adopted by Turgot. Mill is here shifting the emphasis towards a continuous, non-proportional relation between labour inputs and quantity produced. Such a relation applies most naturally to the case of intensive cultivation of a given plot of land; but Mill gives the extensive case a similar formulation too:

When for the purpose of raising an increase of produce, recourse is had to inferior land, it is evident that, so far, the produce does not increase in the same proportion with the labour. The very meaning of inferior land, is land which with equal labour returns a smaller amount of produce.   (Mill, 1965 [1848]: i. 174)

The study of 'limits to production' evolved through a sequence of theories, each characterized by a particular concept of 'scale'. In Serra, and to a lesser extent in Smith, the technological characteristics of agricultural operations determine the *level of output* uniquely on a given plot of land per unit of time. They do so for these writers because, in an agricultural process consisting of a fixed sequence of operations of the kind Serra and Smith had in mind, the output that can be obtained from the available land in an agricultural year is, in general, also fixed or, at most, subject to relatively small fluctuations unless exceptional climatic conditions interfere with the production process.[6] In Malthus, Ricardo, and West, by contrast, 'scale' is the *number of agricultural processes* that can be simultaneously carried out in the economy as a whole. Here, limited land availability in the whole economy determines an upper bound on the number of land-using processes, whereas the level and composition of agricultural output is allowed to vary depending on the number and type of agricultural processes in operation. A third scale concept is characteristic of Turgot and of post-classical writers starting with Mill. In their case, the 'scale' of the production process is the scalar by which the vector of input–output coefficients is multiplied in order to get the input quantities delivering a certain level of output. Turgot and, to a lesser extent, Mill assume that each vector of input–output coefficients is 'scale-specific', and that a continuous scale increase is possible only if input–output coefficients are continuously varied.

To summarize, in Serra and Smith the extent of a given plot of land determines 'scale of production' uniquely. It is not so with the other authors considered in this section, who define 'scale' in terms of the variable number of processes, or of the variable input quantities, that are simultaneously making use of the same fixed inputs. In Malthus, Ricardo, and West, 'scale' is identified with the number of processes using land anywhere in the economy as an input, so that this scale is unrelated to the 'size' of any particular establishment and measures rather the scale of the agricultural industry. On the other hand, Turgot and the post-classical writers define 'scale' in terms of the quantities of the variable inputs that are used in combination with a certain amount of fixed inputs in a single productive establishment. But the quantities of these latter inputs determine in a natural sense the *size* of the establishment. This makes any upper bound on 'scale' in Turgot's sense depend on the size of the establishment under consideration.

---

[6] This distinguishes agriculture from manufacturing, in which the division of labour does make it possible to increase the output delivered during a working day, even if technical knowledge and input endowment are given. This difference may be related to the fact that the efficiency improvements associated with division of labour are often the result of a greater degree of input utilization through time (see ss. 3.2.2 and 3.2.3). For, in manufacturing, it is often necessary to employ inputs (such as workers and tools) that are only intermittently used in the production process. Agriculture, on the other hand, generally requires the utilization of land throughout the *whole duration* of each process. As a result, in agricultural processes, efficiency improvements due to a better time-scheduling of productive operations are more difficult and often impossible.

3.4. LARGE-SCALE PRODUCTION, TASK-SPECIALIZATION, AND PRODUCTIVE SIZE: FROM MILL TO MODERN THEORY

3.4.1. *Division of labour, technology, and scale: alternative patterns of productive organization*

A general characteristic of the economic theories of production formulated round the middle of the nineteenth century is the interest in the relationship between technical practice and the size of the productive establishment. In these theories, scale is an establishment-related concept, and is often identified with the numer of *identical* operations carried out in the establishment at any given time.

An early application of this scale concept to the study both of decreasing and of increasing efficiency is to be found in Mill's *Principles* (1848). Mill's theory established a definite connection between the output of a given commodity, the 'size' of the productive establishment delivering this output, and the internal organization of this establishment (see the previous section).

Later research took up again the relationship between the scale of 'production' and the 'size' of productive establishment. In particular, Nikolaj Gavrilovich Chernyshevskij pointed out that the dependence of the division of labour on the extent of the market does not mean that division of labour necessarily requires large establishments:

Let us assume that a textile factory requires 100 workers to achieve maximum division of labour, thus obtaining the most efficient organization of production. Let us also assume that, in a given community and under given historical conditions, production technology is such that a worker employed in silk-weaving is unable to do anything else, and that the same is true of any worker employed in wool-weaving. In this case, it would clearly be necessary to set up two different factories, one for wool and one for silk fabrics, and it would be necessary to have a market large enough to permit the purchase of the yearly output of both. But let us now assume that the extent of the market is twice as small: in this latter case, if we consider the type of production technology permitting only task-specific jobs, the two factories cannot survive by maintaining 100 workers each: for they could not employ more than 50 workers each, so that division of labour will be much less developed. However, let us now assume that we have, in the same community, a different type of production technology, permitting the utilization of the same worker in a number of alternative tasks. In this latter case, it would be most appropriate to have a single factory that could employ the same 100 workers in producing wool fabrics for half the year, and silk fabrics for another half-year. It is true that a certain expenditure would be necessary in order to transform a factory producing wool fabrics into a factory producing silk fabrics; but such an expenditure would definitely be negligible with respect to the advantage of the greater division of labour. (Chernyshevskij, 1886 [1860]: 830–1; my translation)

The introduction of a technical practice which allows both a great division of labour at any given time and the switching of workers from one productive operation to another from time-to-time is regarded as advantageous because of the 'enormous saving of fixed capital' and the possibility of 'increasing the division of labour, and thus improving production methods, for any given extent of the market, to a much higher degree than would be possible when the same worker cannot be switched from one operation to another' (ibid. 831).

One important element of Chernyshevskij's argument is the idea that, at any given level of output, the employment of workers capable of switching from one type of operation to another allows the same degree of division of labour which fully specialized workers could only achieve at a considerably higher output level. Francesco Ferrara considered the related issue of how far task-specialization can improve productive efficiency, and found that it is not an advantage in production processes consisting of operations that are 'simple and similar to one another' (Ferrara, 1860: 53). Agricultural processes are, in Ferrara's view, an important example of processes of this kind:

If we consider them [agricultural processes] from the point of view of final output, we shall certainly find great differences between what is needed to prepare the ground, to sow it, and to collect the harvest; and all such operations would greatly vary from one product to another. But if we examine the aspect of human effort (which is important to consider here) we would hardly find ten different movements which are repeated all the time. (ibid.)

The consideration of agricultural processes draws Ferrara's attention to a technical limit to the division of labour which was overlooked by Smith (see section 3.2.2). For the limit to the division of labour in agriculture is due, in Smith's opinion, to the impossibility of the continuous employment of workers who are fully specialized in particular tasks. On the other hand, Ferrara argues that there is no return in restricting certain workers to task A and certain others to task B (i.e. there is no return to task-specialization), if tasks A and B, though very different from some points of view (e.g. their outputs), require very similar skills for their execution. Ferrara's discovery highlights an important necessary condition for the type of technical flexibility considered by Chernyshevskij, for the cost of employing versatile workers and of adjusting the productive structure to fluctuations of demand may preclude such flexibility unless the different tasks are 'simple and similar to one another'.

Karl Marx and Henry Sidgwick called attention to the fact that the minimum number of operations simultaneously performed in a given establishment depends on certain technical relationships between the operations of which the production processes are composed. In particular, Marx distinguished between heterogeneous manufacture and serial manufacture. In the former case, each article 'results from the mere mechanical fitting together of partial products made independently'; in the latter, the article 'owes its completed shape to a series of connected processes and manipulations' (Marx, 1983 [1867]: 323). In heterogeneous manufactures, it is only 'a matter of chance whether the detail labourers are brought together in one workshop or not' (p. 324). In other words, the co-operation of workers engaged in different operations does not necessarily require large-scale production in the sense of many operations in one establishment. On the other hand, serial manufacturing is generally associated with the operation of large productive establishments (see pp. 325–8).

A similar point was made by Sidgwick, when considering how the division of labour might affect the 'size' of productive establishments:

> The division of employments has different economic effects according as the co-operating workers are organized under one management, or under several different managements. So far as the simultaneous, or nearly simultaneous, combination of a number of different acts is required for the accomplishment of a single result, it is necessary that the labourers should be in one place, and obviously expedient that their work should be under the direction of one mind.   (Sidgwick, 1883: 112)

Sidgwick also recognized that large-scale production might increase productive efficiency even in cases in which it is not technically necessary to execute a number of operations simultaneously:

> [E]ven when the operations to be performed on the same material, before it becomes a finished product, are merely successive, there is still a considerable

economic advantage in uniting the labourers under one management, and, so far as is possible, either in one building or buildings nearly adjacent. For in the first place the most difficult and valuable kind of labour, that of management, is thus both economized and made more efficient in important respects, e.g. it is easier to adapt the product to the changing needs and tastes of society when all the required changes in production can be carried out under one direction; again, a more exact adjustment is possible of the supply of each kind of labour required, so that every class of producers can be kept in full work; and further, there is less loss of labour and time in carrying the product in different stages from one set of producers to another, and taking care of it till it is wanted. (ibid. 112)

An interesting feature of Sidgwick's argument is the distinction between the technical and the economic factors influencing the 'size' of a productive establishment, and the idea that, 'when the operations to be performed on the same material . . . are merely successive', production within large establishments is an 'economic advantage' rather than a technical requirement. This latter case is given prominence in Marshall's theory of large-scale production, which we shall examine in the following section.

3.4.2. *Large-scale production and the industrial district in Marshall's* Pure Theory of Domestic Values *and the* Principles

An early attempt to apply the classical theory of division of labour to the network formed by a system of interlinked productive establishments is to be found in Marshall's paper *The Pure Theory of Domestic Values*:

[T]he customary method of treating the advantages of division of labour and of production on a large scale appears . . . to be in one respect defective. For the manner in which these advantages are discussed in most Economic treatises is such as to imply that the most important of them can as a rule be obtained only by the concentration of large masses of workmen in vast establishments. If this were the rule, it would be reasonable to object that the introduction of economies into the process of manufacture does not depend directly and in the main on the magnitude of the total amount of the commodity produced. It may indeed be argued that an industry which gives employment to only some twenty thousand men altogether may happen to be concentrated in the hands of a few large firms, and may thus have command over most of the more important advantages of production on a large scale. And it may be argued that industries of far larger dimensions may be conducted almost entirely by small masters.   (Marshall, 1930 [1879]: 7)

The possibility mentioned in the last part of the above passage gives Marshall the clue to explaining the survival of small establishments:

[T]he advantages of production on a large scale can in general be as well attained by the aggregation of a large number of small masters into one district as by the erection of a few large works . . . [T]he advantages which are generally classed under the heads of division of labour and production on a large scale can be attained almost as fully by the aggregation into one district of many establishments of a moderate size as by the erection of a few huge factories. (ibid.)

Marshall gives three reasons for the existence of industrial districts:

Firstly, with regard to many classes of commodities it is possible to divide the process of production into several stages, each of which can be performed with the maximum of economy in small establishments . . . If there exist a large number of such small establishments, specialised for the performance of a particular stage of the process of production, there will be room for the profitable investment of capital in the organising of subsidiary industries adapted for meeting their special wants. The most important of these subsidiary industries fall chiefly into two groups. One of these groups is occupied with making the special tools and machinery required for this stage of the production . . . The other group of subsidiary industries is occupied with collecting and distributing the various materials and other commodities which are required by the small establishments in question, and with collecting and distributing the produce of their work . . . Secondly, among the most important of the economies which are available in the production of many classes of commodities are those which are concerned with the education of specialised skill. When large masses of men in the same locality are engaged in similar tasks, it is found that, by associating with one another, they educate one another. To use a mode of speaking which workmen themselves use, the skill required for their work 'is in the air, and children breathe it as they grow up' . . . Thirdly, if the total number of firms engaged in a particular industry is small, there are but few men in a position to make improvements in the processes of manufacture, to invent new machines and new methods. But when the total number of men interested in the matter is very large there are to be found among them many who, by their intellect and temper, are fitted to originate new ideas. Each new idea is canvassed and improved upon by many minds; each new accidental experience and each deliberate experiment will afford food for reflection and for new suggestions, not to a few persons but to many. Thus in a large localised industry new ideas are likely to be started rapidly: and each new idea is likely to be fertile of practical improvements. (ibid. 8–9)

The idea that, in the case of certain commodities, a large output can be obtained by dividing the production process into specialized operations and processes, and that these latter may be operated either in large or in small establishments, is taken up again in Marshall's *Principles*:

Many of those economies in the use of specialized skill and machinery which are commonly regarded as within the reach of very large establishments, do not depend on the size of individual factories. Some depend on the aggregate volume of production of the kind in the neighbourhood; while others, especially those connected with the growth of knowledge and the progress of the arts, depend chiefly on the aggregate volume of production in the whole civilized world. And here we may introduce two technical terms. We may divide the economies arising from an increase in the scale of production of any kind of goods, into two classes—firstly, those dependent on the general development of the industry; and, secondly, those dependent on the resources of the individual houses of business engaged in it, on their organization and the efficiency of their management. We may call the former *external economies*, and the latter *internal economies*. (Marshall, 1961 [1891]: i. 265–6)

In particular, there are production processes in which the internal economies due to the use of specialized machinery may be achieved at quite moderate scales:

There are . . . some trades in which the advantages which a large factory derives from the economy of machinery almost vanish as soon as a moderate size has been reached. For instance in cotton spinning, and calico weaving, a comparatively small factory will hold its own and give constant employment to the best known machines for every process: so that a large factory is only several parallel smaller factories under one roof . . . In such cases the large business gains little or no economy in machinery. (Marshall, 1961 [1890]: i. 281)

Marshall's treatment of the minimum economic size of a productive establishment is based on the idea that, in any given state of technical knowledge, there is a maximum feasible specialization of 'skill and machinery'. In such circumstances, any further increase of production scale would result, in Marshall's opinion, in the mere repetition of the basic unit of production in which maximum internal economies are already achieved ('a large factory is only several parallel smaller factories under one roof'). Marshall's opinion partly reflects the analysis of Babbage (see section 3.2.3), but no mention is made of Babbage's own 'law of multiples'. In particular, the idea, characteristic of Babbage, that, in any given state of technical know-ledge, the maximum feasible division of labour can be maintained only if production scale is increased stepwise, is not given any prominence in Marshall's analysis of large-scale production, which he considers to be a necessary and sufficient condition for greater division of labour and higher efficiency, rather than a simple pre-requisite of it, as in the theories of Gioja, Babbage, and Marx.

The core of Marshall's argument may be found in *The Economics of Industry*:

It will be useful to refer to the Law of Division of Labour, which may be stated thus:

When the demand of a commodity becomes very large, the process of making it is generally divided among several distinct classes of workers, each with its proper appliances, and each aided by Subsidiary industries; for such a division diminishes the difficulty of making the commodity.

Anticipating a term which will be defined later on, we may say:

The Cost of production of a manufactured commodity is diminished whenever an increase in the demand for it leads to an increased division of labour in making it. The Law of Division of Labour implies that an increase in the amount of capital and labour which is applied to any process of manufacture is likely to cause a more than proportionally increased return. It is therefore sometimes called the Law of Increasing Return, so as to bring out the contrast in which it stands to the Law of Diminishing Return which applies to agriculture.   (A. Marshall and M. Marshall, 1879: 57)

The idea that the unit cost of production of many commodities is a continuous, monotonically decreasing function of the scale of pro-duction is further developed in book iv of the *Principles*:

The general argument of the present Book shows that an increase in the aggregate volume of production of anything will generally increase the size, and therefore the internal economies possessed by . . . a representative firm; that it will always increase the external economies to which the firm has access; and thus will enable it to manufacture at a less than proportional cost of labour and sacrifice than before.   (Marshall, 1961 [1891]: i. 318)

The *law of increasing return* may be worded thus: An increase of labour and capital leads generally to improved organization, which increases the efficiency of the work of labour and capital.   (Marshall, 1961 [1890]: i. 318)

3.4.3. *The 'law of multiples', productive size, and the structure of industry*

The introduction of the factory system, in which a single machine, or a system of machines, takes on most of the tasks that were previously done by specialized operators, induced a number of writers to consider large establishments as a permanent feature of modern industry (see in particular Ure, 1835; Marx, 1983 [1867]). But closer study of machinery led technologists and economists to revise this judgement. Franz Reuleaux, one of the founders of modern kinetics, pointed out that the evolution of machinery is characterized by the simultaneous action of two distinct factors:

the widespread, or rather dominant, view that machinery was born of the need to use motive force . . . As I have shown, the idea of designing a machine was, rather, inspired by the need to obtain a certain definite motion. Of course, the question of force was always of importance in the history of mechanical progress, but it was always expressed through the kinetic relationships on which that progress is based. There are thus two strands of thought underlying the need for machinery; the more important and earlier one is the need to obtain a series of distinct motions; the other is the need to have motive force available . . . Even in our times, and notwithstanding the principle that force and motion should never be considered separately, the above distinction is necessary, since for machines of one kind the dominant characteristic is the abundance of force, while for machines of the other kind it is the richness of motions.   (Reuleaux, 1876: 220–1; my translation)

Reuleaux applied the distinction between machines designed to deliver a certain amount of force and those designed to produce certain movements, in his study of the relationship between the introduction of machinery and the size of productive establishments:

A close examination of the textile industry shows that the dominant element in this industry is not the operating machine, the loom, which can be bought at a low price, but rather the steam engine. Only a large amount of capital permits the purchase and utilization of a powerful motor, around which the remaining parts of the plant are organized, even if their association with the motor is not a technological necessity. . . . This is clearly an instance of a general principle. The operating machine, in many cases, is not a unity, but can be divided and applied in many repeated units within the same productive establishment. The steam-engine keeps all these machines together, without forming of them an indivisible unit. The single operating machine is not too expensive; indeed the 'machinofacture' tries to provide it at increasingly lower price and higher quality.   (ibid. 480–1)

The difference between operating machines and power-generating machines with respect to the dimension of divisibility allows Reuleaux to draw important consequences about the prospects of small and medium-size establishments:

In order to eliminate the ill-effects of centralization [of production], the science of mechanics ought to provide *small and economical motors*. Let us provide the small entrepreneur with the same cheap motive power, which the large steam-engine provides to the large-scale capitalist, and we shall establish an important social class, we shall reinforce it where it already exists, we shall bring it to new life where it is disappearing. (ibid. 482)

Reuleaux's argument that large productive units are not a necessary outcome of technological development was reinforced by a number of studies on the relationship between machinery and the division of labour. Ure and Marx had noted that the pattern of specialization considered by Smith and Babbage tends to disappear in modern industry (Ure, 1835; Marx, 1983 [1867]). Marshall followed their lead by arguing that 'machinery constantly supplants and renders unnecessary that purely manual skill the attainment of which was, even up to A. Smith's time, the chief advantage of division of labour' (Marshall, 1961, [1890]: 256). Paul Leroy-Beaulieu countered this argument by pointing out that 'division of labour . . . is a phenomenon completely different from the simple division of professions, and has deeper effects' (Leroy-Beaulieu, 1896: 334–5; my translation). As a result, he claims, we may find important applications of the basic principles of division of labour not only in the type of manufacturing considered by Smith but in modern industry as well. The reason is that 'division of labour is, so to speak, a process of analysis which, by breaking down the most complex production activities into increasingly simple elementary constituents, induces and permits the introduction of machines' (p. 338).

Division of labour was thus coming to be considered a much more general phenomenon than the one originally studied by Smith, Gioja, and Babbage. This led Pasquale Jannaccone to stress that the 'Gioja–Babbage principle' applies not only to the case of human labour but also 'to any other element of a production process' (Jannaccone, 1904: 248; my translation). In this context, Jannaccone called attention to an important application of Babbage's law of multiples for the explanation of the size of productive establishments:

An increase in the level of output brings about a decrease in unit cost as long as it is possible to maintain the maximum utilization of productive factors, particularly of fixed capital . . . But if the return from an arbitrary factor of production is already associated with maximum utilization, a further output increase requires the employment of an additional unit of that factor; and if the quantity of output delivered by this second unit cannot be equal to the maximum quantity delivered by the first unit, the unit cost of the whole produce will increase . . . Now, this also applies to the concentration of many stages of production in the same establishment, for it is likely that the quantity of semi-finished output which is needed to obtain the most economical quantity of final output does not allow maximum utilization of the factors needed to obtain the semi-finished output. It follows that the concentration of production affects only some of the operations needed to obtain the final output; and such a concentration normally follows the sequence of production operations, and very seldom affects what we have called side-factories. For the quantity of goods and services that side-factories must deliver for the production of final output would not allow, in the case of concentration, their maximum utilization. As a result, only exceptionally will any given enterprise find it advantageous to have its own railway, its own source of electric power, and so forth. (Jannaccone, 1904: 311–12; my translation)

In Jannaccone's analysis, productive size is explained by technical factors. For in a large establishment both the following conditions must be satisfied: (i) the maximum feasible division of labour, which requires a large number of simultaneous operations in a single establishment; (ii) the full-capacity utilization of all the inputs used in making any 'semi-finished' output. As a result, the semi-finished outputs that cannot fully employ the inputs in question if they are made within the establishment are likely to be produced in separate establishments.

The technical influences affecting the size of productive establishments are also considered in Marshall's *Industry and Trade* (1920 [1919], esp. bk. ii. ch. 3). Marshall's argument there may be summarized as follows:

(i) Production processes which need to handle large single masses of homogeneous material are generally carried out in large establishments.

(ii) Production processes in which a continuous stream of homogeneous materials is automatically carried from one operation to the next are also performed, in general, in large establishments.

(iii) Production processes in which it is desirable to switch resources from one specialized use to another, in order to meet fluctuations of demand, are generally performed in large establishments.

(iv) Production processes which do not permit a great division of labour are generally performed in small establishments.

(v) Production processes characterized by the use of many task-specific inputs may be carried out either in large or in small establishments, depending on the special characteristics of each process.

Case (i) is illustrated by the heavy steel industries: 'There is no other group of industries, in which the forces making for the increase of the business unit are promoted in like degree by the magnitude of the aggregate volume of the homogeneous fluid material which has to be produced, and by the magnitude of the individual masses to be handled. Further, there is no other group of industries in which the higher and lower stages work for one another so steadily and on so large a scale' (Marshall, 1920 [1919]: 218–19). An important consequence of the technical indivisibility which is thus introduced is that full-capacity utilization is possible on condition that scale is varied discretely: 'a furnace is not amenable to discipline. It will not work economically except at nearly full pressure: it must be laid by for repairs occasionally; and, therefore, *complete efficiency is to be obtained only by the presence in a single establishment of a good many blast furnaces that are individually of the modern pattern*, in order that a business may be able to adjust total output to varying activities of demand' (ibid. 219; my italics).

Case (ii) is considered to be of particular importance in 'setting up the component parts of an intricate mechanism' (ibid. 237). A 'striking instance' of this type of productive organization is found by Marshall in the Ford automobile factory, where,

[a] standard form and size of chassis having been adopted, all its component parts are made to standard shape by automatic machinery. These appendages, etc., are stored, each in a separate compartment, connected by a slide running down to an appropriate place in a central room. Here is an endless conveyer, which completes a round in about an hour. A frame is put on this: as it reaches each slide, the appropriate part is fixed on it, by men who act . . . automatically, promptly and easily . . . [A]t the end of its round the frame is a complete chassis . . . [T]he method is likely to put a large part of the industries that are most characteristic of the modern age, almost exclusively under the control of giant businesses. (ibid. 237–8)

The production of textiles presents a wide range of productive organizations, from small establishments requiring individual care for certain delicate tasks, and thus offering little scope for division of labour (case (iv)) to large establishments equipped with a vast pool of specialized inputs and permitting a certain degree of flexibility in the productive structure (case (iii)). An example of the former type of organization is found in the woollen and worsted industries. Such industries 'deal with materials which are very variable in character: and nearly all their products, except such things as blankets, are made for consumers who are under the influence of western fluctuations of fashion . . . As a rule all the various stages of woollen cloth making (exclusive of dyeing and finishing), are carried on together in rather small factories: for they yield no very great economies of production on a large scale, and individual care and judgement as to details are incessantly required' (Marshall, 1920 [1919]: 231).[7] But an example of the latter type of productive organization (large and flexible establishments) is given by the final operations of textile production (dyeing and finishing). The reason for this is that

[i]t soon became clear that the resources of a cloth factory could not offer nearly as great a variety of refined finish, as could be got by large firms, each of which gave its whole energies to a particular form of finishing. Every such firm, or rather company, is equipped with vast and various special apparatus, and with high technical skill. It can thus bring the appropriate part of extensive technical forces to bear on each task, which it undertakes: the same highly specialized task often needs to be performed at about the same time on a great variety of goods, coming from many customers and designed for many purposes; and thus it is able to obtain

---

[7] The fact that division of labour might conflict with the need to control the execution of productive operations had already been stressed by Sidgwick: 'In industries whose produce tends to be largely, yet somewhat indefinitely, increased or preserved by minute and vigilant attention to details, together with occasional intensity of effort to meet emergencies, the keen interest which the employer feels in the result is a peculiarly important spring of effective labour. In such industries, therefore, it may be economically best—even at a partial sacrifice of the advantages of division of labour—to organize the separate businesses on a scale so small as to enable the employer's supervision to be everywhere effective, or even to render oversight almost unnecessary, the chief labour being that of the employer himself and his family' (Sidgwick, 1883: 113–14). Sidgwick's remarks had been anticipated in Mill's analysis of *grande* and *petite* culture: 'The most apparently impartial and discriminating judgement that I have met with is that of M. Passy, who (always speaking with reference to *net* produce) gives his verdict in favour of large farms for grain and forage; but, for the kinds of culture which require much labour and attention, places the advantage wholly on the side of small cultivation; including in this description, not only the wine and the olive, where a considerable amount of care and labour must be bestowed on each individual plant, but also roots, leguminous plants, and those which furnish the materials of manufactures' (Mill, 1965 [1848]: 151).

many of the advantages of continuous process, even in regard to small transactions. (ibid. 232)

Standardization (the production of a single type of component used as an input in several different processes) makes it possible to increase division of labour by splitting a complex production process into a number of separate tasks, and having each such task performed in a special establishment. This phenomenon may be found in either large or small establishments, depending on the characteristics of each separate operation (case (iii)) (see also Becattini, 1987: 890–1). But modern technology often makes small and medium-sized establishments possible, provided they adopt an appropriate pattern of specialization:

The same standard girders are used with advantage in thousands of different sorts of buildings, and appliances for use on land and sea: while the same standard screws are used for hundreds of thousands of different purposes: and this contrast is of special significance in regard to the contest between giant businesses and those of moderate size. For even the largest business has but a small output as compared with that of an industrial country; and therefore the small producers can often buy particular components, that have been made for open market by aid of larger economies of massive production than are at the command of any single business. (Marshall, 1920 [1919]: 227)

In particular, Marshall points out that standardization sometimes made it possible to have medium-sized establishments in productive branches that had previously seen vertical concentration in large productive units:

We have seen how the application of water power to spinning collected that branch of the industry into factories, while hand-weaving remained in the cottages: but the power-loom needed factories. At first it was a rough and untrustworthy instrument, likely to deal harshly with the yarn; and the only people who had the technical knowledge and other facilities for the management of textile factories were master spinners. So the growth of machinery seemed at once to crush out the small man, and to bring under one roof the successive processes of a great industry. But all the while machinery was preparing the way for undoing this vertical consolidation: for improvements in spinning gradually enabled yarn to be made with such absolute certainty and precision to any standard requirement, that the weaver could buy it in open market, or even contract for it in advance, with confidence that he could get what he needed; and the loom became both more powerful and gentler. (ibid. 229–30)

Marshall's attempt to give a comprehensive account of the technical factors influencing the size of productive establishments was followed by a number of contributions in which particular aspects of Marshall's analysis are emphasized and extended.

E. A. G. Robinson stressed the importance of two distinct factors: division of labour and integration of processes. Division of labour is considered, as in Marshall, to be a phenomenon that might give rise both to large establishments permitting the full utilization of inputs fully specialized in particular tasks and to establishments specializing in a particular process. This makes it possible to have small productive establishments, even when 'some given process requires a scale of production considerably greater than the smaller firms in an industry can achieve' (Robinson, 1931: 26). The reason for this is that the above process

tends to be separated off from the main industry, and all the smaller firms . . . get this particular process performed for them by an outside specialist firm. Thus the industry becomes broken up into two or more industries, and each is enabled to work at its most convenient scale of production. The specialist firm, working for a number of the smaller firms, is on a larger scale than any of the individual firms could have achieved for that particular process or product. Examples of this principle may be found in the finishing stages of the textile industries, and in the manufacture of various component parts, such as radiators, electrical equipment wings, chassis-frames, and crankshafts and other forgings, in the motor industry. (ibid.)

The integration of processes, on the other hand, is associated with the mechanization of a sequence of productive operations, and is thus similar to that 'economy of consecutive highly specialized operations' to which Marshall had already called economists' attention. In this case, '[t]he process of the division of labour is being reversed: one large machine can be designed to take over what has hitherto been done by a series of manual, or less completely mechanical operations' (ibid. 25). A characteristic example of the integration of processes is found in productive establishments where 'two or three or more consecutive processes are performed by a more complicated machine which thereby eliminates the labour and time required to set up the work on each of the successive earlier machines' (ibid.). The integration of processes normally requires large establishments. An additional principle working in favour of large establishments is the need to maintain a balance between different processes so that all units of productive factors 'can conveniently be used approximately to their full capacity' (ibid. 33). This latter influence on the determination of size explains why '[a] mill of about 100,000 mule spindles will employ, perhaps, one bale breaker, two double openers, four single scutchers, one hundred carding engines, some twelve drawing frames, eight slubbing frames, nineteen intermediate frames, fifty-two jack frames, eighty mules' (ibid. 33–4). The reason for this is that '[a] cotton firm must be of such size that all these various units may be conveniently combined without any wastes from partially employed equipment' (ibid. 34). Robinson's balance of processes calls attention to a factor which is at the root of Babbage's law of multiples, and stresses a phenomenon which was largely overlooked by Marshall.

The simultaneous existence of small and large establishments in the same productive branch was also examined by P. Sargant Florence. In this author's view, the existence of small establishments is explained by two factors: (i) the difficulties of supervision and management, which tend to increase with size; (ii) the existence of a network of establishments, each specializing in a single operation or in a small number of operations. Florence's analysis of this latter issue recalls Marshall's study of the industrial district:

in the extraction-to-consumer sequence of production, the Western economy allows the widest variety of division of labour and function. A small firm may be relieved of its marketing by large wholesale houses, and of its finance and capital-raising by banks, by landlords (e.g. rented shops and farms), or in other ways such as free roads for road transport, or the shoe industry's rental of machines; may be relieved of earlier or later processes by neighbouring factories in a localized production centre, of research by trade associations, universities or the State. In short, a group of specialists may grow up around the small firm either locally or (like publishers of trade journals) nationally, yielding external economies, which allow that firm to operate a single process or product on a large scale.   (Florence, 1961 [1953]: 65)

Florence's stress on the similarity between division of labour in an individual establishment and inter-establishment specialization of production is based on a general formulation of the law of multiples, which applies to any network of productive operations:

Any given specialization of equipment or men involves for balanced production a large scale of operation or production; but conversely it is only a large scale of operation or production that admits of specialization with all its well-known economic advantages. It is only large-scale production that will justify a special research organization, intensive costing, or the working up of by-products able to occupy researchers, cost accountants or by-product plant profitably for their full time. Thus a *virtuous circle* is established. Specialization leads to higher common multiples, higher common multiples to greater specialization.   (ibid. 52)

An important application of the above law of multiples is found in the case of division of labour between establishments in the same area:

what has not been valued at its true importance in a large localization of an industry is the possibility of division of labour between plants in 'linked' processes, products and service industries. The advantage of full use of specialist plants can be combined with proximity. Several specialized plants, if close enough together, may have much the same economies as the separate departments of a large plant.   (ibid. 85)

Both Robinson and Florence stress that the most efficient division of labour may in principle be achieved either by operating large establishments or by having a network of establishments, usually of different sizes, and specialized in a limited number of productive operations. In both cases, the division of labour permits any establishment to take advantage of the principle that 'by dividing the work to be executed into different processes, each requiring different degrees of skill or of force', it is possible to 'purchase exactly that precise quantity of both which is necessary for each process' (Babbage, 1835: 175). Both types of organization presuppose large-scale production, in the sense that, in both cases, a large number of different operations have to be performed at the same time by a certain number of specialized inputs.

Both Robinson and Florence associate large-scale production with a large output per unit of time of a given commodity or commodity basket. In other words, both these authors overlook the possibility, which had been stressed by Marshall, that the scale of production associated with maximum division of labour might be compatible with a *flexible* composition of output. (Consider Marshall's example, quoted above, of the large firm specializing in the final tasks of textile production and able 'to obtain many of the advantages of continuous process, even in regard to small transactions', because of the flexibility of its capital equipment.) Edith Penrose further examined this latter issue, pointing out that the process by which any given firm expands its size normally provides opportunities for output diversification. The reason for this is as follows. First, a growing specialization in the use of productive resources (itself a consequence of large size) tends to lead to further expansion (due to the law of multiples). But the expansion required by the availability of specialized inputs is not always possible when a single commodity is being produced (this is because the demand for it might be too low). This provides an incentive for output diversification, since the multi-product firm might more easily satisfy the law of multiples while producing limited amounts of any particular commodity. The relationship between output diversification and input specialization is described as follows:

the advantage of using the specialized services of resources may themselves lead a firm to diversify its final output. It often happens, for example, that there are 'stages' in the process of production in which significant economies can be obtained if sufficient use can be made of specialized resources. This may promote diversification of final output by encouraging a firm to produce a group of products which require the same productive services at some stage, for example, products that use raw materials processed in common, or products that are sold through the same channels of distribution. In other words, if a group of products have costs in common, specialization at the point of common cost may reduce the cost of production of any one of them.   (Penrose, 1959: 73)

In Penrose's approach, the law of multiples is not only 'one cause of the great size of manufacturing establishments, which have increased with the progress of civilization' (Babbage, 1835: 213). For what is necessary in order to take advantage of the law of multiples is a sufficiently large output level; but in some cases the 'output' in question need not be of a single commodity, but rather of a group of commodities with similar input requirements. This brings about an incentive to output diversification, permitting a firm to use idle resources in the production of new commodities, and thus to maintain the full (or nearly full) utilization of productive resources.[8]

We may conclude that modern theories of division of labour

---

[8] Edith Penrose also pointed out that the combined action of the law of multiples and of the need to avoid idle resources brings about a special association between the expansion of a firm and the change in its product-mix: 'very few of the older and larger firms in the economy have continued to produce the same type of product throughout their lifetime, even when the demand for that product has risen substantially over the period. Conversely, where demand for the original products has fallen or disappeared, firms have still continued to expand. The growth of almost all large firms has been accompanied by far-reaching changes in the *composition* of the demand which the firm has considered relevant for its operations' (Penrose, 1959: 83).

share the view that the size of productive establishments is partly determined by the way in which the operations needed to produce any given commodity are combined or separated from each other, so as to become parts of a single establishment or of different establishments. This point of view is common to all the economists considered in this section, from Jannaccone to Penrose. However, Marshall's *Industry and Trade* stresses technical influences independent of the need to ensure the full utilization of inputs that have differing productive capacities, whereas all the other works call attention to this latter prerequisite, and thus also to the special type of indivisibility on which the law of multiples rests.

3.5. VARIABLE RETURNS AND INPUT PROPORTIONS: A SPECIAL CASE

Mill's formulation of the classical theory of decreasing efficiency, as a theory of the relationship between size of productive establishment and technical practice, had an important influence on the subsequent literature. In this section we shall follow the development of this literature, pointing out the difference between two fundamental models of decreasing efficiency: (i) a model in which certain inputs may be actually fixed for a producer (or a group of producers, such as an industry) in a particular real situation; (ii) a model in which a producer may 'hold an input constant' in some virtual experiment such as maximization.

Model (ii) underlay Turgot's formulation of variable returns to input scale, and becomes explicit again in Marshall's *Principles*. There we find the following formulation of the '*law of* or *statement of tendency to Diminishing Return*': '[a]n increase in the capital and labour applied in the cultivation of land causes *in general* a less than proportional increase in the amount of produce raised, unless it happens to coincide with an improvement in the arts of agriculture' (Marshall, 1961 [1890]: i. 150). This statement is followed by an example which is almost identical with Turgot's case. For, in Marshall's account, the purpose of every agriculturist

is to get as large a total crop as possible with a given expenditure of seed and labour; and therefore he sows as many acres as he can manage to bring under light cultivation. Of course he may go too far: he may spread his work over so large an area that he would gain by concentrating his capital and labour on a smaller space; and under these circumstances if he could get command over more capital and labour so as to apply more to each acre, the land would give him an *Increasing Return*: that is, an extra return larger in proportion than it gives to his present expenditure. But if he has made his calculations rightly, he is using just so much ground as will give him the highest return: and he would lose by concentrating his capital and labour on a smaller area. If he had command over more capital and labour and were to apply more to his present land, he would gain less than he would by taking up more land: he would get a *Diminishing Return*, that is, an extra return smaller in proportion than he gets for the last applications of capital and labour that he now makes, provided of course that there is meanwhile no perceptible improvement in his agricultural skill.   (ibid. 151; from the 3rd edn. of the *Principles* (1895), the word 'applications' replaced the word 'doses', dating from the 1st edn.)

This focus on the individual establishment led Marshall to adopt the same attitude as Turgot to the assumption that one essential input is fixed. For, in general, any input might be considered to be either variable or fixed, from the point of view of an individual producer, depending on the special criterion that the producer follows in determining his technical practice (in other words, any input is variable or fixed as a result of the producer's behaviour, and independently of the characteristics of individual inputs). This is shown, in Marshall's case, by the fact that the situation initially considered is one in which 'seed and labour' are given and land is variable. Such a situation, which Marshall associates with increasing returns, is clearly different from the situation considered in the second part of the passage quoted above (beginning 'If he had command over more capital and labour and were to apply more to his present land'). For in this latter case land is fixed, and 'seed and labour' are variable.

Marshall's approach was taken up and generalized by Thomas Nixon Carver, who studied the role of scarce inputs in production without giving any special emphasis to land and agricultural activities:

In the creation of any product where there are various factors employed, usually classified as labor, land, and capital, the amount of the product does not depend wholly upon any one or any two of these groups of factors, but upon all three. Consequently, if any one or any two groups are varied in amount, the rest remaining the same, the product will vary, but not in exact proportion to the variable factors. In all normal cases—that is, where the various factors have been combined in profitable proportions—if some of the factors are increased, the increase in the product will not be so great as the increase in these factors. Thus, if the land remains the same while the labor and capital are increased, the product will increase, but not in proportion to the labor and capital. Or if the labor and capital remain the same while the land is increased, the increase in the product will not be so great as the increase in the land. (Carver, 1904: 94)

The above formulation is similar to Marshall's treatment, but one important difference is now introduced: the influence of the limited availability of certain inputs is considered in terms of a general model of input co-ordination, irrespective of the particular scarcities that might arise in actual production processes. As a result, Carver makes one important step in the generalization of diminishing returns. For, in Carver's view, the law of diminishing returns is 'as true of a factory as of a farm, and, by a change of terms, all that has been said of the ratio between farm land and the labor which cultivates it could be repeated of the ratio between a manufacturing plant and the labor which operates it' (p. 74).

In this way, the groundwork was prepared for Edgeworth's statement that diminishing returns 'always rule, provided that we take sufficiently large doses' of the variable input (Edgeworth, 1911: 552). The new approach also considered increasing and diminishing returns as special cases of a general law of input co-ordination, by explaining both cases of variable returns as situations which a producer could meet when the quantity of a single input is increased and all other inputs are kept constant (i.e. by following the approach originally due to Turgot) (cf. Edgeworth, 1911: 349–52).

Both the generalization of diminishing returns and their co-ordination with increasing returns presuppose a shift from model (i) to model (ii) (see above), as well as a shift of emphasis from the consideration of a network of productive tasks (the national economy, the industry, the 'industrial district') to the consideration of the productive establishment as the fundamental unit of observation.[9] Marshall himself became aware of this change in the 1910 edition of his *Principles*. There he noted an important difference between the classical and post-classical theories of diminishing returns:

[9] Any productive establishment can also be considered as a network of productive tasks. But the economists of the period under consideration described the establishment as a *combination of inputs* rather than as a *network of operations*. This made it easier to think of variable returns as a property of the input-mix rather than as a consequence of changing technical practices.

[W]hen the older economists spoke of the Law of Diminishing Return they were looking at the problems of agriculture not only from the point of view of the individual cultivator but also from that of the nation as a whole. Now if the nation *as a whole* finds its stock of planing machines or ploughs inappropriately large or inappropriately small, it can redistribute its resources. It can obtain more of that in which it is deficient, while gradually lessening its stock of such things as are superabundant: *but it cannot do that in regard to land*: it can cultivate its land more intensively, but it cannot get any more. And for that reason the older economists rightly insisted that, from the social point of view, land is not on exactly the same footing as those implements of production which man can increase without limit.   (Marshall, 1961 [1910]: i. 170)

This discovery led Marshall to a critical view of the attempts to formulate a general law of diminishing returns, attempts to which he had himself contributed in the earlier editions of the *Principles*:

If a manufacturer expends an inappropriately large amount of his resources on machinery, so that a considerable part of it is habitually idle; or on buildings, so that a considerable part of his space is not well filled; or on his office staff, so that he has to employ some of them on work that it is not worth what it costs; then his excessive expenditure in that particular direction will not be as remunerative as his previous expenditure had been: and it may be said to yield him a 'diminishing return'. But this use of the phrase, though strictly correct is apt to mislead unless used with caution. For when the tendency to a diminishing return from increased labour and capital applied to land is regarded as a special instance of the general tendency to diminishing return from any agent of production, applied in excessive proportion to the other agents, one is apt to take it for granted that the supply of the other factors can be increased. That is to say, one is apt to deny the existence of that condition—the fixedness of the whole stock of cultivable land in an old country—which was the main foundation of those great classical discussions of the law of diminishing return, which we have just been considering.   (ibid. 169)

The assumptions underlying the classical and post-classical theories of variable returns were also examined by Piero Sraffa. In particular, Sraffa noted:

If we define each particular industry as the exclusive consumer of a given *factor of production* (like agriculture or the iron industry) then we are certainly introducing an assumption which tends to give rise to a tendency to increasing costs in that industry, since the factor characteristic of that industry (productive land, iron-mines, etc.) remains, in general, constant when production is increased.   (Sraffa, 1925: 320; my translation)

Such an assumption is sufficient to generate a tendency to increasing cost, if we consider the classical theories (which are theories of diminishing returns for whole productive sectors). But the same assumption might not generate diminishing returns, if we adopt the point of view of the post-classical theories (in which the variable returns studied are those of individual establishments). In this latter case, diminishing returns can be explained in terms of a 'scarce factor', on condition that 'the number of producers is fixed and that each of them, by increasing his output, cannot increase the quantity employed by him of the productive factor which is given for the whole industry' (ibid. 301). Such an assumption implies that 'the identity of each firm is not only determined by the unit of management, i.e. by the entrepreneur, but also by the consideration of one unit of the "constant" factor' (ibid.). In the absence of the 'constant factor' assumption, production in the individual establishment might take place under conditions of constant or diminishing unit cost, even in production processes using an input that is given for the whole industry:

it is . . . possible that, while the industry faces conditions of increasing costs, the individual producer could increase his output, up to a certain point, by diminishing his particular cost of production, provided that he may take advantage of the economies of large scale production; and, rather than being forced into utilizing the constant factor more intensively, he might get a larger amount of this factor by depriving his competitors of it.   (ibid.)

Sraffa also stressed one important difference between the classical and post-classical theories of increasing efficiency, when he noted that post-classical theories focus on the functional relation between the output of particular commodities and their unit cost, whereas in the classical theory of increasing efficiency 'the functional relation between quantity produced and production cost (itself the expression of the law of non-proportional productivity) was never in the foreground' (p. 279).[10] (See also Bullock, 1902.)

---

[10] Sraffa's remark applies strictly only to the treatment of increasing efficiency in Smith. A number of writers of the classical period (such as Gioja, Babbage, and Mill) treated the case of scale-dependent increasing efficiency. However, 'scale' refers, in their writings, to the 'size' of the productive establishment rather than to the quantity produced. In addition, the functional relation between 'scale' and production cost which they consider is discrete rather than continuous (with the exception of Mill). In this century, the Smithian approach has been taken up by Young (1928), Stigler (1951), and Kaldor (1966). The latter, however, has combined Smith's emphasis

The post-classical theories of decreasing and increasing efficiency gave prominence to a type of relation (continuous cost–quantity functions) different from the phenomena considered in the classical theories. After the first formulations of the post-classical approach, a number of economists (including Marshall) became aware of the shift that had occurred in the transition from the classical to the post-classical approach, and pointed out that the apparent generality of the post-classical approach is itself the result of a particular view of the production process: the view focusing on technical practice as a particular input combination in a single productive establishment. But this latter view has maintained its prominence in modern economic theory, as is shown both by the recent literature on scale–efficiency relations and by the treatment of variable returns in the general equilibrium literature. In the former case, the relation of scale to efficiency is associated with special assumptions concerning the way in which inputs are co-ordinated with one another in a single establishment (see e.g. Menger, 1954; Carlson, 1956; Frisch, 1965; Frank, 1969; Shephard, 1970; Färe, 1988).[11] In the latter case, scale–efficiency relations are described by means of assumptions about the production possibility set (the set of all feasible input–output vectors). This approach adopts the Turgot–Edgeworth model of scale–efficiency within a single productive unit to derive scale–efficiency

upon division of labour in manufacturing with the consideration of the positive influence of a high rate of growth of output upon the productivity of labour, which was originally discussed by Verdoorn (1949).

[11] Frank derives increasing returns to scale from the consideration of an input–output set characterized by 'integer convexity' (a set Y is integer-convex if, whenever y belongs to the convex hull of Y and y_i is an integer for all indivisible commodities, then y belongs to Y). In this case, an input–output combination shows increasing returns for integer changes in scale: 'any output may be more than doubled with a doubling of all other inputs and outputs or . . . any input may be less than doubled (in absolute value terms) with a doubling of all other inputs and outputs' (Frank, 1969: 43). Shephard derives weak and strong forms of a physical law of diminishing returns from certain properties of the production function, after noting that 'a law of diminishing returns in the physical output of production has played a central role in the marginal analysis of economic theory, stating in some fashion that the output from production will eventually suffer decreasing increments or decreasing average return if the inputs of some factors of production are fixed and the others are increased indefinitely by some equal increments. Divorced of its reference solely to agriculture, diminishing returns are taken as a fundamental law for technology to support economic theories of equilibrium and price determination' (Shephard, 1970: 7). The relationship between the law of variable proportions and the requirement of *fixed* proportions between certain inputs is considered in Danø, 1966 (an early treatment of the corresponding 'law of definite proportions' may be found in Valenti, 1905; see also Baldone, 1990).

relations for the whole economy. An example is provided by Debreu's *Theory of Value*, in which the input–output possibilities of individual establishments are related to the input–output possibilities of the whole economy in the following way:

For a producer, say the *j*th one, a production plan . . . is a specification of the quantities of all his inputs and all his outputs; *outputs* are represented by *positive* numbers, *inputs* by *negative* numbers. With this convention a production plan, or more briefly a *production*, is represented by a point y_j of R^l, the commodity space. A given production y_j may be technically possible or technically impossible for the *j*th producer. The set y_j of all the productions possible for the *j*th producer is called his *production set* . . . Given a production for each producer, the sum

$$y = \sum_{j=1}^{n} y_j$$

is called the *total production* . . . In forming this sum one cancels out all commodity transfers from producers to producers (each such transfer appears once as an output with positive sign and once as an input with negative sign); *y* describes therefore the *net* result of the activity of all producers together. That is to say, the positive coordinates of *y* represent outputs of producers not transferred to the productive sector; the negative coordinates represent inputs of producers not transferred from the productive sector. The set

$$Y = \sum_{j=1}^{n} Y_j$$

is called the *total production set* . . . The last set describes the production possibilities of the whole economy.   (Debreu, 1959: 37–8)

The assumption that each producer works under conditions of decreasing or constant returns to scale is expressed by assuming the convexity of all individual production sets. But this assumption implies the convexity of the total production set Y (cf. de Montbrial, 1974: 18–19). Decreasing or constant returns for the whole economy are thus derived by assuming that *individual* production sets possess the same property.

PART II

A Task–Process Theory of Production

4

The Elements of Production Processes and the Role of Time

4.1. INTRODUCTION

In the course of this research it was found that the analysis of the relationship between scale and technical practice often requires a more detailed representation of production processes than is normally given in the economic literature. Both 'neoclassical' production functions and linear production models focus on the relationships between input quantities and output levels, and tend to overlook the complex organization of productive operations that is needed in actual processes. But there are important links between output levels and technical practices which cannot be seen at all, unless one looks behind the input–output relationships and examines how changes in output levels may depend on changes in the organization of productive operations within each productive establishment, or within any other type of productive unit.

The range of feasible technical practices may vary because of the influence of output levels on input shortages and on the time-arrangement of productive operations. (As will be seen in Chapter 4, the time-arrangement of productive operations in an establishment may depend on the output level per unit of time.) By *technology expansion*, I shall mean an addition to the range of feasible practices. By *technology contraction*, I shall mean a subtraction from the range of such practices. (Formal definitions of these two concepts are given in sections 5.1 and 6.2 respectively.) By *scale-dependent technical change*, I shall mean the change of technical practice that results from (i) a change in some output levels and (ii) technology contraction or technology expansion. The *network description* of production allows for a detailed consideration of the relationships among the operations carried out within a productive unit, including the 'precedence relations' among these operations.[1]

---

[1] The 'network' approach is seldom used by economists, but is generally followed in the literature on production-control problems; see e.g. Bryton (1954), Kilbridge and Wester (1962), Abruzzi (1965), and Bakshi and Arora (1969).

To a network description of a given productive activity there corresponds a unique input–output description of the same activity, whereas a given input–output pattern is compatible with more than one network of productive operations (see section 4.4). It follows that the network description provides the more general framework for the analysis of production phenomena. This should not be seen as introducing unnecessary complications, since the input–output description may be used whenever we do not need to focus on the time-arrangement of productive operations.

4.2. TASKS AND TOOLS

The network description of production is based on the concept of *productive task* (or simply *task*). A task is a completed operation usually performed without interruption on some particular object. It is not further divisible (at least for the purposes of the analysis in hand).[2]

An expression such as 'cutting a piece of wood of type A' is an example of a description of a task. The name of a task always has a verb component (performing a task implies an action or a change from one state to another), but the verb is not a sufficient description of the task: 'cutting' describes a general action, not a task. In order to describe a task completely we need to consider the object on which the action is performed or the object that is undergoing a change. The reason for this is that human production is generally an activity designed to serve particular purposes, so that 'cutting' as a general action would not be a task. Under most circumstances, even 'wood-cutting' (i.e. cutting *any* piece of wood) would not be a task, for the objective under consideration would generally require cutting a piece of wood of given characteristics. 'Cutting a piece of wood of type A' is thus, in general, a different task from 'cutting a piece of wood of

---

[2] The identification of tasks is always arbitrary, at least to a certain degree. There may, however, be some 'natural characterization' of tasks. In this connection, it has been noted that if 'an input is observed to perform some action several times, it is "natural" to define such an action, performed once, as an activity [a task], and to say that it was performed several times. Thus, if the actions of each input are observed in the process (during T) in sequence, a "natural" set of activities {a} performed by all employed inputs is defined such that all repetition within each activity is eliminated. For example, if an input attaches a bolt to a wheel 100 times, the action of attaching a bolt is defined as a natural activity; this activity is performed 100 times' (Ippolito, 1977: 491).

type B', unless, for the objective under consideration, it is immaterial what piece of wood is being cut.

It often happens that a tool is needed in order to perform a task: 'cutting a piece of wood of type A' may require the use of a lathe. But the task is completely identified without mentioning which tool is used. This is illustrated by the fact that producers may perform the same task ('cutting a piece of wood of type A') by using tools of different kinds.

A statement like 'cutting a piece of wood of type A with lathe x' is not simply the description of a task, but the description of a task *and* of the way in which it is performed. In general, there is no one-to-one correspondence between tasks and tools: it is possible to perform a given task by using tools of various kinds, and to use a given tool in order to perform different tasks, at the same time or at different times.[3]

The relationship between tasks and tools is essential to understanding the problem of tool utilization. The lack of a one-to-one correspondence between tasks and tools makes it possible to distinguish two dimensions of tool utilization: (i) the number of tasks performed by a given tool at the same time; (ii) the fraction of the working day during which a given tool is active.

Utilization in the former sense is involved in saying that a tool is *fully used*: we may say this when it performs, at a given time, the maximum number of tasks. Utilization in the latter sense is involved in saying that a tool is *continuously used*: we may say this when it is used (not necessarily always fully) at every moment of the working day. Full utilization throughout the working day implies continuous utilization, but continuous utilization does not imply full utilization. In other words, any given tool may be under-utilized for two different reasons: (i) the number of tasks that the tool performs at any given time is too small; and (ii) the tool remains idle (i.e. it does

---

[3] The above relationship between tasks and tools has been recognized also in the theory of machinery: 'Even spade . . . derives its identity not from itself alone but from its mechanical contact with what it digs . . . Since Reuleaux (1875) we have known how to regard the motion of any part of a machine as occurring against a frame attached to any other part of the same machine. The idea of frame itself, of course, came very much earlier from Descartes' (Phillips, 1984: 1). In the present formulation, the general concept of tool also refers to a machine. An early distinction between tools and machines from the point of view of their respective operational principles may be found in Ampère (1834: 50–1); see also Rolt (1986). A classical treatment of the common analytical features of tools and machines from the point of view of economic theory may be found in Rae (1834).

not perform any task) during parts of the working day. Economies of speed may be achieved both by shortening the duration of tasks and by reducing (or eliminating) fund-input idleness. But if task durations are parametrically given, economies of speed may only be achieved by reducing fund-input idleness.

4.3. ELEMENTARY PROCESSES AND PRODUCTION PROCESSES

4.3.1. *The basic framework*

The productive activities carried out within any given productive unit consist of arrangements of tasks over time. Such arrangements may be represented as task networks having *terminal nodes* or *sinks*.[4]

We shall call an *elementary process* (e.p.) any time-arrangement of tasks operated between two consecutive terminal nodes of the same task network.[5]

The e.p. is an arrangement of tasks leading to what might be considered as one output unit from the point of view of the productive unit under consideration. (This is a consequence of the fact that task-definitions are 'scaled', due to the size of the object descriptions appearing in each definition.) Such an output unit would often be a *batch* of marketable goods, and should not be confused with an output unit from the buyer's point of view. Within any given e.p. there may be precedence relations between tasks. Such relations define the precedence pattern characteristic of the e.p. under consideration.

A *production process* (or simply a *process*) is the arrangement of e.p.s operated within a productive unit during the working day. Such e.p.s may be of the same type or of different types. The number of e.p.s simultaneously operated within a productive unit is the *scale* of the process (even if simultaneously operated e.p.s are of different types). A special case would be that of a process consisting of a single e.p. at any given time.

---

[4] *Terminal node* or *sink* is the task that 'completes a job', in the sense that, once it is performed, another identical job (corresponding to an identical-task network) may be started.

[5] An elementary process (e.p.) is a way of producing some product so that a change in product-description is likely to bring about a change in the task-composition of the e.p. (a certain arrangement of tasks may be an e.p. in one type of production but not in another). E.g. making matches is not an elementary process in a plant whose output is *boxes of matches*.

4.3.2. *Straight-line and job-shop production processes*

The relationship between tasks and e.p.s within a process, and the way in which workers and tools execute them in a productive unit, may differ greatly from one type of productive organization to another (see also Perrin, 1990). In this study we shall assume that, in spite of this variety, all production processes are of the *straight-line* type, of the *job-shop* type, or a combination of them. 'Straight-line' and 'job-shop' will be treated as ideal cases permitting us to identify the 'logic' operating behind the variety of actual productive organizations. Consequently, either case will be described as a cluster of features chosen so as to bring to the fore, in the clearest possible way, a distinctive organizational logic. However, the application of either category will be flexible enough to accommodate situations in which certain features of the ideal case are absent and yet a given organizational logic is clearly distinguishable. This flexibility is essential if abstract categories are to be used in order to understand the variety of 'productive forms' in economic history.

Processes of the straight-line type may be characterized as follows:

(1) workers and tools tend to be task-specialized (they generally perform a single task or a small number of tasks);

(2) all the e.p.s carried out within any given productive unit have the same precedence pattern (even if they do not need to be the same type of e.p.);

(3) if τ is a given task carried out in e.p.s 1 and 2 respectively, then a given worker or tool may either perform τ first in e.p. 1, then in e.p. 2 or vice versa.

This latter property is a result of the fact that all e.p.s have the same precedence pattern, as can be seen in the following example. In a process consisting of the operation of two e.p. types (an e.p. of type 1 requiring 'wood-cutting', performed on machine A, before 'wood-assembling', performed on machine B; an e.p. of type 2 also requiring 'wood-cutting', performed on machine A, before 'wood-assembling', performed on machine B), machine A may either perform 'wood-cutting' first in e.p. 1 and then in e.p. 2, or it may perform 'wood-cutting' first in e.p. 2 and then in e.p. 1. The same is true for 'wood-assembling' performed by machine B.

Straight-line production may be illustrated by a car-assembly factory in which tasks are executed by task-specific *work stations* (each work station is a combination of workers and machine tools which may execute a certain task independently of the other work stations in the same establishment). The task executed by each work station is rigidly identified in terms of content and duration and the sequence of tasks in each e.p. is also fixed. (A further discussion of this paradigm case may be found in sections 5.5.1–2.)

Straight-line processes characterize certain types of manufacturing, particularly where the assembly line is used, such as the automotive and consumer electronics industries. They are not, however, peculiar to manufacturing. Indeed, it is tempting to say that mining activities provided for a long time, even before the first Industrial Revolution, an important example of the straight-line arrangement of productive tasks.

Processes of the job-shop type may be characterized as follows:

(1) workers and tools tend to be 'universal' rather than specialized (they are generally employed to perform a whole range of tasks);

(2) the e.p.s operated within any given productive unit may have different precedence patterns (for example, 'wood-cutting' precedes 'wood-assembling' in e.p. 1, whereas 'wood-assembling' precedes 'wood-cutting' in e.p. 2);

(3) if a given task τ forms part of two e.p.s, 1 and 2, then there are only some orders in which a given worker (or tool) can perform τ in 1 and τ in 2.

This last property is a consequence of the difference in the precedence patterns of the various e.p.s, as can be seen from the following example. In a process consisting of the simultaneous operation of two different e.p.s (e.p. 1 requiring 'wood-cutting', performed on machine A, before 'wood-assembling', performed on machine B; e.p. 2 requiring 'wood-assembling', performed on machine B, before 'wood-cutting', performed on machine A), not all the sequences in which a given worker or machine might 'operate' the e.p.s are compatible with the continuous utilization of the worker or machine, for it is impossible to have machine B performing 'wood-assembling' first in e.p. 1, then in e.p. 2. The reason for this is that, with such an operating sequence, 'wood-cutting' would be performed before 'wood-assembling' in e.p. 2, and 'wood-assembling' would be performed before 'wood-cutting' in e.p. 1. Such a situation would make the continuous utilization of A and B impossible.

Job-shop production may be illustrated by a tailor's shop in which workers, pairs of scissors, and sewing machines may execute tasks belonging to a number of different e.p.s (such as suit-making, shirt-making, and ribbon-making). In this case, task durations are not rigidly determined and the different e.p.s may be executed by the various productive factors in an interlocking way. (A further discussion of this paradigm case may be found in section 5.4.1.)

Job-shop processes characterize the manufacturing activities in which demand is low and/or discontinuous and seldom allows for the simultaneous operation of a large number of identical e.p.s (the production of turbines may be an example). This might explain why, before the first Industrial Revolution, job-shop processes were more common than straight-line processes in the production of manufactured goods.

Job-shop processes are not peculiar to manufacturing: agricultural processes may often be considered as special cases of job-shop production, where machines are relatively specialized but workers are 'universal', the e.p.s normally have different precedence patterns, and the operations by workers and machines have to follow a relatively determined sequence.

Straight-line processes and job-shop processes tend to be associated with very different operating criteria. In the straight-line case,

the process is subdivided into component parts which are as elementary as is operationally feasible; at the individual work cycle level these become operation elements or even simple hand motions. The subdivision logic . . . also defines elementary connecting operations between the elementary process operations, which are conceived so as to be functionally independent of one another. The elementary operations, being independent, are also immutable and inelastic. It is these properties, at bottom, which necessitate the connecting operations, which, having the same properties, define a production sequencing order which is essentially fixed, with linkages based eventually on work pace rather than work content.   (Abruzzi, 1965: B101)

In the job-shop case,

the process is . . . segmented into linked organic work phases, each as functionally unified as is operationally feasible. Also, each of these phases is decomposable into individual work cycles having the same characteristics, which vary in number and quality according to particular job orders. The organic work phases thus have variable contours, which means that they are mutable and elastic. With these properties, there is no necessity for defining separate connecting phases; successive phases, being organic and variable, have internal connecting operations with the quality of being fully sequential in the functional sense. In sum, then, the organic work phases . . . are mutually interdependent to the point that their very structures are functionally linked. It follows that the production sequencing order is variable rather than fixed, with linkages based eventually on work content rather than work pace.   (ibid. B101–2)

The distinction between job-shop and straight-line production may primarily be applied to the arrangement of tasks and processes within an individual establishment. However, this distinction is also important if we consider productive units consisting of a plurality of establishments, such as an industrial district. As a matter of fact, constraints upon the scale and composition of the production processes operated within individual establishments may be gradually lifted if establishments organized according to the job-shop or straight-line patterns are combined into a mixed form of productive organization. A case in point could be the 'putting-out' organization, which amalgamates different establishments (some of the job-shop type, others of the straight-line type) into a complex productive network co-ordinated by means of inventories (see Landesmann and Scazzieri, 1991*b*).

Another case could be that of networks supporting 'just-in-time' manufacturing (with zero inventories). Here again, individual units may be of the job-shop or straight-line type, depending on the particular way in which each technical recipe, as implemented by means of specific fund-input capabilities, is associated with a particular scale and composition of the production process. The zero-inventories goal may be achieved by operating a network of job-shop and straight-line establishments, even if the internal organization of the latter has to follow the principles of 'cellular manufacturing' rather than those of 'the traditional process layout' (Schonberger, 1987 [1984]: 5).[6] Job-shop and straight-line units co-operating within the same 'just-in-time' network would have one important feature in common. For fund inputs should have a flexible endowment of capabilities, so that, for example, temporary shortages of intermediate products will be dealt with by stretching certain capabilities of existing fund inputs rather than transforming the production set-up in a more fundamental way.

---

[6] In cellular manufacturing systems, 'the manufacturing processes and systems [have to be designed so that] *small lots* can be produced. The ideal "lot size" is one. Small lots smooth the production flow' (Black, 1987 [1983]: 29). The compatibility between cellular manufacturing and straight-line organization is discussed in s. 5.5.4.

4.3.3. *The allocation of workers and tools to productive tasks in straight-line and job-shop production*

The problem of which workers and tools execute which tasks is dealt with differently in the various types of productive organization. Let us define *division of labour* as a function from the set of tasks to the set of task-performing capabilities, or *skills*, of workers and tools (including machines): any skill may be associated with one or more tasks, and any task with only a single skill (see also Landesmann, 1986: 228–9, where the concept of a 'job-specification programme' is introduced to describe a similar mapping). Division of labour thus allows for 'versatile' inputs (workers or machines capable of performing two or more separate tasks), but no task is 'indifferent' with respect to the skill. Any given pattern of division of labour presupposes a particular way of identifying skills and tasks, and consists of a particular way of relating skills to tasks. As a result, inputs that are 'versatile' under a certain division of labour can only become specialized on condition that a different division of labour is established. (We must note, too, that the evolution of technology brings about new tasks, and often requires the formation of skills that had not previously existed.)

If we examine the necessary conditions for division of labour, it turns out that it might work in a rather different way from the pattern that economists who have read Smith in the conventional way have come to consider normal. The central issue is whether the set of tasks executed at any given time allows the full and continuous utilization of all the existing skills.

Any pattern of division of labour is economically viable on condition that the demand for the existing skills is sufficient to keep workers and tools (including machines) in a state of full (enough) and continuous (enough) utilization throughout the working day. Smith's condition on the 'extent of the market' (see section 3.2.2) can be reformulated in terms of the minimum number of tasks needed to ensure full and continuous utilization of workers and tools. The minimum number of tasks permitting continuous utilization varies according to whether production follows the straight-line or the job-shop model. In the former case, workers and tools tend to be task specific, even if the same task may be executed in a variety of e.p. types. This feature of straight-line production has one important shortcoming: the scale condition for continuous utilization can be satisfied even when the production process delivers a heterogeneous product-mix, but only provided that all e.p.s have the same precedence pattern (see section 4.3.2). It follows that straight-line production allows for change in the product-mix only provided the condition of uniform precedence pattern continues to be satisfied. However, changes in the specifications of given products can be accommodated more easily than a radical innovation in the types of products. (The shift from one product-variant to another often does not affect the sequencing of tasks in the e.p.)[7] If production follows the job-shop pattern, workers and tools need to perform different tasks in different types of e.p. (See also section 5.4.2.) Continuous utilization is possible on condition that workers and tools be 'versatile' (at least to a certain extent), and that division of labour be one in which the same general skill can be applied to a variety of tasks. Versatility of skills means that the producer can continue to meet the scale condition for continuous utilization even when there are changes in the pattern of 'concentration of demand' upon tasks of different types.

There are cases in which a more effective utilization of workers and tools can be achieved through division of labour independently of any direct condition on process scale (e.g. when division of labour facilitates 'learning by doing' and 'learning by using'—as defined, respectively, in Arrow, 1962, and Rosenberg, 1982). The reduction of idle time and unused capacity cannot be achieved, however, unless certain scale conditions are satisfied (see section 3.2.3).

We may now state the following propositions concerning the relation of division of labour to the degree of utilization of workers and tools:

(1) Division of labour permits the producer to avoid idle time and unused capacity through concentration of demand upon specific tasks (see also Hicks, 1969: 23).

(2) Concentration of demand upon specific tasks may be obtained in two different ways, depending on whether the production process is organized on the straight-line or the job-shop pattern.

---

[7] When the condition of a fixed sequencing of tasks is satisfied, continuous utilization can be maintained even if the product-mix is varied, provided scale is adjusted according to the task-lengths of the e.p.s in the new product-mix. From the producer's point of view, a straight-line process takes its shape when task-sequencing is determined, regardless of the commodities actually produced. This feature distinguishes straight-line from job-shop production, in which the structure of the production process remains 'open' until the commodity-mix is determined.

In the straight-line case, task-specific workers and tools are continuously used in executing certain tasks, either in identical e.p.s or in different e.p.s that have the same precedence pattern. In the job-shop case, 'universal' workers and tools are continuously used in executing tasks that may belong to e.p.s having different precedence patterns. In either case, the continuous and full utilization of workers and tools requires that the demand for tasks be concentrated upon the workers and tools employed in an establishment. However, the straight-line organization brings about a one-to-one relationship between concentration of demand for tasks and concentration of demand for single commodities (or for 'technologically homogeneous' commodity groups). The job-shop organization is free from this constraint, and this makes it possible to have a 'concentrated' demand for tasks, even if the demand for each particular commodity is low and subject to fluctuations.

To sum up, straight-line production is characterized by a 'content-specific' division of labour between workers and between tools: the production process is divided into elementary components consisting of the specific operations executed in each e.p. (or *tasks*), regardless of the general abilities that may be required by these operations. Job-shop production is characterized by a 'functional' division of labour between workers and between tools; the production process may be divided into elementary components consisting of the abstract functions performed (*skills*) rather than of the special operations executed in each process (*tasks*).

Consider an establishment following the straight-line pattern. The production process would be divided into elementary components given by particular tasks such as 'cutting a piece of wood of type A' or 'assembling pieces of wood of type B', regardless of whether the same skill or different skills were required. Consider, on the other hand, the workshop of a wood artisan organized on the job-shop pattern. The production process would be 'divided' into elementary components given by general skills such as 'wood-cutting' or 'wood-assembling', regardless of which particular task requiring these skills was being performed. (In general, human and non-human capabilities may be exerted in a plurality of ways, provided any given capability is identified as a general skill and not as a specific task-performing capacity; see also Sen, 1985.)

4.3.4. *Time-arrangement of elementary processes*

Each production process may contain several or many e.p.s of the same type or of different types. In principle, such e.p.s may be arranged along the time-dimension in one of the following ways:[8] (a) *in series*, so that one e.p. follows the other, and there is no systematic overlapping of e.p.s over time (this is always the case with productive establishments in which a single network of tasks is being operated); (b) *in parallel*, so that in all the task networks the e.p.s start at the same time and are then repeated according to the same time-pattern (there is thus a complete overlapping of e.p.s over time); (c) *in line*, so that 'the time of production is divided into equal intervals and one elementary process (or a batch of such processes) is started at each division point' (Georgescu-Roegen, 1971: 238). Any such interval corresponds to the time needed to perform a certain task (or a set of tasks). A consequence of this last arrangement is that the e.p.s are partially overlapping over time.

The arrangement of e.p.s over time is an essential feature of productive organization whenever tasks have a fixed duration and e.p.s consist of an uninterrupted sequence of tasks. Consequently, the time-arrangement of e.p.s is an essential feature of straight-line production but not of job-shop production. Indeed, in a straight-line process the time-arrangement of e.p.s has a critical importance in determining whether workers and tools are fully/continuously utilized or not (see Chapter 5).

4.3.5. *The elements of a production process*

A production process is characterized by the following elements:

(1) the properties of the e.p.s (task characteristics, precedence patterns);
(2) the general pattern according to which the tasks are arranged into e.p.s, i.e. whether the e.p. is of the straight-line or job-shop type;
(3) the arrangement of e.p.s over time;
(4) the allocation of workers and tools to the various e.p.s;
(5) the 'levels of utilization' of workers, tools, and raw materials

---

[8] The distinction between the 3 fundamental patterns according to which the e.p.s may be arranged over time was originally presented in Georgescu-Roegen (1969: 516).

(such levels depend on how often these inputs take an active part in the production process);

(6) the scale of the process, as defined above.

Our definition of 'scale' is process-based, rather than output-based. As a consequence, it may also cover the case of joint production (where two or more commodities are delivered by the same e.p.) and the case in which e.p.s of different kinds are simultaneously operated within the same productive unit (think of an artisan's shop, in which different e.p. types may be simultaneously operated in order to obtain a range of different commodities).

Our concept of scale implies that we cannot talk of 'large-scale production' in the case of processes in which a great number of e.p.s are carried out throughout the working day, by operating, at any given time, a single e.p. or a small number of e.p.s. (A single worker producing one thousand nails in a day would not be a case of large-scale production.) It would also be impossible to describe as 'large-scale production' productive activities that require inputs of large size, or large quantities of inputs, but such that no more than one output unit is processed at any given time. (This is often the case with shipbuilding, the building of bridges, and so on.)

Process scale is determined in two different ways, depending on whether the establishment follows the straight-line or the job-shop model. In the former case, scale reflects the time-arrangement of e.p.s. In the latter case, scale derives from the use of a certain number of general skills in a variety of tasks. In the straight-line establishment, a given scale is associated with a given *productive capacity* (this is the maximum number of e.p.s that can be simultaneously operated in a given establishment) and with a certain arrangement of tasks. (Variations of product-mix are still possible by changing proportions between e.p.s, but these must have the same precedence pattern.) In the job-shop organization, a given scale is associated with particular ranges of variation in the number of e.p.s of different types, so that the same scale would be compatible with a variety of productive arrangements and product-mixes. (Scale in this sense reflects the stock of workers, tools, and 'general skills' available in the productive unit, but is only indirectly associated with the types of commodities produced and their output levels.)

That the production process has a certain scale has quite different implications according to whether the establishment follows the straight-line or the job-shop pattern. In the former case, process scale determines the output of each commodity, or at least the output of each 'technologically homogeneous' group of commodities. In the latter case, no fixed relationship whatsoever can be detected between the scale of a process and the output levels of individual commodities, for task-lengths may be varied according to the need for the continuous utilization of workers and tools, and a given e.p. is generally executed in an interlocking way with other e.p.s. This contrast has a number of interesting implications, which we shall examine in the following chapters.

The above definition of scale is particularly helpful in the analysis of cases in which a 'more efficient' organization of the production process appears to be related to higher output levels. We shall be able to explain such cases by showing that, at certain scales of the production process, the number of e.p.s that are simultaneously operated enables producers to increase the levels of utilization of workers, machines, and raw materials (see Chapter 8). In this connection, it is worth noting that the above distinction between fund utilization at a given point of time and fund utilization over time (see section 4.2) may be related to the distinction between 'speed' of capacity utilization and duration of productive operations within the day (see Betancourt and Clague, 1981; Winston, 1982; Betancourt, 1986). However, our distinction is process-based rather than output-based, so that higher speed would here be associated with the operation of a great number of e.p.s per unit of time, regardless of whether such processes are of the same type or not. In addition, the duration of the utilization period within the day is here related to the pattern of task-arrangement over time, as well as to the level of output. As a result, an increase in daily output (that is, an increase in the number of e.p.s operated within the day) may not lead to a significant reduction in fund input idle time, unless it is associated with a change in the way tasks are arranged over time.

In the present theoretical framework, any scale-induced switch to higher levels of input utilization is, at least in principle, independent of the production of large quantities of any particular commodity; for a high scale of production in our sense implies high commodity outputs only in the special case in which a large number of e.p.s all delivering the *same* commodity are simultaneously operated within the productive unit. Our process-based definition of scale is also helpful in analysing certain cases in which a 'less efficient' organization of the production process seems to be related to higher output levels.

It also enables us to analyse situations that seem difficult to treat if attention is limited to the production of individual commodities.

Elements 1–5 of the production process determine the *technical practice*, i.e. the pattern of task-organization and input utilization adopted in the productive unit. The technical practice may or may not change when there are changes in the scale of the production process. The structure of a production process is shown in Fig. 4.1.

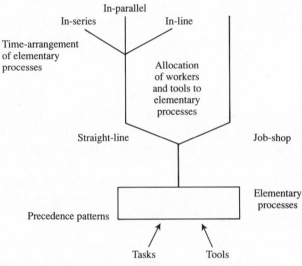

Fig. 4.1. *The production process: scale and technical practice*

Tasks and tools are the fundamental concepts in our description of production processes. The consideration of precedence relations among tasks is logically prior to the analysis of task networks and e.p.s. The precedence pattern is not sufficient to determine the duration of an e.p. It is also necessary to consider which type of task-organization is adopted (straight-line or job-shop), for the type of 'organization' determines whether a given e.p. is executed without interruption or, instead, in an interlocking way with other e.p.s. In the latter case, the interval of time during which the e.p. is executed is obviously longer than in the former case. Finally, the allocation of workers and tools to the various e.p.s, and the arrangement of e.p.s over time, determine which technical practice is followed at any given scale.

4.4. THE DESCRIPTION OF PRODUCTION PROCESSES: NETWORK OF TASKS AND INPUT–OUTPUT RELATIONSHIPS

In modern economics, production phenomena are often considered as relationships between input and output quantities. This has led to three different, though connected, descriptions of the production process:

(1) the *production function*, where a set of input vectors is mapped into the output set;

(2) the *productive activity*, i.e. a vector of input and output quantities relating to a given period of time (this concept was originally used in Koopmans, 1951);

(3) the vector of *input–output coefficients*, i.e. a vector of real numbers expressing input quantities per unit of output.

None of the above descriptions of the production process makes it possible to compare the effectiveness of alternative arrangements of tasks and e.p.s in terms of the total time in which workers, machines, and raw materials are actually used during the working day. It is this criterion, however, that is the most relevant when we come to consider alternative ways of co-ordinating the tasks. For, when the tasks are given, it is normally possible to sequence them in a number of different ways. Moreover, even when the sequence of tasks is fixed in an e.p., it is possible to arrange the sequences according to different patterns, depending on whether and how they overlap in time. Differences of this kind are normally reflected in the time in which workers, machines, and raw materials are actually involved in productive operations.

A production process may be represented by the vector of 'use-times' T_j (I shall suppress the subscript j when this creates no ambiguity):

$$T_j = \begin{bmatrix} t_{1j} \\ t_{2j} \\ \cdot \\ \cdot \\ \cdot \\ t_{nj} \end{bmatrix}$$

The elements of T_j include: the total labour-time employed in process j for any given type of skill, the lengths of time worked by machines of different types, and the lengths of time for which the various raw materials actually take part in the production process.

The vector **T** will normally change whenever there is a change in the tasks performed within the productive unit. It will also change when changes in the sequencing of tasks, or in the time-arrangement of the sequences, involve changes in the levels of utilization of workers, machines, and raw materials.

Given the vector **T**, it is possible to compute the number of workers, machines, and batches of raw materials needed for the corresponding amount of activity. In the case of each labour-skill, we may divide the labour-time in **T** (say, t_{1j}) by the duration of the working day, T_w. If t_{1j} is an integer multiple of T_w, we immediately obtain the necessary number of workers employed during one day; otherwise, the number of workers is given by the smallest integer multiple of T_w that exceeds t_{1j}/T_w. The same criterion may be applied to obtain the number of machines.

In the case of raw materials, we may divide the overall time taken during a day by the processing of any material by the time needed to process one conventionally defined unit of that material. The quotient is the quantity of raw material needed to keep the process going for one day.

The above mentioned method permits us to associate with any time vector **T**, a vector of physical input requirements. We shall denote this latter vector by v_j. The elements of v_j are hence the input quantities necessary to maintain a given level of utilization for fund inputs and materials (they would be the input quantities necessary to obtain the required amount of active time from workers and machines). We may now obtain a set of standard input–output coefficients by dividing the vector v_j by the output q delivered from production process j during the working day:

$$\frac{v_j}{q} = \begin{bmatrix} a_{1j} \\ a_{2j} \\ \cdot \\ \cdot \\ \cdot \\ a_{nj} \end{bmatrix}$$

Our focus on the production process as a network of tasks performed by human beings and machines permits us to identify certain limits intrinsic to the input–output description of production. In particular.

a change in the sequencing of tasks, such as may sometimes considerably reduce the length of an e.p., is not always associated with changes in the input–output coefficients. The labour coefficients, for instance, do not vary if a change in active labour-time is not accompanied by changes in the number of employed workers. (This could happen because the reduction in e.p. duration is too small to release one entire worker, or because there are reasons for retaining workers other than technical needs.) The same applies to machines.

In general, changes in the input–output relationships follow from changes both in the characteristics of tasks and in the way the tasks themselves and the e.p.s are sequenced over time. Changes of the latter type cannot be adequately analysed, however, unless we go beyond the input–output relationships and deal explicitly with the special problems of production as a time-consuming activity.

4.5. NOTE ON THE LITERATURE

An early attempt to analyse production in terms of observed input–output relationships is to be found in Leontief (1941), in which the set of producers' practices is described by production coefficients computed from inter-industry commodity flows. The same approach was followed in the subsequent literature on inter-industry transactions, whose theoretical foundations have been recently analysed in Pasinetti (1977). Leontief's book also contains a discussion of the relationships between the input–output model and the traditional production function. A subsequent paper by Leontief (1947) considers the related issue of how to break down 'overall' production functions into several simpler relationships, each involving fewer variables.

The empirical input–output models, based on observed inter-industry flows, are presented in terms of *ex post* production coefficients. In modern economics, there is an older tradition of describing production processes as vectors of *ex ante* coefficients, which goes back to Walras (1874–7). The *ex ante* approach was later developed by von Neumann (1937) and Koopmans (1951).

A common feature of the approaches we have mentioned is the representation of production as a set of input–output relationships without considering the actual network of tasks needed in each production process. This latter issue is, by contrast, at the forefront of the literature concerned with production-control problems. A basic distinction that is made in this literature is that between production processes of the straight-line type and production processes of the job-shop type (Abruzzi, 1965). The general problem considered in the production-control literature is how to reduce the time needed to perform any given set of tasks. In certain processes of the straight-line type, this problem takes the special form of 'line-balancing', and leads to the assembly line (see Bryton, 1954; Kilbridge and Wester, 1962).

The first explicit attempt in modern economic theory to analyse the production process as a network of tasks was made by Georgescu-Roegen (see *inter alia* 1969; 1971), who used this framework to study alternative time-arrangements of e.p.s and their relative efficacy in achieving the continuous use of workers and tools. Anticipations of this latter approach can be found in Smith's and Babbage's analysis of the division of labour in manufacturing (Smith, 1976 [1776]; Babbage, 1835), as well as in Marx's study of the links among tasks in so-called 'serial manufacture' (1983 [1867]). Tani (1986) has recently developed Georgescu-Roegen's approach to show how it may be related to the input–output description of production processes.

5

Scale-Technology Expansion

5.1. TECHNICAL PROGRESS AND TECHNOLOGY EXPANSION: THE FEASIBILITY ELEMENT IN TECHNICAL INNOVATION

The economist's consideration of technical progress is often characterized by the idea that the discovery and use of new and 'better' technical practices are to be explained by purely economic incentives. Such an approach is apparent in the explanations based on the 'factor-augmenting' bias of technical change, which assume that new technical practices are characterized by a higher proportional rate of reduction in labour or capital costs, depending on relative factor shares in total cost.[1]

This emphasis on purely economic factors in explaining changes of technical practice has been criticized by various authors. Among them, W. E. Salter stressed that 'the entrepreneur is interested in reducing costs in total, not particular costs such as labour costs or capital costs' (1960: 43). An important implication of Salter's proposition is that the influence of cost minimization on technical behaviour is of a general kind, and that it is often impossible to explain by cost minimization the 'factor-augmenting' bias of technical progress.

The need for an alternative explanation of technical progress has also been urged by Nathan Rosenberg, who has maintained that 'economic incentives to reduce cost always exist in business operations, and precisely because such incentives are so diffuse and general they do not explain very much in terms of the *particular sequence and timing of innovative activity*' (Rosenberg, 1969a: 3). Also, according to Rosenberg, 'technology is much more of a cumulative and self-generating process than the economist generally recognizes' (ibid.), particularly because 'complex technologies create internal compulsions and pressures which, in turn, initiate exploratory activity in particular directions' (ibid. 4). In Rosenberg's view, many

---

[1] This line of thought was started by Kennedy (1964) and Weizsäcker (1966). It led to the consideration of a 'technical-progress frontier', based on the idea that there is a trade-off between the rate of labour-augmenting and the rate of capital-augmenting innovation.

important instances of technical progress may be explained by 'technological disequilibria' among elements of the production process, seen as a system of interdependent tasks having its own internal 'logic' and its own internal standards of satisfactoriness (see also Gibbons, 1983). Such imbalances tend to be corrected by new technical practices, which may in turn produce technological disequilibria of a different kind.[2] Cost-minimizing choice, in the sense of a comprehensive and timeless deliberation, is, in Rosenberg's interpretation, almost irrelevant in so far as the actual course of technical change is concerned. In particular, actual production processes are not seen, in this interpretation, as resulting merely from the behaviour of producers combining input quantities in a rational manner: rather, production processes are seen as having an internal dynamic which strongly affects the direction producers follow in modifying their technical practice (see also Basalla, 1988).

This conception leads to a model of technical progress in which the introduction of new technical practices consists of three distinct phases: (i) new practices are conceived, often as a result of problem-solving activity; (ii) some practices are excluded as not technically feasible (note that this exclusion is neutral as to whether there is a deliberate feasibility study by humans); (iii) one of the new practices is adopted.

This picture of technical progress implies that the introduction of new and 'better' technical practices has two separate sets of causes: on the one hand, the technical (non-human) factors that determine the problems to be solved and the range of feasible solutions; on the other hand, the problem-solving activity and the solution that is actually adopted by producers. The usual model of the relationship between technical discovery and technical practice is thus partly

---

[2] The evolution of metal-cutting devices provides an interesting example: 'it was impossible to take advantage of higher cutting speeds [using high-speed steel] with machine tools designed for the older carbon steel cutting tools because they could not withstand the stresses and strains or provide sufficiently high speeds in the other components of the machine tool. As a result, the availability of high-speed steel for the cutting tool quickly generated a complete redesign in machine tool components— the structural, transmission, and control elements' (Rosenberg, 1969a: 8). In addition, 'the need to adapt speeds and feeds to the enlarged cutting capacity of the tool was a major stimulus to the development of new speed-changing devices' (ibid.). A sequence of changes in technical practice was thus generated by a sequence of 'disequilibria' among components of the machine tool. In Rosenberg's view, the former sequence is 'compulsive' because any change of practice can be seen as an attempt by producers to eliminate an imbalance characteristic of the current practice.

reversed: technical progress is no longer seen as a process in which discovery affects technical practice in a one-way direction, since the imbalances that often characterize current practices have a decisive influence in determining the nature of the new technical device.

This explanation of technical progress is thus characterized by an 'internal' approach to *technical practice* and an 'external' approach to the technological environment within which a certain technical practice is adopted. In other words, each new practice appears as the result of producers' problem-solving activity, whereas the problem space and the range of feasible solutions depend on technical factors, which are independent of producers' behaviour.[3] Technical progress is of the 'induced' kind, in the sense that any particular change of practice is explained as a result of producers' actions (their problem-solving activity). However, there are important differences from other theories that adopt an 'internal' explanation of technical practice. In particular, technical innovation is not explained by the theory of 'learning by doing', in which a change of technical practice is seen as a direct result of the expertise acquired by producers while engaged in production activity.[4] For in a learning-by-doing explanation, the problem-solving aspect of technical change plays no explicit role. As a consequence, changes in the problem space and in the range of feasible solutions are not part of the explanation of technical change either. The above model of technical change also differs from the model of induced technical progress based on the consideration of factor prices and of the 'factor-augmenting' bias of innovation. In particular, there are three important differences from the approach of C. Kennedy (1964) and Weizsäcker (1966): the problem space is not limited to finding the cost-minimizing innovation at given input prices; the problem space may vary from one case of technical progress to another; and changes in the problem space are explained by the internal dynamics of technical practices (the existence of imbalances and the drive to eliminate them in a 'satisfactory' way).

An essential element of the above model of technical change is the feasibility stage. The consideration of this stage permits us to

[3] The concept of 'problem-space', in connection with the study of learning behaviour, was first used by Newell and Simon (1972). In this work, the problem-space is identified as 'the space in which . . . problem solving activities take place' (p. 59). See also s. 7.1.3 below.
[4] This line of thought was suggested by Verdoorn (1949) and Alchian (1963). A well-known development is to be found in Arrow (1962).

explain technical change as a consequence not only of technical discovery but also of an expansion in the number of feasible practices. An important implication of this is that a change in process scale may explain the direction of technical progress by generating an expansion of the set of feasible practices.

Let $\phi(s)$ be the set of technical practices feasible at scale s. We shall define a *scale-technology expansion* to be a situation in which s and s' are two scales such that $s < s'$, and there is at least one technical practice θ such that $\theta \notin \phi(s)$ and $\theta \in \phi(s')$. Scale-technology expansion implies $\phi(s) \not\supseteq \phi(s')$; on the other hand, it is not required that $\phi(s') \supseteq \phi(s)$. In short, not all the technical practices feasible at s have to be feasible at s'.

This chapter considers the feasibility stage. It is intended as a contribution to the study of the technological factors that determine which practices are feasible at a given scale. The content of the chapter is thus logically prior to the study of producers' adoption of a technical practice, which will be the subject of Chapters 7 and 8.

In the present chapter, the imbalances argument for technical change will be reformulated within the framework of task–process theory. A remarkable outcome of such a reformulation is that information about technological imbalances may be derived from the knowledge of basic characteristics of production technology, such as the structure of fund-input capabilities or the structure and length of e.p.s, once process scale is known. In addition, the imbalances argument is here related to the feasibility stage of technical adoption, rather than to the complete process of technical change. It should thus be free from the analytical weaknesses of the induced-innovation argument, for which it may be argued that an imbalance can be identified only after the relevant invention is made. The analysis of this chapter also aims at providing a theoretical background to the contributions in applied literature that have considered the importance of 'scaling up' (or 'scaling down') as a source of information for changing the technical practice (see e.g. Sahal's emphasis upon the relationship between scale and technological capabilities in Sahal, 1981*a*; 1981*b*).

The chapter is organized as follows. Section 5.2 introduces the distinction between two cases of scale-technology expansion: those due to the impossibility of reducing the scale of a production process below the unit scale at which an e.p. is defined; and those due to imbalances of a technical kind (such as mismatches between the capacity, speed, or strength of the various inputs, or the discontinuous utilization of inputs that are not continuously needed in an e.p.). Section 5.3 examines the above technical imbalances, distinguishing between: (i) the case in which one or more inputs are under-utilized because too few tasks are performed per unit of time with respect to a given technical maximum; (ii) the case in which one or more inputs are under-utilized because they are completely idle during parts of the e.p. (this may happen with the *fund inputs*, which are continuously available willy-nilly in the productive establishment, even if the length of the task in an e.p. for which they are used is less than that of the whole e.p.).[5]

In case (i), scale-technology expansion can be seen as a result of the general 'law of multiples' (see section 5.3.1). In case (ii), scale-technology expansion may follow a number of different patterns, depending on (a) the organization of the production process (whether the job-shop or the straight-line model is adopted) and (b) the degree of specialization of workers and tools (whether they are 'special-purpose' or 'multi-purpose'). Section 5.4 examines scale-technology expansion in the case of job-shop production (5.4.1 describes a paradigm case of job-shop production; 5.4.2 discusses general facts about fund-input utilization when production follows the job-shop model; and the implications of these facts for scale-technology expansion are examined in 5.4.3). Section 5.5 examines scale-technology expansion in the case of straight-line production. (In particular, 5.5.1 outlines a paradigm case; 5.5.2 presents a general condition for continuous fund-input utilization; the two alternatives available for reducing fund-input idleness—the in-line arrangement of a sufficient number of e.p.s and the specialization of the e.p.—are presented in 5.5.3; 5.5.4 compares the relative advantages of these two alternatives, by distinguishing between production processes using special-purpose and multi-purpose fund inputs).

---

[5] The notion of *fund input* (or 'fund factor') was introduced by Georgescu-Roegen (1969; 1970; 1971; 1972) while making the distinction between flow factors and fund factors. *Flow factors* enter the elementary process as inputs and disappear within that process. Solar energy, rainfall, coke used in a foundry, and lubricating oil belong to this category (see Georgescu-Roegen, 1971: 231–2). *Fund factors* enter the elementary process as inputs and may still be described as productive factors after leaving that process. Agricultural land, workers, and machinery belong to this category (see Georgescu-Roegen, 1970: 4). Most fund factors involved in a given elementary process are idle during a great part of the duration of that process (see Georgescu-Roegen, 1971: 236). (See also Scazzieri, 1979: 44–92; 1981: 55–100.)

Section 5.6 brings the chapter to a close by discussing the major implications for the analysis of technical change.

5.2. MINIMUM SCALE AND TECHNOLOGY EXPANSION: THE GENERAL ISSUES

An increase in output may involve the 'expansion' of the set of feasible practices for one of two reasons: (i) no e.p. can exist unless the outputs of its constituent tasks attain certain minimum levels; (ii) for given task-definitions, certain technical practices can only be operated at certain process scales.

Case (i) follows from the definition of 'productive task' given in Chapter 4 ('a completed operation usually performed without interruption on some particular object'). This definition implies that any task has a certain scale, owing to the size dimensions in the object-descriptions appearing in the task's definition. An elementary process (e.p.) is a time-arrangement of tasks. Any e.p. thus has a certain minimum scale, which derives from the particular way in which tasks are defined.

One example of case (i) is a production process in which the quantity of the commodity produced increases more than proportionally with respect to the physical capital needed in the process. Consider, for instance, a chemical process that has to be carried out within a spherical container, and in which the relationship between output and volume is described by the formula $q = ar^3$, where q denotes the output level, r the radius of the sphere, and a is a constant parameter. The relationship between the physical capital and the output level is a result of the fact that the former is proportional to the area of the surface of the sphere, whereas the latter is proportional to its volume (an analysis of scale effects due to the minimum size of certain tasks may be found in Enos, 1962). Now, once an e.p. that uses the smallest feasible plant has been defined, the level of output can be expanded either by having several small spheres in one location or by operating a single sphere of greater radius. In the former case, there is no change in the e.p. type. In the latter case, there is a change in the e.p. type because e.p.s are defined in terms of their constituent tasks, and these are defined in relation to the size of the associated objects. (A sphere of greater radius thus involves different task-definitions.) A higher level of output may be associated either with the operation of more 'small-size' e.p.s or with the operation of a single e.p. involving a sphere of greater radius. It may still be useful to describe this latter case as an instance of scale-technology expansion, provided we bear in mind that here the scale expansion is of a virtual kind. For the greater output would be associated with an increase in the number of simultaneous e.p.s if 'small-size' e.p.s are operated, but the introduction of a sphere of greater radius makes an output increase compatible with a *contraction* in process scale, if process scale is measured by the number of simultaneous e.p.s using the larger sphere (see the definition of 'scale' in 4.3.1 above). Here the previous definition of scale-technology expansion applies only in the sense that an increase in process scale, defined in terms of the old e.p. type, ought to enable a change of e.p. type to take place.

Case (ii) above follows from technical reasons which mean that not all process scales allow for the full and continuous utilization of all the inputs needed in the e.p.s involved. First, differences in the maximum number of e.p.s that can be carried out in parallel on the various inputs mean that the full utilization of these inputs is possible only at certain process scales (see section 5.3.1). Secondly, the need to use *fund* inputs is responsible for the fact that *continuous* input utilization is only possible at certain process scales (see section 5.3.2).

5.3. TASKS, INPUT UTILIZATION, AND SCALE-TECHNOLOGY EXPANSION

5.3.1. *Technology expansion and full utilization of productive capacity*

Scale-technology expansion may be the result of reducing or eliminating, by increasing process scale, the technical imbalances due to differences among the maximum number of e.p.s that can be carried out in parallel on the various inputs. Such differences are due to mismatches between the size, speed, or strength of the various inputs and can normally be reduced or eliminated, if the production process is operated at a sufficiently high scale.

This point was made by Gioja, Babbage, and Hermann (see section 3.2.3). More recently, E. A. G. Robinson maintained that, in such cases, 'the best solution may be a kind of least common multiple of all the various outputs, in which three units of one machine, four of another, five of a third, give a balance in which all the units can conveniently be used approximately to their full capacity' (Robinson, 1931: 33).

Robinson's proposition was corroborated in E. Schneider's *Theorie der Produktion* (1934). Schneider's analysis considers a production process that uses inputs that can only be varied by discrete amounts. More specifically, Schneider examines 'a production process requiring the following indivisible inputs . . . : one machine A and one subsidiary machine B, which helps the working of A. Let the minimum available size of B be such that it permits the operation of three machines of type A' (Schneider, 1942: 95; my translation). In this case,

The minimum plant that is conceivable, if the given method of production is to be applied, is thus 1A +1B. Let the capacity corresponding to this fixed input set be $x' = 100$. At any output level below $x' = 100$, the plant is clearly being utilized below full capacity. If output 110 has to be produced, we need plant 2A + 1B, having capacity $2x' = 200$. If output 220 has to be produced, we need to operate plant 3A + 1B, having capacity $3x' = 300$. If output 320 has to be produced, we shall have to build plant 4A + 2B, having capacity $4x' = 400$, and so forth. (ibid.)

In Schneider's example, machinery of type A is fully utilized if plant 1A + 1B is producing output $x' = 100$. The same plant is utilized below its full capacity if the output level is below $x' = 100$. The full utilization of machinery of type A can be maintained if the output level is 100 or 200 or 300, and so forth. On the other hand, the full utilization of machinery of type B can be maintained only if the output level is 300 or 600 or 900, and so forth. Let the *own capacity* of an input be the maximum number of parallel e.p.s that it is technically possible to operate using one unit of that input. An input is fully utilized when process scale coincides with its own capacity. We shall henceforth denote by c_i the own capacity of input i $(i = 1, \ldots, r)$.

The following proposition can now be derived.

Proposition 5.1. If a set of inputs i have own capacities c_i $(i = 1, \ldots, r)$, a technical practice permitting the full utilization of all inputs is feasible only if process scale is equal to an integer multiple of the lowest common multiple of the c_i.

This proposition follows from the fact that, for any input i, the own capacity c_i is defined as the maximum number of parallel e.p.s that can be operated using that input. A process scale permits the operation of all inputs at their respective own capacities only if it allows, for each input i, the simultaneous operation of this maximum number c_i of e.p.s. This condition is satisfied if process scale is the least common multiple of all the own capacities, or an integer multiple of that number.

An important implication of proposition 5.1 is that an increasing process scale involves an addition to the number of feasible practices whenever it rises to a level that is an integer multiple of lowest common multiple $\{c_i\}$ from a level that is not. For, at the higher scale, it is possible to adopt a technical practice that enables the full utilization of all the inputs needed in the production process.[6]

5.3.2. *Technology expansion and continuous utilization of productive capacity*

Scale-technology expansion may also be the result of reducing or eliminating, at a higher process scale, the idleness of inputs that are continuously available in the productive unit, but are only needed, in each e.p., for a period of time shorter than the duration of the whole e.p. (This situation is characteristic of fund inputs such as workers and tools. Land is different in this respect, since it is a fund input that is continuously needed in any agricultural e.p.).[7]

The problem of the utilization of fund inputs over time is different from the problem of the utilization of inputs at any point of time. (As we pointed out in section 4.2, the *full* utilization of a given input throughout the working day implies that the input is *continuously* used during that period, but continuous utilization does not imply full utilization.) The utilization of fund inputs over time may be analysed by using the conceptual framework proposed by Georgescu-Roegen,[8] who pointed out that the tasks performed in an arbitrary e.p. may require, at least in principle, the contribution of different inputs for different lengths of time. Inputs belonging to the category of *fund inputs* may tend to be left idle for some time, since a single e.p. seldom requires the continuous operation of any given fund input.

The way in which a fund input is utilized in an e.p. may be

---

[6] A parallel result concerning technology contraction is presented in s. 6.3.2.

[7] The link between scale-technology expansion and the existence of differences among input 'use-times' was clearly described by Babbage in the passage quoted in s. 3.2.3 (n. 3).

[8] See esp. Georgescu-Roegen (1969; 1970; 1971; 1972; 1986; 1990).

analytically represented as a function of time. Let the *utilization function* $F_i(t)$ denote the amount of fund input i's services that are needed by the e.p. at time t. Let T denote the total duration of the e.p. In most cases, $F_i(t) > 0$ at some times $t \in [0,T]$, and $F_i(t) = 0$ at some other times $t \in [0,T]$. For example, if a fund input is only ever used over the time-interval $[0,t_1]$ where $0 < t_1 \le T$, the utilization function satisfies:

$$F_i(t) > 0 \text{ for } 0 \le t < t_1 \quad \text{and} \quad F_i(t) = 0 \text{ for } t_1 \le t \le T.$$

Let $\bar{F}_i$ denote the amount of services provided by fund input i when it is being used at full capacity. ($\bar{F}_i$ is thus the amount of services provided by fund input i when the number of parallel e.p.s using this input coincides with the input's own capacity c_i.) We must have $TF_i \le T\bar{F}_i$, where the equality sign holds in the case in which the fund input is continuously utilized at full capacity during the whole duration of the e.p. On the assumption that the fund input under consideration is only utilized at full capacity or not at all, the amount of 'unused services' due to the time-intervals over which it remains idle may be measured by the expression:

$$T\bar{F}_i - \int_0^T F_i(t) \, dt, \, t \in [0,T]$$

The patterns of fund-input utilization may vary widely, depending on the nature of the e.p. under consideration. For instance, we may assume that land, regarded as a fund input, contributes to production in a more continuous way than fund inputs such as machines or workers. Various possible patterns of fund-input utilization are illustrated in Fig. 5.1.[9] Land is assumed to be continuously utilized from 0 to T. In addition, its rate of utilization is constant through time. On the other hand, workers and machines appear to be active in an intermittent way, so that there are time-intervals over which the e.p. is carried out without their participation.

When a fund input is needed in an e.p. for a period shorter than the whole e.p., a special kind of 'technological disequilibrium' is brought about. This disequilibrium involves fund-input idleness over certain intervals of the working day, unless certain technical practices are adopted, which will be described in sections 5.4 and 5.5. This type of fund-input idleness is thus to be distinguished from the cases of under-utilization that may arise when, because of a low

---

[9] This figure is based on Georgescu-Roegen (1969: 515).

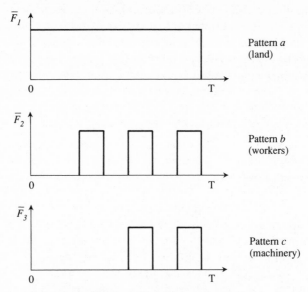

Fig. 5.1. *Alternative patterns of fund-input utilization*

process scale, certain fund inputs are idle throughout the working day. (Underutilization of this latter type could be eliminated simply by increasing the number of e.p.s that are simultaneously operated, without any change in the technical practice.) In the present study, we shall consider only fund-input idleness of the former type.

Fund-input idleness due to the discontinuous utilization of fund inputs in an e.p. can be reduced or eliminated in a number of ways, depending on the characteristics of the tasks and on the precedence relations between them. These ways of dealing with fund-input idleness also depend critically on whether the production process follows the job-shop or the straight-line model of organization (see sections 5.4 and 5.5).

5.4. FUND-INPUT UTILIZATION AND JOB-SHOP PRODUCTION

5.4.1. *A paradigm case*

Throughout this section, we shall refer to the analysis of job-shop production in section 4.3.2. In particular, we shall build on the idea that the fund inputs employed in production processes of the job-shop type are generally able to execute various different tasks, and are involved in the production of different commodities. (Note that in this case different types of e.p. may be carried out in the same production unit.) Another characteristic of job-shop production that we shall use in the present analysis is that the e.p.s operated in a single productive unit may have different precedence patterns between tasks executed by the same fund inputs.

A paradigm case of job-shop production is a tailor's shop. Let the fund inputs employed in the shop be workers (W), pairs of scissors (M_a), and sewing-machines (M_b). Assume that three e.p. types are operated in the shop: suit-making (e.p. I), shirt-making (e.p. II), and ribbon-making (e.p. III). Suit-making requires that 'cloth-cutting' be performed (by W and M_a) before 'cloth-sewing' is performed (by W and M_b). Shirt-making also requires that 'cloth-cutting' be performed (by W and M_a) before 'cloth-sewing' is performed (by W and M_b). Ribbon-making requires that 'ribbon-sewing' (sewing pieces of cloth left from suit-making and shirt-making) be performed by W and M_b before 'ribbon-cutting' (cutting ribbons of the required length) is performed by W and M_a.

In this example, all fund inputs are multi-purpose, since a worker can perform either cutting or sewing tasks, a pair of scissors can perform either cloth-cutting or ribbon-cutting, and a sewing-machine can perform either cloth-sewing or ribbon-sewing. The e.p.s operated in the tailor's shop have different precedence patterns ('cloth-cutting' precedes 'cloth-sewing' in suit-making and shirt-making, whereas 'ribbon-sewing' precedes 'ribbon-cutting' in the ribbon-making process). Finally, the allocation of e.p.s to fund inputs has to follow a given time-sequence. For example, a pair of scissors has to be used first in suit- and shirt-making and then in ribbon-making, whereas a sewing-machine has to be used first in ribbon-making and then in suit- and shirt-making. (It would be impossible to start a working day by using a given pair of scissors first in ribbon-making, then in suit- or shirt-making, since in this case, contrary to assumption, 'ribbon-cutting' would be performed before 'ribbon-sewing' in the ribbon-making process, and 'cloth-cutting' would be performed after 'cloth-sewing' in the suit- and shirt-making processes.)

In our paradigm case (and in job-shop production generally, in practice) the links between tasks in any e.p. are 'functional' rather than based on work-pace (see section 4.3.2). As a result, the time taken by any task is flexible, and may be adjusted according to the operations needed in the shop. It follows that productive organization determines the *order*, but not the *lengths*, of the various tasks. Another important result is that there may be intervals in which a given e.p. type is not operated at all (the production of the corresponding commodity is discontinued), even if all fund inputs are continuously used by being switched from one e.p. type to another.

5.4.2. *A general condition for continuous fund-input utilization*

The flexibility of job-shop production over task-lengths and precedence patterns allows a given fund input to be used in different tasks figuring in different e.p. types. However, fund-input idleness is still possible, if the number and types of the commodities produced, and the proportions between their respective output levels, do not allow producers to exploit fully the differences in the precedence patterns of the various e.p. types.

The special problems raised by fund-input utilization in job-shop production may be illustrated by considering our paradigm case. In that example, two types of machines (denoted respectively by M_a and M_b) are used in three different e.p. types (I, II, III). We assume that e.p.s I and II (suit-making and shirt-making respectively) use M_a first, then M_b, and that e.p. III (ribbon-making) uses first M_b, then M_a. Labour services are needed in each task in each e.p.

One pair of scissors and one sewing-machine are continuously used, if the following sequences of operation are adopted:

(1) machine M_a is used first in e.p. I, then in e.p. II, and finally in e.p. III;

(2) machine M_b is used first in e.p. III, then in e.p. I, and finally in e.p. II.

This situation is depicted in Fig. 5.2. Each line of Fig. 5.2 corresponds to an e.p. of a distinct type. Each interval $(M_a)_i$ and $(M_b)_i$, $(i = 1, 2, 3)$, shows the period for which M_a or M_b is used in e.p. *i*. The index *i* indicates that this is the *i*th use of M_a or M_b. (For instance, the interval $(M_a)_1$ of the line labelled I shows the period for which M_a is used in e.p. I, and the index 1 indicates that this is the first use of M_a.)

Fig. 5.2 describes a case in which, for each machine, the endpoint of a task coincides with the starting-point of another task in e.p.

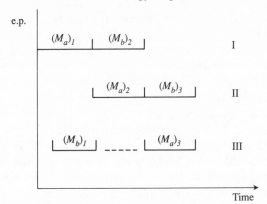

Fig. 5.2. *Fund-input utilization in a 'job-shop' production process*

another e.p. (The end-point of 'cloth-cutting' in e.p. I coincides with the starting-point of 'cloth-cutting' in e.p. II, and so on.)

This characteristic is a general feature of job-shop production, where task-lengths are not fixed a priori, but may always be varied in order to improve co-ordination between tasks, thus decreasing or eliminating fund-input idleness over time. (Any given task may be slowed down or speeded up, depending on the requirements for co-ordination. This change of task-lengths does not necessarily affect the number of tasks executed by fund inputs at any given point of time. In general, the 'stretching out' of tasks is not related to the degree of capacity utilization of fund inputs at a given point of time. Indeed, the degree of capacity utilization cannot be unambiguously determined in the case of job-shop production, for *maximum* capacity varies with the type of task, and fund inputs are clusters of different skills.)

If production is organized according to the job-shop model, fund-input idleness can be avoided, provided the following three conditions are satisfied: (i) the differences in the precedence patterns of the e.p.s carried out in the productive unit permit producers to switch fund inputs from one e.p. type to another; (ii) there is enough scope for the 'stretching out' of tasks; (iii) the number of e.p.s of each type is sufficient.

This result is a straightforward generalization of properties of our paradigm case. The differences in the precedence patterns of e.p.s I, II, and III permit producers to switch machines M_a and M_b from one e.p. type to another. Continuous utilization of M_a and M_b is achieved if such machines can be switched from one task to another as soon as the former task is completed. That this situation can arise is due to the fact that the length of each task does not exceed a certain maximum, and that a sufficient number of e.p. types are simultaneously operated in the productive unit. (It is easy to see from Fig. 5.2 that fund-input idleness cannot be avoided if, for instance, only two e.p. types are being operated.)

The main implications of this result can also be seen from Fig. 5.2. Continuous fund-input utilization is compatible with changes in the scale of certain e.p.s. In particular, it is possible for there to be a small increase/decrease in the 'scale' of e.p. I (i.e. the number of e.p.s of type I simultaneously operated in the productive unit), provided there is a corresponding decrease/increase in the 'scale' of e.p. II (similarly defined). For e.p.s I and II have the same precedence pattern, and it is possible to substitute the use of M_a or M_b in e.p. I for the use of the same inputs in e.p. II (and vice versa) without changing in other ways the structure of the production process. (Similarly, a small increase/decrease in the scale of e.p. II can be realized on condition that there is a decrease/increase in the scale of e.p. I.) On the other hand, it is impossible to vary the scale of e.p. III without changing the scale of the whole production process and the total number of fund inputs employed in the productive unit. The change of process scale and of the number of fund inputs is also necessary, in the tailor's-shop case, if three or more e.p.s of type I or II are to be operated.

As process scale increases, continuous fund-input utilization can only be maintained if it increases by integer multiples of the minimum scale compatible with continuous utilization. For a certain pattern of fund-input utilization is associated with a given combination of e.p.s, and can only be maintained by adding further identical combinations of e.p.s. (However, the pattern of fund-input utilization may be changed to allow continuous increases in scale.)

5.4.3. *Variations of scale and variations of practice in job-shop production*

Two different types of changes in technical practice may accompany a change of process scale. In the first case, one practice may be substituted for another in an establishment organized on the job-shop model; in the second case, straight-line organization may be substituted for job-shop organization (or vice versa).

The first case may be explained by looking at Fig. 5.2 above. Let the production process consist of two e.p.s, of types I and II respectively. As can be seen from the figure, M_a can then be continuously operated as long as e.p.s of types I or II are started in the establishment. On the other hand, M_b will be idle over a certain interval at the beginning of the working day. An increase in process scale has a different effect, depending on which additional e.p.s are operated in the establishment. For example, if process scale is increased by adding one e.p. of type I or II, one additional unit of inputs M_a and M_b is needed, and fund-input idleness is also increased. On the other hand, if process scale is increased by adding one e.p. of type III, no change of the fund-input endowment is necessary and both M_a and M_b can be continuously used.

The second case may be understood by recalling that, in a job-shop process, continuous fund-input utilization can only be maintained if process scale increases by integer multiples of the minimum scale compatible with continuous utilization. This property introduces a certain degree of rigidity in the production process. On the other hand, contrary to what happens in the case of straight-line production (see section 5.5), a given process scale is compatible with almost continuous change in the output levels of individual commodities. For, at a given process scale, continuous fund-input utilization is compatible with changes in the proportions between the different e.p. types operated in the establishment, as long as it is possible to substitute certain e.p.s for other e.p.s which, though they produce different commodities, have the same precedence pattern. This feature makes it possible to adjust the structure of the production process, without changing the degree of fund-input utilization, in the case of changes in the composition of demand that do not affect the range of precedence patterns involved in the various e.p. types being operated. But it also makes job-shop production particularly vulnerable to a contraction in the range of the commodities produced, for the disappearance of certain final products might enforce the disappearance of certain precedence patterns between tasks, and thus the temporary idleness of certain fund inputs. This vulnerability may explain why job-shop processes are more common in establishments that produce a wide variety of products, even if the composition of the demand for them is frequently changing, than in establishments that produce a variety of products for which demand is steady, but which is limited in range. In particular, this characteristic of the 'job-shop' organization may explain why job-shop production was the more common pattern of organization before the first Industrial Revolution, and why it was subsequently superseded by straight-line production in many important branches of mass production. It may explain, too, the recent appearance of job-shop processes in productive branches (such as the electronic data-processing industry) that are particularly affected by changes in demand structure and product innovation.

5.5. FUND-INPUT UTILIZATION AND STRAIGHT-LINE PRODUCTION

5.5.1. *A paradigm case*

Throughout this section, we shall refer to the outline of straight-line production presented in section 5.3.2. It is worth recalling the essential points made there. A productive unit organized on the straight-line model can only operate e.p.s that have the same precedence pattern (though they do not need to be the same type of e.p.). In the case of establishments where different e.p. types are carried out, a fund input x may either perform the ith task first in e.p. I then in e.p. II, or it may perform the ith task first in e.p. II then in e.p. I. (Note that this is impossible in the case of job-shop production, where the difference in precedence patterns obliges producers to use fund inputs in the different e.p.s only in a particular sequence—or, at most, in a restricted range of sequences.) Finally, workers and tools typically perform a single task or a small number of tasks.

A paradigm case of straight-line production is the car-assembly factory. Let the fund inputs be workers and machine tools, organized into *work stations* along the assembly line. (Each work station is a combination of workers and machine tools, which may perform some group of tasks independently of the operations of other workers and machine tools employed in the same establishment.) For the sake of simplicity, we shall assume that only one type of e.p. is carried out in the establishment, and that such e.p. consists of two tasks, 'car-assembling' and 'wheel-screwing', each of these tasks being performed by a separate work station. In each e.p. 'car-assembling' must be performed before 'wheel-screwing'.

In our paradigm case—and in straight-line production generally—

the time-schedule of the tasks making up any e.p. is determined by work pace. The productive organization lays down both the ordering and the lengths of the different tasks, and the tasks making up a given e.p. follow one another without break. (We may note in this connection that the waiting periods necessary to the starting or the completion of certain tasks, for instance in processes of the chemical type, ought to be considered as constituent elements of the e.p., rather than 'breaks' of particular e.p.s such as those that take place with the job-shop model of production.)

5.5.2. *A general condition for continuous fund-input utilization*

A characteristic of straight-line production is that every task of a given type takes the same fixed time. Let t_1 be the fixed length of 'car-assembling' and t_2 that of 'wheel-screwing'. The work station(s) performing 'car-assembling' and the work station(s) performing 'wheel-screwing' can be continuously employed throughout the working day, provided that the number of e.p.s carried out in the day requires from each work station a number of tasks whose corresponding durations add up to the length of the working day. The following proposition generalizes this statement for all straight-line processes. (We shall denote by n_i/p_i the fraction α_i of the working day T_w taken by fund input F_i to execute its particular task or set of tasks. Let p_i be the number such that T_w is divided into a certain number of equal time-intervals. The reason for this notation will become apparent below.)

Proposition 5.2. If production is organized according to the straight-line model, F_i is any fund input and F_i performs m_i times in immediate succession a set of tasks lasting $(n_i/p_i)T_w$, then fund-input idleness can be eliminated provided, during a working day,

$$m_i = (p_i/n_i). \qquad [5.1]$$

It is clear that F_i cannot repeat its tasks more than m_i times in a day and that, if the number of repetitions is $m_i < (p_i/n_i)$, F_i is employed each day only for the period $m_i(p_i/n_i) T_w < T_w$.

An important implication of this result is that, in the case of straight-line production, continuous fund-input utilization is not always possible. For, if a set of tasks is not further divisible (as in the case of a unit set), condition [5.1] can be satisfied only if m_i is a positive integer (obviously only an integer number of tasks can be operated in an establishment). If m_i is not a positive integer, fund-input idleness can be reduced, but never entirely eliminated.

5.5.3. *In-line arrangement and the specialization of elementary processes: two alternatives for continuous fund-input utilization*

In a productive establishment organized on the straight-line pattern, condition [5.1] above can be satisfied in one of two ways: (i) by arranging 'in line' a sufficient number of e.p.s (each consisting of one or more tasks); (ii) by arranging 'in series' a sufficient number of e.p.s each consisting of a single task (*specialized* e.p.s). (The 'in-line' and 'in-series' arrangements of e.p.s over time have been presented in section 4.3.4).

The way in which an 'in-line' arrangement of e.p.s can reduce fund-input idleness can be illustrated by our paradigm case. Assume that the time taken by 'car-assembling' is α_1/T_w, and that the time taken by 'wheel-screwing' is α_2/T_w. A necessary condition for continuous fund-input utilization is that a work station can be switched from one e.p. to another as soon as the first e.p. is completed. (Note that it is possible to do this by changing the e.p. that is processed at a given work station, without changing the location of the work station itself.) This condition can be satisfied only if each work station performs a certain number of tasks during a working day.

This situation is represented in Fig. 5.3. It is assumed that $\alpha_1 = 1/8$ and $\alpha_2 = 2/8$. As the figure shows, an in-line arrangement of e.p.s permits producers to switch each work station from one e.p. to another, provided at least 8 e.p.s are simultaneously carried out in the establishment. In this case, the car factory needs the simultaneous employment of one work station performing 'car-assembling' and two work stations performing 'wheel-screwing'.

Fig. 5.3 also shows that in general only approximately continuous utilization of fund inputs can be achieved by the in-line arrangement of the e.p.s. This is because the 'staggering' of e.p.s entails time-intervals at the beginning and at the end of the working day during which certain fund inputs cannot be used at all. In particular, of the two work stations specializing in 'wheel-screwing', the one that starts to operate at time 0 is idle both at the beginning and at the end of the day for periods of $(1/8) T_w$ each. The other 'wheel-screwing' work station is idle at the beginning of the day for a period of $(2/8)$

e.p.

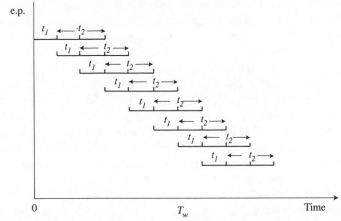

Time

0   T_w

Fig. 5.3. *Fund-input utilization in a 'straight-line' process: the in-line arrangement case*

T_w. On the other hand, the work station specializing in 'car-assembling' is kept continuously employed throughout the day except for a period of $(1/8)$ T_w at the end of the day. (Note that this period of idleness would disappear if tasks could be executed in a way disconnected from the other tasks of the same e.p.)

Thus we see that condition [5.1] above is not, in general, satisfied by arranging the e.p.s in line. The in-line arrangement permits the continuous utilization of all the work stations throughout the working day only in the hypothetical case of a production process that goes on without interruption all day and night. This special situation draws attention to the possibility of combining the advantage of an in-line arrangement with that of shift-work. In general, however, shift-work influences the total number of e.p.s. operated within the day but not the arrangement of e.p.s. over time. As a result, the introduction of shift-work will not, in general, determine any significant reduction of fund-input idle time unless the time-arrangement of e.p.s. is also transformed. (A careful analysis of the relationship between shift-work and capacity utilization may be found in Marris, 1964.)

Fund-input idleness can be reduced, and eventually eliminated, in a different way: the use-times of fund inputs can be increased by separating off one or more tasks, which thus become independent e.p.s. We shall refer to this latter phenomenon as an increase in the *degree of specialization* of the e.p. (An e.p. is more specialized the fewer the tasks required for its operation). The way in which a higher e.p. specialization may reduce fund-input idleness can be illustrated by considering again our paradigm case.

Assume that 'car-assembling' and 'wheel-screwing' can be executed as two separate e.p.s, so that the output of each can vary independently of that of its previously complementary task. Condition [5.1] above implies that the fund inputs specializing in 'wheel-screwing' are continuously active throughout the working day, provided that four 'wheel-screwing' tasks are executed each day, whereas the fund inputs specializing in 'car-assembling' are continuously active provided eight 'car-assembling' tasks are executed each day. In this case, the 'loose-ends' problem characteristic of the in-line arrangement disappears altogether, since each e.p. is started at the very beginning of the working day and the working day can be divided an exact number of times by the length of time it takes to perform each task (now, each e.p.).

The two examples above help us to derive the general conditions for minimum fund-input idleness in the two cases of an in-line arrangement of e.p.s and of complete e.p. specialization. In the rest of this section, we shall consider a production process in which n e.p.s are operated by a sequence of s tasks. (Note that not all tasks have to be performed in each e.p.) Let the task-lengths t_i be expressed as fractions of the working day, $T_w : t_i = (n_i/p_i) T_w, i = 1, \ldots, s$. Let e be an e.p. consisting of all s tasks, and $e_i, i = 1, \ldots, s$ an e.p. consisting of task i only. We assume that all fund inputs are special-purpose (so that s different types of fund input are needed in the establishment). The following proposition can be derived.

Proposition 5.3. In a straight-line production process which uses s types of single-purpose fund inputs, fund-input idleness can be reduced to a minimum in either of the following two ways: (i) by arranging e.p.s of one or more types in line, and operating these e.p.s at time-intervals equal to $T_w/\text{l.c.m.} \{p_i\}, i = 1, \ldots, s$; (ii) by operating, for each task i, a specialized e.p. e_i, and performing in each working day a number of e.p.s equal to p_i/n_i if p_i/n_i is a whole number, otherwise a number of e.p.s equal to the maximum integer less than p_i/n_i.

This proposition follows from condition [5.1] in proposition 5.2. The in-line arrangement referred to in case (i) above involves the 'staggering' of e.p.s in the establishment, thus permitting a reduction in the idle time of fund inputs by switching them from one task to another. The more often a certain task is required, the shorter will be the idleness of the corresponding fund input. If the e.p.s are started at time-intervals equal to $T_w/$l.c.m. $\{p_i\}$ from each other, each division of T_w, when T_w is divided by any one of $p_1, p_2, \ldots, p_s$ is also a division point of T_w when T_w is divided by l.c.m. $\{p_i\}$. Hence any task i ($i = 1, \ldots, s$) can be repeated at time-intervals $(n_i/p_i)\ T_w$ apart and so condition [5.1] above is satisfied (see proposition 5.2). This same condition is obviously satisfied, for each task i, if (p_i/n_i) e.p.s of type e_i are operated, one after the other, in a single working day.

The main implication of proposition 5.3 is that the minimum fund-input idleness made possible by an in-line arrangement of e.p.s (of the same or different types), if each e.p. consists of two or more distinct tasks, is generally different from the minimum fund-input idleness made possible by operating specialized e.p.s of type e_i. For any in-line arrangement involves the 'staggering' of e.p.s, and this implies the existence of idle times both at the beginning and at the end of the working day. This source of fund-input idleness may disappear altogether in the case of specialized e.p.s, for the operation of (p_i/n_i) tasks permits tasks of type i to be continuously executed from the beginning to the end of each working day, if (p_i/n_i) is a whole number.

Minimum fund-input idleness requires that a certain number of tasks be performed every day by each fund input. If the in-line arrangement is adopted, proposition 5.2 implies a condition of minimum process scale (approximately continuous fund-input utilization is possible, provided the number of e.p.s simultaneously operated in an establishment is at least equal to the lowest common multiple $\{p_i\}$). On the other hand, if specialized e.p.s are introduced, condition [5.1] from proposition 5.2 can be satisfied independently of any condition on process scale (for the required frequency of tasks can be obtained even in an establishment operating a single e.p. per unit of time).

The process scale that minimizes fund-input idleness with an in-line arrangement of e.p.s can itself be reduced to a minimum by an even distribution of work between fund inputs (or work stations). For a production process in which each fund input (or work station) contributes the same fraction of total work time (say, $(1/m)\ T_w$, where m is equal to the number of fund inputs needed in the e.p.), gives minimum fund-input idleness, if m e.p.s are simultaneously operated in the establishment. An uneven distribution of the same total work implies that certain fund inputs contribute a fraction, $(n_i/v_i)\ T_w$, greater than $(1/m)\ T_w$, whereas other fund inputs contribute a fraction $(n_j/v_j)\ T_w$, less than $(1/m)\ T_w$. But in this case, the lowest common multiple $\{v_i\}$, $i = 1, \ldots, s$, exceeds m, so that minimum fund-input idleness would require a higher process scale.[10]

5.5.4. *In-line arrangement and the specialization of elementary processes: the cases of special-purpose and multi-purpose fund inputs*

In general, any task may be executed by *special-purpose* or *multi-purpose* fund inputs, according to whether the fund inputs are employed in executing a single task or a variety of tasks in the *same* production process. Obviously, this distinction only applies to the case of a production process whose e.p.s consist of two or more tasks each, for, in the case of a completely specialized e.p., which consists of a single task, even a fund input which is potentially multi-purpose would be employed in executing that task only.

(*a*) *Special-purpose fund inputs*. In a production process in which only *special-purpose* fund inputs are employed, the least idleness permitted by an in-line arrangement of e.p.s can be achieved by starting the e.p.s at time-intervals $T_w/\text{l.c.m.}\ \{p_i\}$ from each other (where T_w is the length of the working day, and $(n_i/p_i)\ T_w$ the length of task i, for $i = 1, \ldots, s$). Assuming that any task i may also be performed independently of the other $(s - 1)$ tasks, the minimum fund-input idleness permitted by complete specialization of the e.p.s can be achieved by operating, each day, a number of e.p.s of type e_i ($i = 1, \ldots, s$) equal to (p_i/n_i), or the highest positive integer less than (p_i/n_i), depending on whether (p_i/n_i) is an integer or not. (The completely specialized e.p. is one in which all fund inputs co-operate in executing a single task.)

If all tasks of a production process have equal or approximately equal length, it is more likely that e.p. specialization would permit continuous or approximately continuous fund-input utilization (in the extreme case qf an e.p. consisting of i tasks, all lasting $(1/m)\ T_w$,

---

[10] This result is consistent with the emphasis on 'line-balancing' characteristic of a number of studies on production management (see 'Note on the literature' at the end of Ch. 4).

continuous utilization can be achieved by operating *m* e.p.s in each working day). On the other hand, if there are considerable differences among task-lengths, continuous fund-input utilization may be impossible, particularly in the case of the fund inputs used in the longest types of task.[11]

We may tentatively say that the nearer a straight-line process is to perfect 'line-balancing' (even distribution of work among fund inputs or work stations), the more likely it is that e.p. specialization would permit the continuous utilization of all the fund inputs. On the other hand, the more unequal the distribution of work among fund inputs or work stations, the more difficult it is to avoid fund-input idleness by e.p. specialization. This result confirms the conjecture of authors such as Gioja, Hermann, and Babbage that, in the case of a 'non-symmetrical' division of labour among workers (such that the product spends unequal cycle times at the different work stations), large-scale production may be necessary in order to avoid fund-input idleness (see section 3.2.3).

We may now compare the number of fund-input units necessary to avoid fund-input idleness by an in-line arrangement or by e.p. specialization respectively. In the case of special-purpose fund inputs, approximately continuous fund-input utilization by an in-line arrangement requires that n_i units of fund input $F_i (i = 1, \ldots, s)$ be employed in the establishment, where $(n_i/p_i)T_w$ is the length of task *i*. For it would be impossible to start e.p.s at the required time-intervals from each other, unless the number of fund-input units executing the longest types of task is higher than the number of fund-input units executing the shortest types of task. (In an e.p. consisting of two tasks τ_1 and τ_2, lasting 1/3 of an hour and 2/3 of an hour respectively, the in-line arrangement ensures approximately continuous utilization provided e.p.s are started at time-intervals of 20 minutes from each other and there are 1 and 2 units of the fund inputs executing tasks τ_1 and τ_2 respectively.) On the other hand, for the operation of specialized e.p.s to enable continuous utilization, it is sufficient that a *single* unit of each fund input is active for a sufficient number of times in each working day, and that a *single* e.p. is operated per unit of time.

[11] An example would be an e.p. consisting of tasks τ_1 and τ_2, lasting respectively $(1/3)T_w$ and $(2/3)T_w$. E.p. specialization permits continuous utilization of the fund inputs specializing in task τ_1, provided 3 specialized e.p.s are operated each day. On the other hand, the fund input specializing in task τ_2 would be idle for $(1/3)T_w$, if this task is executed as an independent e.p.

(*b*) *Multi-purpose fund inputs.* The employment of *multi-purpose* fund inputs makes several considerable differences to the previous analysis. The minimum scale allowing continuous utilization is generally lower with multi-purpose than with special-purpose fund inputs. This can be seen by considering a production process in which *s* tasks are required and the *j*th fund input, F_j, is able to execute k_j different and *consecutive* tasks ($j = 1, \ldots, r$). The general condition [5.1] from proposition 5.2 may now be expressed as follows.

Proposition 5.4. In a straight-line production process employing *r* types of multi-purpose fund inputs, fund-input idleness can be avoided, provided that the *j*th fund input F_j ($j = 1, \ldots, r$) is used on each working day a number of times equal to

$$1 / \sum_{i \in T_j} (n_i/p_i) \qquad [5.2]$$

where T_j is the set of tasks done by F_j.

Proposition 5.4 follows directly from proposition 5.2 above, together with the assumption that the *j*th fund input can be used to perform k_j alternative tasks.

To make notation simpler, let α_j denote the fraction of T_w that the set of tasks T_j takes to be executed. An in-line arrangement of e.p.s permits approximately continuous fund-input utilization provided the e.p.s are started at time-intervals equal to $T_w/$l.c.m. $\{1/\alpha_j\}$, $j = 1, \ldots, r$. For any division point of T_w, if T_w is divided by $1/\alpha_j$, is also a division-point of T_w if T_w is divided by l.c.m. $\{1/\alpha_j\}$. (See the discussion of proposition 5.3 above.) In this case, each group of consecutive tasks T_j is repeated at time-intervals equal to

$$\alpha_j T_w \qquad [5.3]$$

Condition [5.2] is approximately satisfied, provided that the process scale is either l.c.m. $\{1/\alpha_j\}$, $j = 1, \ldots, r$, or an integer multiple of this number. (Exact fulfilment is impossible due to the 'loose-ends' problem characteristic of the in-line arrangement of e.p.s.) An example is given in Fig. 5.4, which depicts a production process consisting of a single e.p. type. Four tasks (τ_1, τ_2, τ_3, τ_4) are executed in a sequence, the working day (T_w) lasts 8 hours, any e.p. lasts 4 hours, and the task-lengths are as follows: $t_1 = (1/8)T_w$, $t_2 = (1/8)T_w$, $t_3 = (1/8)T_w$, $t_4 = (1/8)T_w$. We assume that 2 multi-purpose fund inputs are used (F_1 and F_2), which are respectively

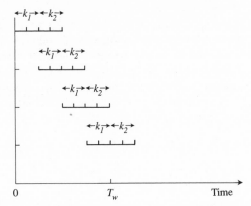

Fig. 5.4. *Multi-purpose fund inputs: the in-line arrangement and the 'loose-ends' problem*

able to perform the groups of tasks (τ_1, τ_2) and (τ_3, τ_4). Each task group k_j is repeated at time-intervals equal to $\alpha_j T_w, j = 1, 2$ (in our example, such time-intervals are of 2 hours each). The minimum process scale permitting the switching of fund inputs from one e.p. to another, as soon as a task is completed in an e.p., is 4 e.p.s. The need to carry out production in day-time only brings about idle times for both fund inputs (F_1 is idle for $(1/8)T_w$ at the end of each working day, and F_2 is idle for $(1/8)T_w$ at the beginning of each working day).

In the special case in which F_j is a general-purpose fund input (so that $k_j = s$) and there is a single e.p. which uses F_j to perform the k tasks once each consecutively, F_j can be continuously utilized by operating a single e.p. at any one time. For, if the 'use time' of a fund input in an e.p. is equal to the length of the whole e.p., that fund input can be kept continuously active by operating α_j e.p.s one following the other (i.e. in a series). In general, however, the length of the e.p. (T_e, say) is greater than $\alpha_j T_w$, for there are stages of the e.p. in which the fund input, even though it is general purpose, is not in use. In this case, condition [5.2] is approximately satisfied by operating in series a number of e.p.s equal to the highest positive integer less than T_w/T_e.

If T_w is 8 hours and T_e is 4 hours, a general-purpose fund input is continuously active provided 2 e.p.s are operated, one following the other, in the establishment. If T_w is 8 hours and T_e is 3 hours, minimum fund-input idleness is obtained by operating in series 2 e.p.s, but the fund input will be idle 2 hours per day. It is easy to see that, in this case, an in-line arrangement of e.p.s would greatly increase the idle times of fund inputs, obliging producers to have 2 fund inputs instead of 1. The two situations (arrangements in series and in line) are depicted in Figs. 5.5A and 5.5B (the dotted lines show periods of idleness).

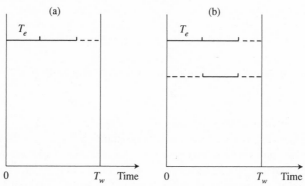

Fig. 5.5A. *Arrangement in series*   **Fig. 5.5B.** *Arrangement in line*

On the other hand, if we consider an intermediate case in which F_j is multi-purpose, but not *general*-purpose, so that $1 < k_j < s$, there is an in-line arrangement of e.p.s using multi-purpose fund inputs (each executing a series of consecutive tasks) which still makes it possible to achieve approximately continuous fund-input utilization at a minimum scale (equal to l.c.m. $\{1/\alpha_j\}$) lower than that required in the case of special-purpose fund inputs (i.e. l.c.m. $\{p_i\}$). This can be immediately seen by noting that, for any $k_j > 1$, the interval $\alpha_j T_w$ is greater than the interval $T_w/\text{l.c.m.} \{p_i\}$).

The advantages of the straight-line model of productive activity with multi-purpose fund inputs may be illustrated by considering the structural and operational characteristics of flexible manufacturing systems. These are production systems in which computer-controlled fund inputs (machine tools) are able to process a variety of parts, and thus to operate a variety of e.p.s, by means of a change of software (see Kalkunte, Sarin, and Wilhelm, 1986: 3). Here, flexibility is associated with the multi-dimensional character of machine-tools capabilities, and leads to the possibility of changing the mix of different e.p. types, without introducing significant delays in the delivery of goods as the system switches from one output-mix to another. Flexible manufacturing systems highlight the advantage of multi-purpose fund inputs when each product variety is produced in batches of medium size, for the continuous utilization of machine tools is achieved at a process scale lower than in the case of single-purpose fund inputs. They also make it possible to avoid idle fund-input capacity when there is a change of the output-mix, for 'in the computer-integrated-manufacturing factory, the existence of multimission machinery means that the excess capacity of [good] A's production can be made available for [good] B's production run, so that excess *demand* for one product can be met by excess *capacity* in another product' (Talaysum, Zia Hassan, and Goldhar, 1986: 49; see also Mermet, 1981; Warnecke and Steinhilper, 1985; Milgrom and Roberts, 1990).

The above features of flexible manufacturing systems draw attention to another result of the utilization of multi-purpose fund inputs: the possibility of significantly reducing the amount of 'work-in-process' by avoiding the formation of stocks of unfinished products of specific varieties. (Note that such stocks would often pile up when it is necessary to maintain separate production lines serviced by different single-purpose fund inputs.) The latter feature of multi-purpose fund inputs provides an important link with the conditions that have to be satisfied to make 'just-in-time' manufacturing possible.

This analysis raises the question of whether the same advantages are to be gained with multi-purpose fund inputs that are able to execute *non-consecutive* tasks. There are cases of advantage, but we shall not pursue this line of inquiry in the present research. (We may conjecture that the type of advantage deriving from multi-purpose fund inputs depends on whether their capabilities are *adjacent* or *non-adjacent*. In the latter case, the tasks which the same fund input may perform are non-consecutive, and it may happen that the advantage of versatility conflicts with the requirement that there are no gaps between tasks in any given e.p.)

(c) *In-line arrangement and e.p. specialization: a comparison.* In the case of e.p. specialization (case 1), continuous fund-input utilization is possible, even if a single e.p. is operated at any one time. (This implies that the corresponding production process is operated at unit scale.) On the other hand, in the case of continuous utilization by an in-line arrangement (case 2), the required scale is greater than 1. But it would be misleading to compare the processes of cases 1 and 2 at a common scale, owing to the different task-composition of the e.p. in the two cases. A proper comparison of the conditions for minimum fund-input idleness with e.p. specialization, on the one hand, and with an in-line arrangement of e.p.s, on the other, requires us to calculate the total number of *tasks* executed in the two cases, counting a given task n times, if the scale is n. Throughout the following analysis, we shall assume that the jth fund input is capable of performing k_j consecutive tasks, with $k_j > 1$.

Consider a production process consisting of s consecutive tasks. Elementary-process specialization involves the operation of each task as a separate e.p. Continuous utilization is possible, if we have s fund inputs each performing (p_i/n_i) tasks each day ($i = 1, \ldots, s$). (Note that this condition follows immediately from the general condition on continuous utilization expressed in proposition 5.2.)

On the other hand, the number of tasks permitting minimum fund-input idleness in the case of an in-line arrangement of e.p.s may be determined as follows. Let $\alpha_j T_w$ be the length of the sequence of consecutive tasks k_j ($j = 1, \ldots, r$). If $(n_i/p_i)T_w$ is the length of each task i ($i = 1, \ldots, s$), an in-line arrangement allows minimum idleness, if it has

$$n_j = \sum_{i=1}^{k_j} n_i$$

units of fund input j performing, in each day, the set of tasks T_j a number of times equal to $1/\alpha_j$. (This condition is an extension of the similar condition for the in-line arrangement with special-purpose fund inputs.) As a result, the total number of tasks is smaller in the case of an in-line arrangement with multi-purpose fund inputs than in the case of e.p. specialization, since $1/\alpha_j$ is obviously less than (p_i/n_i). If, on the other hand, fund inputs are special purpose, we have $(1/\alpha_j) = (p_i/n_i)$, so that the same number of tasks would be required with the two methods.

The foregoing analysis has shown that an in-line arrangement using multi-purpose fund inputs allows minimum fund-input idleness at a lower scale than any *in-line arrangement* using special-purpose fund inputs. Furthermore, multi-purpose fund inputs enable continuous utilization for a lower number of tasks performed in each working day than in the case of complete e.p. specialization (when any fund input can be used to perform only a single type of task).

An in-line arrangement can only permit *approximately* continuous fund-input utilization, because of the 'loose ends' at the beginning and end of each day. These 'loose ends' are impossible to avoid, regardless of whether special-purpose or multi-purpose fund inputs are used, as long as we consider production processes consisting of a single e.p. type. On the other hand, the elimination of all idle times may be possible in a production process consisting of e.p. types that have different precedence patterns. However, the elimination of idle times generally requires that task-lengths can be varied, and that time-lags between tasks are admissible. Both these possibilities are a characteristic feature of actual job-shop production: in a job-shop organization, fund-input continuous utilization is typically made possible by the employment of multi-purpose fund inputs in tasks of variable length, in e.p.s with different precedence patterns. Fig. 5.6 shows how an actual productive arrangement, which may be regarded as a combination of the straight-line and job-shop models of organization, can eliminate fund-input idleness.

Elementary process I consists of tasks τ_1 and τ_2 which are performed in a sequence. Task-lengths are as follows: $t_1 = (1/4)T_w$ and $t_2 = (1/4)T_w$. Fig. 5.6 shows an in-line arrangement of e.p.s of type I, which permits minimum fund-input idleness. On the assumption that $T_w = 8$ hours, fund inputs F_1 and F_2 would remain idle for

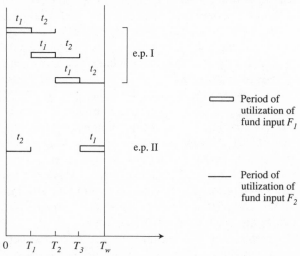

Fig. 5.6. *Continuous fund-input utilization in a combination of straight-line and job-shop processes*

the time-intervals $[T_3, T_w]$ and $[0, Ts_1]$ respectively, unless one e.p. of type II is also operated.

The characteristic of e.p. II that makes continuous fund-input utilization possible is that such an e.p. type permits time-lags between tasks.

5.6. CONCLUDING REMARKS

The foregoing argument suggests that the phenomena of scale-dependent technology expansion, in spite of their apparent hetero-geneity, can be reduced to a common set of causes. In particular, we have argued that these phenomena can be explained by the existence of gaps between the task-performing capacities of the different inputs and the levels of their utilization. Such gaps are due to the existence of indivisible inputs or fund inputs. Both these categories of inputs are capable of idleness along one dimension or another of utilization. The dimension in question is generally the capacity to be used in parallel e.p.s in the case of indivisible inputs, and time in the case of fund inputs. (Of course, it is also possible for fund inputs to operate a number of parallel e.p.s and so to be used below full capacity with respect to this dimension too.)

A general feature of the feasibility problems considered in this chapter is that the operation of a 'balanced' technical practice (in which under-utilization and idleness are eliminated or reduced to a minimum) is only possible when the production process delivers a given minimum output; only then can there be a coincidence between input 'productive potentials' and the levels of their utilization. Furthermore, the maintenance of full and continuous utilization as the output of the process is expanded is normally possible only if the output is expanded in a series of discontinuous steps.

In the present chapter, we have paid special attention to the relationship between fund-input utilization and technology expansion. In particular, we have found that a technical practice permitting continuous or approximately continuous fund-input utilization is feasible only if a certain number of tasks are performed in a given sequence in the productive establishment.

If the job-shop model of organization is adopted, task-lengths are not fixed. Continuous utilization can then be achieved by maintaining certain proportions between e.p. types characterized by different precedence patterns. (Note that, in this case, the number of tasks that any given fund input must perform in order to be continuously utilized is variable, depending on the particular e.p. combination operated in the establishment.) This condition can generally be satisfied at a low scale of production, provided that the variety of products permits the e.p.s to be combined in the required pattern.

In the straight-line model of organization, on the other hand, task-lengths are fixed. In this case, continuous fund-input utilization requires that at least a certain number of tasks be performed each day (see condition [5.1] in proposition 5.2). In an establishment organized on the straight-line model, minimum fund-input idleness can be achieved in one of two ways: (i) by e.p. specialization; (ii) by large-scale production. Both methods deal with the same problem (how to reduce the periods of fund-input idleness). Furthermore, the solution criterion is the same. In both cases, minimum idleness is obtained by having each fund input perform, in each working day, a number of tasks (or a number of groups of tasks) which approximately satisfies the condition expressed in proposition 5.2.

However, e.p. specialization and large-scale production involve technical practices that appear to differ markedly. In particular, a completely specialized e.p. is often operated in workshops in which a single e.p., or a small number of e.p.s, is operated per unit of time.[12] On the other hand, large-scale production permits continuous fund-input utilization only if a minimum number of e.p.s are in simultaneous operation in the productive establishment. This condition may require that a considerable scale of production is reached before continuous utilization is possible.

The analysis of this chapter has shown that the minimum number of tasks needed for continuous fund-input utilization also depends on the number of different tasks that each fund input is able to perform. With special-purpose fund inputs, the same number of tasks is required in a day, either with e.p. specialization or with large-scale production. On the other hand, the required number of tasks decreases as a fund input becomes more and more versatile (less specialized), by taking on more tasks in the same e.p. In this case,

[12] This characteristic implies small-scale production, if scale is defined as the number of e.p.s in simultaneous use. However, this kind of 'small-scale production' is not necessarily carried out in a small establishment, for process scale may be low, even if the size of the objects appearing in each task-definition is large. A blast-furnace may be an example of a production process that consists of few simultaneous e.p.s operating in a large establishment.

large-scale production permits continuous utilization with a lower total number of tasks performed in each working day than is required with complete e.p. specialization. However, as the number of different tasks performed by a single fund input approaches *s* (the total number of tasks needed in a single e.p.), continuous fund-input utilization can be achieved by operating a single e.p. per unit of time, thus going back to a situation characteristic of complete e.p. specialization. We may conclude that large-scale production is the method that permits the attainment of minimum idleness of the fund inputs with a minimum number of tasks per day only in the case in which the following three conditions are satisfied: (i) straight-line organization is used; (ii) multi-purpose fund inputs are employed; (iii) the number of different tasks performed by any fund input is sufficiently small in relation to the total number of tasks needed in an e.p.

It has also been shown that, if the type and sequence of tasks to be executed in an establishment is fixed, there are in general strict conditions governing the output levels that allow full and/or continuous utilization of inputs. In the case of full input utilization, the condition on the output level(s) yields a condition on process scale (for full utilization requires that a minimum number of parallel e.p.s be operated per unit of time). In the case of continuous fund-input utilization, the condition on the output level(s) may not always entail a parallel condition on process scale (viz. on the number of e.p.s taking place simultaneously in the establishment). For, in the case of e.p. specialization, the requirement that a minimum number of e.p.s be executed, one after the other, may be satisfied by operating a single e.p. at any one time (i.e. at the minimum process scale). In job-shop production, on the other hand, continuous fund-input utilization is possible on condition that a certain minimum process scale is attained, even though various proportions between e.p. types (and thus also between the output levels of different commodities) are consistent with this. It is only in the case in which producers achieve approximately continuous utilization by an in-line arrangement of e.p.s that there is a one-to-one correspondence between minimum process scale and minimum output level(s).

The operation of a technical practice permitting full and/or continuous input utilization often requires that the production process attains a certain minimum scale, and that the process scale then be expanded in a discrete way. However, this condition on process scale can sometimes be satisfied even if the outputs of some of the commodities are reduced or varied in a continuous way. Moreover, e.p. specialization allows the continuous utilization of fund inputs, even if a production process is operated at unit scale.

The above set of results clarifies the distinction between the present theory of the economies of scale and product diversification and recent contributions on 'economies of scope' (see, in particular, Baumol, Panzar, and Willig, 1982). If the scale of a process is measured by levels of output, the economizing of shareable inputs requires the consideration of multiple products. However, if scale is measured in terms of processes utilized, it appears that productive facilities may be shared by productive processes in a number of different ways. For example, a machine may be shared by processes that are using it at the same time or in a sequence, and this may be done independently of whether the processes sharing a common input are producing different commodities.

The present theoretical framework suggests that diversification of production is a special device whose relevance and mode of operation have to be assessed by considering how the network of e.p.s is organized in each productive unit. (For example, the diversification of production is subject to different constraints depending on whether we consider job-shop or straight-line establishments.)

We may conclude that scale-technology expansion is an important element in explaining the changes of practice that may accompany an increasing process scale. In certain cases, however, large-scale production is not a necessary condition for the continuous utilization of fund inputs. The adoption of a technical practice that requires the simultaneous operation of a large number of e.p.s can therefore be explained in one of two ways: either the characteristics of the various inputs make full utilization possible only in the case of large-scale production; or producers prefer large-scale production, regardless of the feasibility problems we have examined so far.

6

Scale-Technology Contraction

6.1. CHANGES OF TECHNICAL PRACTICE AND TECHNOLOGY CONTRACTION

Since the writings of the classical economists, changes of technical practice due to upper bounds on the scale of the production process have been thought to be a major cause of decreasing productive efficiency as the output scale expands.[1] However, it seems to have passed unnoticed that the change of practice and the decline in efficiency have two quite distinct causes: the contraction of the set of feasible technical practices as the output scale expands, and the substitution by producers of a less for a more 'efficient' practice.[2]

This distinction lies behind another, which has been noted by various authors: the distinction between the 'agricultural' and the 'economic' laws of diminishing returns. An early formulation of this distinction is to be found in the following passage by Étienne Antonelli:

Is it not possible to admit the agricultural law of diminishing returns while rejecting the corresponding economic law? This is what we shall now try to do, by showing, on the one hand, that the link established by the classical school between the two laws is artificial, and on the other hand that agricultural production, from an economic point of view, follows complex laws in which the agricultural law of diminishing returns plays the role of an ordinary technical factor . . . If we consider agricultural production in a given economic framework, it is possible to say that the agricultural law of diminishing returns will certainly have an economic influence, but *it is impossible to determine exactly the direction and intensity of such an influence.* (Antonelli, 1910: 538, 544; my translation)

The distinction between the 'agricultural' and the 'economic' cases of diminishing returns was also made by Maurice Byé when describing

---

[1] Early formulations of the classical theory of decreasing efficiency, in connection with the theory of rent, are to be found in Malthus (1815*a*; 1815*b*), and Ricardo (1815; 1817). A recent appraisal of the technological basis of classical rent theory may be found in Quadrio-Curzio (1987).

[2] The 'less efficient' practice may sometimes be interpreted as the *choice* of the 'best' of the remaining practices according to the 'economic' preferences of the producer. (See Ch. 8.)

the choice of agricultural practices: 'The agriculturist is in fact choosing the most productive way of employing his endowment [of productive resources]. The way in which this choice is made is arbitrary, that is to say it depends on causes that are complex and entirely external to the technical laws of productivity change' (Byé, 1928: 422; my translation). In Byé's view, technical choice is not merely the result of technical laws, and the factors that bring about 'productivity change' may not be sufficient to explain the course of technical change on any given occasion.

Common to Antonelli and Byé is the idea that changes in productive efficiency, as output scales expand, are the result of an interaction between producers' actions and certain non-human factors that determine the set of practices feasible at each scale. It is thus no wonder that authors such as Antonelli and Byé thought it impossible to formulate in a precise form a law of decreasing productive efficiency: for, in their opinion, technical *choice* is an 'arbitrary' element which obscures any tendency towards diminishing efficiency due to technical laws *per se*.

The idea that both producers' behaviour and non-human factors underlie decreasing productive efficiency was also expressed by Piero Sraffa, who linked decreasing efficiency to the existence of a choice criterion, and to a 'certain degree of *variety and independence*' among the feasible technical practices (Sraffa, 1925: 288; my translation). However, the 'arbitrary' element introduced by producers' preferences and behaviour is not seen by Sraffa as an obstacle to the formulation of a law of decreasing efficiency. For, according to Sraffa, 'decreasing efficiency is a necessary outcome', since 'the producer himself, following his own advantage, will rank the factor doses and their modes of use along a decreasing scale, from the best to the worst, and will start production by using the best combinations, and then moving to the inferior ones when the former are no longer available' (ibid.).

The distinction between the feasibility element and the action element in decreasing productive efficiency throws light on the distinction between various cases of decreasing efficiency found in the economic literature. This chapter deals with the cases in which increasing process scale narrows the set of feasible technical practices. Section 6.2 introduces the problem of the existence of an upper bound on the 'scale' of a technical practice, by distinguishing between the 'engineering' case (in which a practice does not work above a certain scale k) and the 'availability' case (in which a practice could work, but does not work above a certain scale because of the limited availability of some essential input(s) x). Section 6.3 deals with the engineering and availability cases due to fund inputs (inputs that remain available in the productive unit after they have been used in a task). There we shall find that the engineering cases are often linked with capacity utilization, and so establish a connection between the engineering and the availability cases. Section 6.4 deals with the engineering and availability cases due to flow inputs (inputs that are normally 'used up' in the course of the production process). The cases due to flow inputs are found to differ sharply from the cases due to fund inputs. Section 6.5 considers the relationship between upper bounds on the process scale and upper bounds on the production levels of commodities. There it is argued that, if the production process is an arrangement of elementary processes (e.p.s) that may not all deliver the same kind of output, then the disappearance of certain practices from the set of feasible practices influences the 'technology in use', but has no implications for the production levels of the individual commodities. Section 6.6 concludes by comparing the results with other treatments in the economic literature.

6.2. SCALE-TECHNOLOGY CONTRACTION AND MAXIMUM PROCESS SCALES: THE GENERAL ISSUES

Let $\Phi(s)$ be the set of technical practices feasible at scale s. (Note that, in section 4.3.1, the *scale* of a production process was defined as the number of simultaneously operated e.p.s.) We shall use the term *scale-technology contraction* for a situation in which, if s and s' are two scales such that $s' > s$, there is at least one technical practice θ such that $\theta \in \Phi(s)$ and $\theta \notin \Phi(s')$. Thus there is a scale-technology contraction if, and only if, $\Phi(s') \not\supseteq \Phi(s)$. (Note that, by this definition, there is a scale-technology contraction if at least one technical practice feasible at s is not feasible at s', *even if* there are practices feasible at s' which are not feasible at s.[3])

---

[3] Scale-technology contraction is related to, but not coincident with, the convexity of the production possibility set considered in activity analysis. As a matter of fact, convexity may be interpreted as a sub-case of technology contraction under special assumptions: it presupposes the law of variable proportions (see s. 3.5), whereas technology contraction is compatible with a more general representation of technology,

Scale-technology contraction is the result of one or more upper bounds on the process scales at which a technical practice is feasible. The classical economists considered cases of scale-technology contraction due to upper bounds on land availability (Malthus, Ricardo, West) or on the availability of other non-produced inputs, such as mineral resources (Ricardo). Other cases of scale-technology contraction derive from upper bounds on the rates of renewal of inputs that can be reproduced only at rates only partially determined by producers' actions (such as fisheries or forests). Finally, a relationship between increasing process scale and contracting technology is also seen when a technical practice can be maintained, as process scale is expanded, only on condition that scale is expanded by discrete steps. (This latter phenomenon reflects the requirements for the full and/or continuous utilization of inputs that were considered in Chapter 5.)

It is worth distinguishing at this point two cases of scale-technology contraction, corresponding to two sources of upper bounds on process scale: (i) the *engineering case*, in which a technical practice does not work above some scale k; (ii) the *availability case*, in which above some scale k a technical practice could work, but does not because of the limited availability of some essential input(s) x. Case (i) divides into two sub-cases: (i.i) the technical practice cannot work above scale k, because above k one of its constituent e.p.s would not work; (i.ii) a technical practice cannot work over a range of scales immediately above k, because the levels of capacity utilization that characterize that practice can only be maintained by increasing scale by a discrete step.

Sub-case (i.i) is a result of the fact that, in general, physical laws, chemical reactions, or biological functions can only work or be performed within certain scale boundaries.[4] Sub-case (i.ii) is a result of the laws governing capacity utilization as process scale is increased (see Chapter 5). In this sub-case, the upper bound on the scale of the practice is explained by one of two reasons: either (a) there are differences in the own capacities of the various inputs (the concept

such that *qualitative* differences across different sets of feasible practices may also be considered (see also, in this connection, Scazzieri, 1982).

[4] As Georgescu-Roegen puts it: '[a]ll individual processes whether in biology or technology follow exactly the same pattern; beyond a certain scale some collapse, others explode, or melt, or freeze. In a word, they cease to work at all. Below another scale, they do not even exist' (1976 [1964]: 289).

of 'own capacity' of an input was defined in section 5.3.1); or (b) the lengths of the tasks performed by the various inputs are less than the length of the whole e.p. In situation (a), full capacity utilization per unit of time can be maintained only if process scale is increased by integer multiples of the minimum scale permitting full utilization (see section 5.3.1). In situation (b), continuous capacity utilization over time can be maintained only if process scale is increased by integer multiples of the minimum scale permitting continuous utilization (see sections 5.4.2 and 5.5.4).

In case (ii) we may also distinguish two sub-cases: (ii.i) the upper bound on the process scale is due to the limited availability of certain fund inputs (such as land, workers, machinery); (ii.ii) the upper bound is due to the limited availability of certain flow inputs (such as fuel, chemicals, and energy). In both sub-cases, the limited input availability may in turn be the result either of technical factors (certain inputs cannot be produced at all, or can only be produced at a rate lower than the required rate) or of institutional factors (certain inputs, regardless of whether they can be produced or not, are available only in limited amounts to the productive unit under consideration).

Technical factors are increasingly important as we move our attention from individual establishments to larger concerns, such as industries or whole economic systems. In addition, technical reproducibility is increasingly important as we move from the short to the long run; in the short run, the limited availability of inputs is not necessarily attributable to their limited reproducibility.

Fund inputs can be a source of upper bounds on process scale both of the engineering type and of the availability type. Accordingly, there are cases of scale-technology contraction that can be explained as the joint effect of engineering upper bounds and availability upper bounds on the rate of utilization of certain fund inputs; for example, a certain machine-using practice may not be operable above some scale k because: (i) only one such machine is available and that machine does not allow the operation of more e.p.s per unit of time; (ii) the practice does not allow the 'staggering' of more e.p.s over the working day.

The relation of fund inputs to technology contraction is studied in section 6.3.

6.3. FUND INPUTS AND TECHNOLOGY CONTRACTION

6.3.1. *Capacity utilization and technical practice: two cases*

Fund inputs can be a source of upper bounds on process scale for reasons associated with: (i) the existence of engineering upper bounds; (ii) the limited availability of fund inputs in the productive unit under consideration. In both cases, the upper bound on process scale derives from an upper bound on some dimension(s) of fund-input utilization. The engineering upper bounds may be due to either of two reasons: (a) if there is to be full utilization of all the fund inputs needed in the process, then the number of e.p.s that are operated in parallel must satisfy a certain condition (this condition is due to the existence of differences in the own capacities of the various fund inputs used in the process); (b) if there is to be continuous utilization of fund inputs over the working day, then the lengths of the time-intervals separating the starting-points of the various e.p.s or batches of e.p.s must satisfy a certain condition (this condition derives from the differences between the various task-lengths in each e.p.).

The availability upper bounds are due to the existence of a technical maximum on the number of identical e.p.s that can be operated in parallel on a single fund input, together with the fact that only a limited number of such fund inputs are available in each productive unit.

Engineering upper bounds and availability upper bounds are often present in the same productive unit, and it is sometimes difficult to say which type of upper bound explains a particular case of scale-technology contraction. Nevertheless, the above distinction provides a guideline to the explanation of some complex cases of technology contraction (see section 6.3.4). The importance of the distinction is shown by the fact that scale-technology contraction due to engineering upper bounds can be avoided, if producers follow a different pattern of scale expansion (for engineering upper bounds on the utilization of fund inputs do not involve any absolute upper bound on the process scale). On the other hand, scale-technology contraction due to availability upper bounds can only be avoided in one of two ways: by a decrease in process scale or by an increase in the availability of fund inputs.

6.3.2. *Engineering upper bounds and scale-technology contraction*

Engineering upper bounds on process scale can be observed in the utilization of all fund inputs. An important distinction, however, has to be made between land, on the one hand, and fund inputs such as machinery and workers, on the other. Land is continuously used in any e.p. in which it is needed (in such e.p.s, land performs a task that lasts the whole length of the e.p.). As a result, a change of process scale does not affect the level of utilization of this fund input *over time*. On the other hand, a characteristic feature of machinery and workers is that, in most e.p.s, they are needed for less than the whole duration of the e.p. As a result, a technical practice continues to permit the continuous utilization of all the fund inputs as scale increases, only if it does so in a discrete way (see sections 5.4 and 5.5). In the case of this category of fund inputs, the following proposition applies. (The relevant notation was introduced in Chapter 4.)

Proposition 6.1. If a fund input is needed, in any e.p., for a fraction (n_i/p_i) of the length T_w of the working day, the following two cases of scale-technology contraction may be distinguished: (a) In a job-shop production process, there are scales that make it impossible to switch fund inputs between e.p.s that have different precedence patterns in such a way as to maintain continuous fund-input utilization. (The technical practice that has continuous fund-input utilization would not be feasible at these scales.); (b) In a straight-line production process, there are scales that make it impossible to satisfy any of the following three conditions for continuous fund-input utilization: (i) process scale is equal either to the l.c.m. $\{p_i\}$ or to an integer multiple of this number (the case of single-purpose fund inputs); (ii) process scale is equal either to the l.c.m. $\{1/\alpha_j\}$ or to an integer multiple of this number (the case of a multi-purpose fund input F_j, performing k_j tasks in any elementary process); (iii) process scale is equal either to (p_i/n_i) or to an integer multiple of this number (the case of a specialized e.p. e_i). If any of the above three conditions is not satisfied, the technical practice that has continuous fund-input utilization would not be feasible.

This proposition follows from the analysis of fund-input utilization in Chapter 5. In particular, case (a) derives from the fact that job-shop production allows continuous fund-input utilization only on condition that a certain combination of e.p.s (which have different precedence patterns) is operated. This implies that a technical practice that has continuous fund-input utilization is feasible only if process scale is increased by adding identical combinations of e.p.s. (Hence there are intermediate scales at which this technical practice is not feasible.) Case (b) derives from the fact that, with straight-line production, continuous utilization is possible only if each fund input performs a certain definite number of tasks in each working day.

An important implication of proposition 6.1 is that the use of fund inputs makes technology contraction likely in a considerable number of cases, particularly if process scale is varied according to 'rules' that do not take into account the requirements for continuous utilization. An example might be when the changes of process scale reflect the changes in final demands.

Engineering upper bounds may also derive from differences in the own capacities of the various fund inputs (see section 5.3.1). The relationship of this type of upper bound to scale-technology contraction is expressed by the following proposition.

Proposition 6.2. Given a production process employing r fund inputs with own capacities c_i ($i = 1, \ldots ,r$), any process scale other than l.c.m. $\{c_i\}$, or an integer multiple of this scale, precludes the full utilization of all fund inputs per unit of time.

This proposition follows from the fact that, for each fund input i, the own capacity c_i can be interpreted as the maximum number of parallel e.p.s that can be operated on this fund input per unit of time. In section 5.3.1, it was shown that the utilization of all fund inputs at their respective technical maxima is possible only if the capacity of the productive unit is l.c.m. $\{c_i\}$ or an integer multiple of this number. This implies the proposition directly.

One important implication of this result is that the upper bounds on the scales at which the 'full utilization' practices are feasible cannot be removed by increasing the number of units of the various fund inputs employed in the productive unit, unless they are all increased by a common integer multiple. For the upper bounds derive from the proportions between the capacities of natural units of the various inputs.

6.3.3. *Availability upper bounds and scale-technology contraction*

Upper bounds on input availability normally take the form of an upper bound on the number of parallel e.p.s (of a given type) that it is technically possible to operate on a fund-input unit. Examples are the upper bound on the land available for cultivation of a particular crop, or the upper bound on the total work a given machine or worker can perform in a given time. Scale-technology contractions due to availability upper bounds follow the pattern described by propositions 6.3 and 6.4 below.

Proposition 6.3. Any technical practice consisting of e.p.s of a type *i* operated in parallel on a fund input of type *h* is feasible, only if the product of process scale and of the fraction of *h* needed to operate one e.p. *i* is not greater than the total number of e.p.s of type *i* that can be operated on *h*.

This proposition is illustrated by considering the following example. Let λ_i^h denote the 'fraction' of fund input *h* needed to operate one e.p. *i* (say, the land necessary for the planting, growing, and harvesting of one potato) and Λ_h the maximum number of e.p.s of type *i* that can be operated in parallel on *h* (say, the maximum number of potatoes that can be grown on the available land). Let q_i^h denote the process scale (i.e. the number of e.p.s simultaneously operated on the given piece of land). Proposition 6.3 implies that the process is feasible only if:

$$q_i^h \leqslant \frac{\Lambda_h}{\lambda_i^h} \qquad [6.1]$$

An important implication of this result is that the upper bound on process scale can be removed by increasing the number of fund-input units available in the productive unit. The next proposition generalizes proposition 6.3 to the case in which e.p.s of several different types make use of a fund input of a given type.

Proposition 6.4. Any technical practice consisting of e.p.s of types 1,2, . . . ,*n* operated in parallel on fund input *h* is feasible, provided that the maximum number of e.p.s operated on *h* is not less than the sum of the products obtained by multiplying the number of e.p.s of each type by the fraction of *h* needed to operate one e.p. of the same type.

This proposition follows directly from the fact that any technical practice consisting of e.p.s of type 1,2, . . . ,*n* (each using fund input *h* and all operated in parallel) is feasible only if

$$\sum_{i=1}^{h} \lambda_i^h q_i^h \leqslant \Lambda_h \qquad [6.2]$$

where q_i^h denotes the number of e.p.s of type i.

As in the case considered in proposition 6.3, the upper bound on process scale can be removed by increasing the number of fund-input units available in the productive unit.

6.3.4. *The relationship between engineering and availability upper bounds*

Engineering and availability upper bounds are sometimes related to each other, so that scale-technology contraction appears to be the joint effect of both. There are two main cases. (i) In a productive unit that uses fund inputs with different own productive capacities, the availability of the fund input that provides minimum capacity for operating parallel e.p.s determines an upper bound on process scale. (ii) In a productive unit that uses a number of fund inputs below full capacity and only discontinuously over the working day, scale-technology contraction may be the result of increasing process scale up to the technical maximum determined by fund-input availabilities and by the length of the e.p. relative to the length of the working day.

From case (i) we can put forward proposition 6.5.

Proposition 6.5. In a productive unit in which n_h units of fund input h ($h = 1, \ldots, r$) are used, and in which $\bar{q}_i^h$ ($h = 1, \ldots, r$; $i = 1, \ldots, n$) is the maximum number of e.p.s of type i that it is technically possible to operate in parallel on one unit of fund input h, the least product $n_h \bar{q}_i^h$ determines an upper bound on the number of e.p.s of type i that can be operated in parallel.

This proposition follows directly from the definition of $\bar{q}_i^h$. By this definition, the number of e.p.s of type i that can be performed in parallel in a productive unit and that have n_h fund inputs of type h cannot exceed $n_h \bar{q}_i^h$. Hence, in the productive unit described, the number of e.p.s of type i that can be performed in parallel cannot exceed any of $n_1 \bar{q}_i^1, \ldots, n_n \bar{q}_i^r$. This result implies that any increase of process scale above $n_h \bar{q}_i^h$ requires either an increase in fund-input availability or a change in the e.p. type.

From case (ii) we can put forward proposition 6.6.

Proposition 6.6. In a productive unit in which Γ_i is the maximum number of e.p.s of type i that can be operated in parallel on the existing fund inputs, T_w the length of the working day, γ_i ($i = 1$,

. . . . ,n) the maximum number of e.p.s of type i that can be performed in parallel, and t_i ($i = 1, . . . ,n$) the time needed to operate one e.p. of type i, the actual number g_i of e.p.s of type i performed in a working day may be increased as long as the following inequality is satisfied:

$$g_i < (\Gamma_i/\gamma_i) \cdot (T_w/t_i) \qquad [6.3]$$

This proposition follows from the fact that the number of e.p.s operated in a productive unit in one working day can be increased, without increasing the number of fund-input units available, in one of two ways: (i) by increasing, up to the technical maximum, the number of e.p.s operated in parallel on the available fund inputs; or (ii) by increasing, up to the full length of the working day, the 'use-time' of the available fund inputs (this can be done by arranging in line a sufficient number of e.p.s). The upper bound given by Γ_i/γ_i can be removed by increasing the number of fund-input units available (this follows from the fact that this is an availability upper bound). The upper bound given by T_w/t_i is independent of the number of fund-input units (this follows from the fact that this is an engineering upper bound).

Proposition 6.6 has different implications, depending on the types of fund input used in the e.p.s. In the case of land-using processes, we generally have

$$t_i = T_w \qquad [6.4]$$

since the time during which one e.p. of any type i is operated on land in a working day is generally the total time for which land can be worked during a working day.[5] When condition [6.4] holds, it is impossible to increase process scale by arranging batches of parallel e.p.s in line. As a result, for any given plot of land, the only upper bound on land utilization that is relevant to technology contraction is that expressed by inequalities [6.1] or [6.2]. As soon as the process scale attains the level $\bar{q}_i^h$ (the scale at which land is fully utilized), any increase in the number of e.p.s requires either an increase in the availability of land or a change in the type of e.p. In particular, since condition [6.4] holds, proposition 6.6 implies that the number of e.p.s of type i operated in parallel may be increased as long as $g_i < \Gamma_i/\gamma_i$.

In the case of machinery, we usually have

[5] This is also true in such cases as double-cropping, where the same plot of land can be used to operate the same e.p. (or the same batch of e.p.s) twice a year.

$$t_i < T_w \qquad [6.5]$$

since the time that an e.p. of type i takes on a machine h is generally shorter than the maximum time that the machine can be in use during a working day. In this case, then, it may be possible to increase process scale using only machine h, even if that machine is already utilized at full capacity during any period in which it is in use at all. In fact, machinery is sometimes used to process, at a given time, a number of parallel e.p.s *below* the technical maximum. In this case, it is of course possible to increase process scale without increasing the 'use-time' of the machine.

The case of workers is, in a sense, opposite to that of land, for there is generally very limited scope for increasing the number of parallel e.p.s operated at a given time by a given worker. However, workers are usually utilized in e.p.s of types i such that $t_i < T_w$. This leaves scope for expanding process scale without any increase in 'payroll' by simply reducing the periods of the day during which the workers are idle.

6.4. FLOW INPUTS AND TECHNOLOGY CONTRACTION

Flow inputs can be a source of upper bounds on process scale for reasons associated with: (i) engineering upper bounds on flow input utilization; (ii) the limited availability of flow inputs in productive units.

Engineering upper bounds may be the result of differences in the own capacities of the inputs needed in a production process, for a process may require inputs (either of the fund or of the flow kind) that have different natural or economic units. The following proposition applies to all cases of scale-technology contraction deriving from this particular type of technical imbalance.

Proposition 6.7. In a production process employing r inputs, each having a different own capacity c_i ($i = 1, \ldots, r$), any process scale not equal to l.c.m. $\{c_i\}$, or an integer multiple of this scale, precludes the full utilization of all inputs per unit of time.

This proposition follows directly from proposition 5.1. It points to the possibility that scale-technology contraction derives from engineering upper bounds involving a certain input, regardless of whether this input remains available in the productive unit after being used in a certain task. This type of technology contraction is possible in establishments using only flow inputs, only fund inputs, or a combination of both.

In the case of flow inputs, there is no equivalent of proposition 6.1, which relates to the existence of upper bounds to the scale of a practice that allows the producer to eliminate fund-input idleness.

Availability upper bounds on flow input quantities may be associated with cases of 'contraction' in feasible technology that differ sharply from the cases due to the limited availability of fund inputs, and that may appear to entail a notion of scale different from the number of e.p.s simultaneously operated in the productive unit. The upper bounds on flow input availability are associated with upper bounds on the *total number* of e.p.s (of any given type) that can be operated during a certain period before using up the total quantity of flow input available in the productive unit at the beginning of that period. (Note that no assumption is made about the time-arrangement of the e.p.s in each period, so that the e.p.s can be arranged in series, in parallel or in line. As a result, any upper bound on the total number of e.p.s is compatible with different process scales, if scale is defined as the number of e.p.s simultaneously operated in the productive unit.)

The following proposition applies to all cases of technology contraction due to limited flow input availability.

Proposition 6.8. A technical practice is feasible only if, for each flow input, the quantity available in the productive unit is not less than the sum of the products obtained by multiplying the number of e.p.s of each type by the flow input requirement for the corresponding type of e.p.

This proposition can easily be made plausible by considering that the total quantity of any flow input cannot be less than the sum total of the 'shares' of this input which are allocated to the various types of e.p. In other words:

$$\lambda_1^h M^h + \lambda_2^h M^h + \ldots + \lambda_n^h M^h \leq M^h \qquad [6.6]$$

$$\text{subject to} \quad \sum_{i=1}^{n} \lambda_i = 1$$

where M^h is the quantity of flow input h available in the productive unit, and λ_i^h ($i = 1, \ldots, n$) the share of M^h used to operate the e.p.s of type i.

Each term on the left-hand side of inequality [6.6] is given by the expression

$$\int_0^T q_i^h(t)\, \mu_i^h, \quad i = 1, \ldots, n \qquad [6.7]$$

where $q_i^h(t)$ is the total number of e.p.s of type i that are operated during the time-interval $[0,T]$ and μ_i^h the quantity of h needed to operate one e.p. of type i. Proposition 6.8 follows directly from the fact that the sum of terms in expression (7) over the various types of e.p. cannot exceed the total quantity of h available in the productive unit.

Proposition 6.8 entails that it is possible to express upper bounds on the total number of e.p.s of each type that can be operated. For if only e.p.s of one type are operated, condition [6.6] reduces to

$$q_i^h \leq \frac{M^h}{\mu_i^h} \qquad [6.8]$$

Condition [6.8] states that, in each period in which the quantity of flow input is given, the total number of e.p.s of a certain type may be less than or equal to the number of e.p.s that would entail the depletion of the flow input. After such an upper bound is attained, the number of e.p.s may be increased in one of two ways: (i) by leaving the e.p. type unchanged and increasing the quantity of input h; (ii) by changing the e.p. type and bringing into operation inputs that are substitutes for h. Upper bounds on flow input endowments may make alternative (i) no longer feasible. In this case, an increase in the total number of e.p.s in operation is necessarily associated with technology contraction, and only alternative (ii) permits producers to increase the number of e.p.s.

A noteworthy feature of the cases of technology contraction due to limited flow input availability is that the depletion of the quantity of a given flow input h makes it strictly impossible to operate any e.p. for which input h is essential. In other words, once the quantity of a certain flow input is depleted, it becomes impossible to increase the number of e.p.s through a more 'intensive' utilization of that input, or by operating in the same productive unit e.p.s using input h and e.p.s using substitutes for h, for no flow input can be used at all after depletion of the corresponding quantity. (Note that this property points to an important difference between flow input depletion and full fund-input utilization: a fund input can generally be used at a process scale higher than that involving full utilization, in some type of e.p. other than that for which full utilization has been defined.[6])

6.5. PROCESS SCALE, COMMODITY PRODUCTION LEVELS, AND TECHNOLOGY CONTRACTION

We have seen that increasing process scale does not necessarily imply increasing the outputs of all the commodities produced. Process scale can be increased by only increasing the number of e.p.s carried out that deliver certain commodities, leaving unchanged or even decreasing the number of e.p.s carried out that deliver the remaining commodities. This property has important implications for the possibility of technology contraction due to upper bounds on input availability.

Piero Sraffa called attention to the fact that it is difficult to find cases in which the production level of any particular commodity is bounded from above because of limited resources:

If we define each particular industry as the exclusive consumer of a given *factor of production* (such as agriculture or the iron industry) then we are certainly introducing an assumption that makes it more likely that we shall find a tendency towards increasing costs in that industry, since the factor characteristic of that industry (arable land, iron mines, etc.) remains, in general, constant when production is increased. If, on the other hand, we define each industry as the exclusive producer of a given *product*, and we identify this latter in a sufficiently narrow sense, we may assume that, in general, each individual industry employs a fraction of each factor of production that is small, and negligible with respect to the quantity employed by all the other industries taken together. This eliminates from the industry under consideration the cause generating increasing costs . . . (Sraffa, 1925: 320; my translation)

[6] Certain processes using flow inputs show a characteristic that is in apparent contrast with this feature of flow input utilization. For instance, there may be a mine in which the extraction activity is simultaneously carried out from different 'stocks' of a given mineral resource (different iron ores, coal fields, etc.). Such cases, however, have nothing to do with the depletion of the quantity of any particular flow input, and are a consequence of the fact that this production process is also subject to upper bounds on fund input utilization. In particular, the simultaneous utilization of different flow input 'stocks' in the same mine follows from the existence of an upper bound on the number of e.p.s that can be operated in parallel on the same flow input stock (for instance, as a result of space limits), and is independent of any upper bound due to the depletion of such stocks.

The analysis of this chapter shows that there is no a priori reason why the production level of any particular commodity should be directly constrained by the limited endowment of any particular input (except in the special case in which a given input is needed in the production of that commodity only).

A relationship between resource endowments and upper bounds on process scales is, in general, compatible with a wide range of production possibilities (more than one output-mix may be compatible with any given process scale). If the production process is an arrangement of e.p.s that do not necessarily deliver the same kind of output, it is reasonable to consider scale-technology contraction as a phenomenon influencing technical practice but having no implications for the production of individual commodities. (Note that, if process scale is defined as the number of simultaneous e.p.s, of the same or different types, a change of scale is neutral with respect to the output composition of the production process: an increase in the scale of a process delivering commodities x_1 and x_2 is compatible with a *decrease* in the production level of either commodity.)

This conclusion corroborates Sraffa's analysis; it also makes scale-technology contraction appear, not as a *curiosum* due to a particular definition of an industry, but as the normal outcome of organizing production as a system of e.p.s that are not necessarily all of the same type, and that partially or completely overlap within the productive unit. As a matter of fact, the borders of productive units are conventional, and our definitions of process scale and scale-technology contraction take this important fact into account by making technology contraction independent of the way in which productive units are defined. In particular, there is no reason to think that taking a larger operation as the productive unit, such as a group of industries, or the whole economic system, makes a one-to-one relationship between upper bounds on process scale and upper bounds on the production levels of individual commodities or commodity baskets any more likely.

This can be seen by considering the example of agriculture. If the production process is defined to include all land-using e.p.s, there is a functional relationship between upper bounds on land and upper bounds on process scale. However, this relationship does not imply another functional relationship between upper bounds on land and upper bounds on the production levels of individual commodities, for increasing process scale is compatible with a situation in which the production levels of certain commodities remain constant, or even decrease, while those of other commodities increase (see above). It would be unwarrantably restrictive to assume that increasing process scale entails increasing production levels for all commodities delivered by the production process (as is implied by a functional relationship between upper bounds on process scale and upper bounds on the production levels of individual commodities or commodity baskets).

Changes in the definition of a production process are, however, important if we ask how likely a given resource endowment is to induce technology contraction. For the more comprehensive the definition of the production process is, the more likely it is that this process will absorb the entire 'productive capacity' of any given input. And if this happens, increasing process scale will involve the disappearance of certain practices from feasible technology.

6.6. CONCLUDING REMARKS

Scale-technology contraction is far more complicated than the simple cases usually considered in economic literature, following a tradition which goes back to Ricardo and other classical economists. In particular, technology contraction in land-using processes is not a paradigm case for technology contraction in general. Land can be an important factor limiting process scale, but its characteristics are rather special: it is a fund input, and one which in most land-using e.p.s is utilized in a continuous way. Hence technology contraction due to upper bounds on land availability is different both from technology contraction due to flow input depletion and from technology contraction due to upper bounds on the utilization of machines and workers (for these are fund inputs that, unlike land, are discontinuously utilized in most e.p.s).

Consideration of the case of land led the classical economists to make the following assumptions. First, scale-dependent technology contraction is always due to upper bounds on resource endowments; second, in the long run only upper bounds on the endowments of non-producible inputs can lead to technology contraction; and third, the characteristics of technology contraction in agriculture can be generalized to other industries using non-producible inputs.

The analysis of this chapter leads us to conclude that scale-dependent technology contraction is not always the result of limited resource endowments in the productive unit under consideration. As a result, technology contraction is possible both in the case of production processes using non-producible inputs and in the case of those in which only producible inputs are needed. Finally, it is wrong to derive any 'general' law of technology contraction from the consideration of land-using processes only. Increasing process scale may lead to technology contraction in a number of different ways and, generally speaking, technology contraction is equally likely in any production process. (Every process uses at least one fund input, quite apart from possible constraints due to limited resources.) Not all cases of scale-technology contraction can be subsumed under a general law. Indeed, there are many actual cases that can only be explained as combinations of the simple abstract cases examined in this chapter.[7]

---

[7] As when process scale is limited by upper bounds on fund input endowments and on flow input stocks.

7

Scale, Technology, and Technical Behaviour

7.1. TECHNICAL ADOPTION, LEARNING, AND SEARCH: A GENERAL FORMULATION

7.1.1. *Scale, technical adoption, and technical choice*

Changes of process scale are often associated with changes in the set of feasible technical practices. However, such changes do not necessarily bring about technical change: in many circumstances technology expansion and technology contraction may leave the technical practice unchanged. This is because the technical practice followed at any given scale of the production process is the result of two separate, though interrelated, causes: the scale, and the behaviour of producers, who each adopt precisely one of the feasible technical practices. Changes in process scale may change the set of feasible practices: new practices may become feasible and other practices may drop out of use. In general, however, more than a single practice is feasible at any given scale. This makes the technical practice in use depend on which practices are excluded by the producer at a given scale. As a result, there are cases in which different sets of technical practices are feasible at each scale but the practice in use is the same. (An example is when the two sets of technical practices are $\{\theta_1, \theta_2, \theta_3\}$, $\{\theta_1, \theta_3, \theta_4\}$ and the producer excludes the subset $\{\theta_1, \theta_2\}$ in one case and the subset $\{\theta_1, \theta_4\}$ in the other case.)

Producers' behaviour is not necessarily best described as choice. For instance, producers may simply find themselves in the position of following a certain practice, without ever considering its advantages and disadvantages compared with other feasible practices. Here, technical practice is not the outcome of deliberation, but appears more or less unintentional. But we shall see that this is not the only kind of case in which it would be inappropriate to describe producers as 'choosing' in the strong sense familiar in neoclassical economic theory. For the strength of the latter notion of choice is due to a combination of two distinct features: (i) scanning all the available alternatives; (ii) intentional adoption of one particular alternative. It would be inappropriate to describe the intentional adoption of a technical practice as technical choice in this strong sense, if that practice were adopted without a prior scanning of the alternatives.[1] If either feature (i) or (ii) above is absent, the set of feasible technical practices is not a choice-set in this neoclassical sense. Rather, the set of feasible practices simply determines the range of possible courses of action. In the following analysis, we shall use the concept of technical adoption to cover all the cases in which the technical practice is determined out of a range of feasible courses of actions, regardless of whether or not the practice is adopted after scanning and intentional choice. When a technical practice is deliberately adopted after comparison of all the technical alternatives (note that this involves both scanning and intentionality), technical adoption takes the special form of *technical choice*.

7.1.2. *A model of technical behaviour*

In the following analysis, we shall consider a situation in which scale does vary, and we shall study how the producer would behave (which technical practice he would follow) if this were to change. Treating scale in this way is an analytical device. Its interest derives from its convenience in studying the relationship between changes in the set of scale-feasible practices and changes in the actual practice adopted by the producer. However, it is not difficult to find real-life cases in which scale actually is a parameter from an individual producer's point of view. An example is a factory manager in a planned economy who has to produce a certain output, the amount of which he is not free to determine (whose 'output target' is determined in the national plan).

In this chapter, technical adoption is assumed to take place in an environment described by the following assumptions: (i) For each scale s, there is a set $\Phi(s)$ of technical practices feasible at s, whose

---

[1] Lack of intentional behaviour and/or of scanning can be found in a wide range of situations. Instances of this are the primitive producer whose practice is determined by custom (received knowledge) and the modern entrepreneur whose practice is determined by the technical facilities already existing in the productive establishment. In such cases, the fact that a given technical practice is followed simply provides evidence that this practice is feasible and was *not rejected* by the producer; but the absence of rejection cannot be taken as constituting evidence for choice.

typical element will be denoted by θ.[2] (ii) At each scale *s*, there is, in any given state of the producer's knowledge, a set *K*(*s*) of technical practices known to be feasible for that scale. That is, *K* is a function from scales to subsets of practices; it may be called the producer's 'knowledge function'. To say that a technical practice θ belongs to *K*(*s*) will also be expressed by saying that the producer knows that the pair (θ, *s*) is feasible. The producer's beliefs are assumed to be true. (iii) Actual scale is equal to assigned scale, so that the producer never considers which technical practice he might adopt at a scale different from the assigned one. This is an analytical device that we shall use in examining the consequences of changes in scale on the adopted practice, disregarding how slow a change of practice may be in real time.

Assumption (ii) implies that θ ∈ *K*(*s*), only if θ ∈ Φ(*s*), so that the set Φ(*s*) non-strictly includes the set *K*(*s*). The relationship between Φ(*s*) and *K*(*s*) can be seen in Fig. 7.1. In any given environment, the

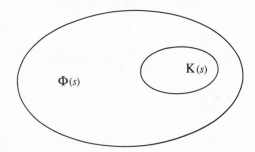

Fig. 7.1. *The relationship between feasible practices and the producer's knowledge*

current technical practice may be found by the producer to be either (a) temporarily or (b) permanently satisfactory. (Note that a technical practice is 'temporarily' satisfactory if the producer continues to search for a more satisfactory practice even after adopting the former practice. On the other hand, a technical practice is 'permanently' satisfactory if its adoption stops the search for a satisfactory practice. Thus our notions of 'temporarily' and 'permanently' are defined in terms of search behaviour, and are only loosely related

---

[2] In formal notation, we have: θ ∈ Φ(*s*) ↔ ∃ *s* such that the pair (θ, *s*) is feasible.

to the standard Marshallian notions of 'short period' and 'long period'.)

Let $\Sigma_1(s)$ and $\Sigma_2(s)$ be respectively the set of temporarily satisfactory practices and the set of permanently satisfactory practices which, at scale s, the producer knows are feasible for that particular scale. By definition, a technical practice cannot be both temporarily and permanently satisfactory at the same time. To say that a technical practice belongs to $\Sigma_1(s)$ or to $\Sigma_2(s)$ is equivalent to saying that the pair (θ, s) is feasible, known and satisfactory. The set $K(s)$ semi-strictly includes the sets $\Sigma_1(s)$ and $\Sigma_2(s)$.

The relationship between the sets $\Phi(s)$, $K(s)$, $\Sigma_1(s)$, and $\Sigma_2(s)$ can be seen in Fig. 7.2. A technical practice θ will be operated at scale s only if $\theta \in K(s)$ and $\theta \in \Sigma_1(s) \cup \Sigma_2(s)$.

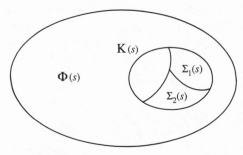

Fig. 7.2. *The relationship between feasible practices, producer's knowledge, and satisfactory practices*

A technical practice that is neither permanently nor temporarily satisfactory will never be adopted. It follows that production can take place at scale s only if there is at least one practice θ for which the above condition holds.

The set $\Sigma(s)$, which is defined as $\Sigma_1(s) \cup \Sigma_2(s)$, may vary under the influence of any of the following causes (some of which may operate simultaneously):

(a) Scale-technology expansion (this concept is defined in section 5.1).

(b) Scale-technology contraction (this concept is defined in 6.2).

(c) *Technical learning*. For scale s, there is technical learning if there is a change in producer's knowledge from $K(s)$ to $K'(s)$, such that, for at least one technical practice θ, $\theta \notin K(s)$ and $\theta \in K'(s)$. Technical learning at s thus implies $K(s) \not\supseteq K'(s)$. This phenomenon may be described as an addition to the set $K(s)$ within the set $\Phi(s)$, in view of assumption (ii).

(d) *Technical unlearning.* For scale s, there is technical unlearning if there is a change in the producer's knowledge from $K(s)$ to $K'(s)$ such that, for at least one technical practice θ, we have: $\theta \in K(s)$ and $\theta \notin K'(s)$. Technical unlearning consists of a subtraction from the set of practices that the producer knows to be feasible for s. This phenomenon may be interpreted as the result of a contraction of the producer's experience in operating technical practices (a practice that is not operated for a long time may be completely forgotten).

(e) *Technical invention.* Under certain circumstances (such as a change from job-shop to straight-line mode of organization, or a scientific discovery) there may be an expansion of the set $\Phi(s)$ because new task-definitions are used by the producer. Technical invention is the discovery of technical practices whose primitive elements (tasks) were, at least partly, unknown beforehand. It may occur whether or not there is a change in process scale. It may or may not be associated with an addition to the set $K(s)$, depending on whether the invention is made by the producer himself (in which case, of course, he knows of the novel practice) or by applied scientists, technologists, etc., who are not directly involved in the production process.

(f) *Technical loss.* A change in the basic organization of the productive establishment (say, from the job-shop to the straight-line model), or the disappearance of certain technical skills, may have the result that certain tasks can no longer be performed. This involves the disappearance of certain technical practices from the set $\Phi(s)$. This phenomenon may occur independently of changes in process scale.

(g) A change in the criterion by which technical practices are considered to be satisfactory or not satisfactory.

A change of $\Sigma(s)$ is related to the changes (a) to (f) in the following way. An addition to $\Phi(s)$ can add to $\Sigma(s)$ only if it adds to $K(s)$. The reason for this is that a change in the set of technical practices feasible at scale s does not change the domain of technical adoption unless the producer's 'true beliefs' about what practices are feasible are also changed. On the other hand, a subtraction from $\Phi(s)$ subtracts from $\Sigma(s)$ only if there is at least one technical practice θ such that the two following conditions are satisfied: (i) initially,

$\theta \in \Phi(s)$ and $\theta \in \Sigma(s)$); (ii) after some change in circumstances (such as a change in the mode of organization of the establishment), $\theta \in \Phi(s)$ and $\theta \notin \Phi'(s)$. (I shall write $\Phi'(s)$ for the new value of $\Phi(s)$ after the change—similarly for $K'(s)$, etc., below.) In this case, a subtraction from $\Phi(s)$ implies a subtraction from $K(s)$. This property follows from the fact that only practices that are known to be feasible for s may be satisfactory for that scale, and that a technical practice that is not feasible may not be known to be feasible by a producer whose beliefs are true by assumption (by virtue of (ii) above). Technical learning produces an addition to $\Sigma(s)$ only if there is at least one practice θ such that the following conditions are satisfied: (i) $\theta \notin K(s)$ and $\theta \in K'(s)$; (ii) $\theta \in \Sigma'(s)$. Technical unlearning subtracts from $\Sigma(s)$ only if there is at least one practice θ for which the following conditions hold: $\theta \in K(s)$ and $\theta \notin K'(s)$; (ii) $\theta \in \Sigma(s)$. Technical invention brings about an addition to $\Sigma(s)$ only if there is at least one technical practice θ for which the following conditions hold: (i) $\theta \notin \Phi(s)$ and $\theta \in \Phi'(s)$; (ii) $\theta \in \Sigma'(s)$. Technical loss brings about a subtraction from $\Sigma(s)$ only if there is at least one technical practice for which the following conditions hold: (i) $\theta \in \Phi(s)$ and $\theta \notin \Phi'(s)$; (ii) $\theta \in \Sigma(s)$. Both technical invention and technical loss may be associated with a change in $\Sigma(s)$ only if there is also a change (addition or subtraction respectively) in the set $K(s)$ of the technical practices known to be feasible for scale s.

For any scale s, the following cases are possible:

(i) $\Phi(s)$ is a unit set, $K(s)$ is also a unit set. In this situation, production at s is possible only if the single technical practice in $K(s)$ is considered to be at least temporarily satisfactory by the producer. Otherwise, scale s is feasible only if an addition is made to the set $\Phi(s)$ by technical invention.

(ii) $\Phi(s)$ is a unit set, $K(s)$ is an empty set. In this case, only technical learning or invention would permit the producer to operate at scale s.

(iii) $\Phi(s)$ is an empty set. This implies that $K(s)$ too is empty. Production at s would presuppose technical invention.

(iv) $\Phi(s)$ is an n-element set, with $n > 1$. In this case, the following alternatives may be considered:

(a) $K(s)$ is an empty set. This assumption makes technical learning or invention a necessary condition for production at scale s.

(b) $K(s)$ is a unit set. In this case, only one technical practice is compatible with the assigned scale. If this practice is not found to be satisfactory, production at scale s presupposes technical learning or invention.

(c) $K(s)$ is an n-element set, with $n > 1$. In this case, production at scale s is possible only if there is at least one technical practice in $K(s)$ which is found to be either temporarily or permanently satisfactory. Production at scale s would normally be followed by technical learning or invention, if scale s is obtained by operating a practice that is only temporarily satisfactory.

7.1.3. *Technical adoption as a problem-solving activity*

Producers' 'adoption' behaviour may be *described*—in any theory of it—by a function from process scale to the technical practice adopted. There is thus no loss of generality in expounding the theory of technical adoption by looking at a 'section' of this function at the—arbitrary—scale s. On the other hand, this analytical device may also sometimes represent *causal* relationships, as in cases when the adoption of a certain technical practice is determined by scale-technology contraction or expansion. In this case, to assume that scale is a parameter for the producer helps one to see more clearly into the structure of the existing causal relationship (see sections 7.2, 7.3, and Chapter 8). The technical practice actually employed at a given time may be considered to be the solution to a particular problem (how to produce at a 'parametric' scale, given the technological and economic environment). If the conceptual framework originally introduced by Newell and Simon (1972) is adopted, it is necessary to describe not only the problem-solver's actual behaviour, 'but the set of possible behaviors from which these are drawn; and not only his overt behaviors, but also the behaviors he considers in his thinking that don't correspond to possible overt behaviors. In sum, we need to describe the space in which his problem solving activities take place. We will call it the *problem space*' (p. 59). The problem we shall consider here is to find a suitable practice for the assigned scale. We may call the problem a *technical-adoption problem*. The producer, as a problem-solver, operates within a problem-space given by a particular set of pieces of knowledge, each relating to a technical practice. The behaviour of a producer who is trying to find a suitable practice in $K(s)$ can be described as a search through the set of practices known to be feasible for scale s.

If search through the problem-space has no solution (as happens when the producer does not know of any feasible and satisfactory technical practice permitting him to produce at scale s), a change in the problem-space is required if the producer is to find a satisfactory practice. The producer must now search through a different set of pieces of knowledge: namely, the *tasks* that are known to him and that represent the primitive elements of any would-be satisfactory technical practice. This new problem is what we may call a *technical-learning problem*. In this case, production at scale s requires the solution of two different, though related, problems: (i) a technical-learning problem, whose solution involves adding to the set $K(s)$; (ii) a technical-adoption problem, whose solution is reached by search through the new 'knowledge set' $K'(s)$.

Technical learning covers all the advances of a producer's knowledge that can be obtained without changing the task-definitions representing the primitive elements of the technical practices in his 'knowledge set' (these are, one might say, expansions of technical knowledge made possible by using the 'language' of received technology). Technical learning is based on human experience in performing productive operations. An important category of technical learning is 'learning by doing'. As Arrow and others have pointed out, learning of this type consists of developing increasing skill in performing the tasks that make up a production process (see Arrow, 1962). Rosenberg has recently identified an important source of technical learning in the increased experience obtained with the repeated use of certain types of input ('learning by using'). Learning by using is characteristic of production processes that require complex capital goods, such as air transport and electronic computing. In Rosenberg's view, the reason for this is that

[f]or a range of products involving complex, interdependent components or materials that will be subject to varied or prolonged stress in extreme environments, the outcome of the interaction of these parts cannot be precisely predicted. In this sense, we are dealing with performance characteristics that scientific knowledge or techniques cannot predict very accurately. The performance of these products, therefore, is highly uncertain. Moreover, many significant characteristics of such products are revealed only after intensive or, more significantly, prolonged use.   (Rosenberg, 1982: 122)

If the technical-learning problem has no solution (as happens when, for instance, no rearrangement of known tasks makes production at scale *s* possible), or if the technical-adoption problem remains insoluble in spite of technical learning, the producer may attempt the solution of his overall problem (how to produce at scale *s*) by considering a more radically different problem-space. This space would now be the set of alternative arrangements of 'productive functions' (such as 'cutting', 'painting', and so forth) that are independent of the particular task-definitions that characterize the 'language' of received technology (an expression such as 'cutting piece of wood A' is an example of a task description, whereas an expression such as 'wood-cutting' would, under most circumstances, describe a general productive function rather than a task). (For a comprehensive treatment of tasks as problem-solving activities, see the essays in Goodstein, Andersen, and Olsen, 1988.) The producer now faces what may be called a *technical-invention problem*. In this case, production at the assigned scale calls for the solution of three different (but related) problems: (i) the technical-invention problem, the solution of which may be represented as an addition to the set $\Phi(s)$ (note that the set $\Phi(s)$ has been defined as the set of all feasible technical practices that may be obtained from a given set of tasks); (ii) the technical-learning problem, the solution of which consists of the expansion of set $K(s)$; (iii) the technical-adoption problem, the solution of which is the technical practice permitting the producer to operate at scale s.[3]

Technological history is rich in cases where a scale variation gave the original impulse to a sequence of changes in $K(s)$ (technical learning) and/or in $\Phi(s)$ (technical invention), which could be considered a sequence of strategic transformations towards solving the problem of how to produce at the different scale. In any such case, the sequence of strategic transformations may be considered to be 'compulsive' in the sense that: (i) the scale variable here is an exogeneous constraint; (ii) at any scale, there is a single technical practice that is known, feasible, and satisfactory to the producer.

An example associated with technology contraction is the sequence of changes in technical practice that was brought about, during the early phases of the first Industrial Revolution in Britain, by the growing scarcity of wood. This circumstance induced the

---

[3] The conceptual distinction between invention and learning may give the clue to the historical distinction between the constraints upon the growth of an economic system that derive from 'limitations in the stock of knowledge' and those associated with 'the extent to which techniques that are possible with a given state of knowledge are actually realized' (see Rosenberg, 1972: 166).

substitution of mineral fuel (coal) for organic fuel (wood) in almost every productive use. However, the substitution took place at different speeds in various branches of production, according to the varying availability of satisfactory alternatives. As a consequence, the substitution of mineral fuel for wood took over 200 years before reaching the stage of near-completion, in spite of the fact that early attempts (mainly in activities such as the evaporation of salt water and brick-making) date back to the beginning of the seventeenth century. One important reason for such differences in the speed of substitution is probably the existence of technical problems that seriously impaired the quality of final output in operations such as the smelting of metallic ores, glass-making, and the drying of malt for breweries. In all such cases, we may assume that the producer knew a single technical practice, which permitted him to obtain a product of the required standard. The increasing difficulty in obtaining vegetable fuel had the consequence either of reducing the scale of certain processes or of significantly increasing production costs per unit of output (by obliging the producer to use the most expensive sources of wood supply). (See Wrigley, 1962; 1988; Deane, 1967: ch. 8; Evans, 1982.)

The case of changing fuel requirements during the first Industrial Revolution may be seen as an instance of scale-dependent technical change, in which the scale variation gave the original impulse and subsequently maintained the 'best' wood-using practices outside the range of feasible technical practices, while new technical solutions were sought, until a satisfactory coal-using practice had been found.

Another example is the mechanization of different branches of agriculture in the US economy. In this case, the opportunity of producing at a higher scale made it feasible to operate mechanized practices in all branches of agriculture (there was a scale-technology expansion). However, machine methods were applied at a much earlier date in the reaping and threshing of wheat than in cotton- and corn-picking, owing to the fact that, in the former case, the use of machine methods was possible without radical alteration of the prevailing practices. In both cases, scale-technology expansion had to be followed by technical learning, but learning was quicker in the cases in which the mechanized practice was nearer to the traditional manual practice (in the reaping and threshing of wheat, the mechanized practices were simply an imitation of the actions of the arm required in the reaping and threshing operations) (see Parker, 1971: 385).

7.1.4. *Search through the space of practices known to be feasible: two models of technical adoption*

In the simplest case of technical adoption, the technical practice is the outcome of a search through the set $K(s)$. This means that a satisfactory practice can be found without technical learning or invention.

In the following two sections, we shall examine two ideal models of technical search. One type of technical search involves producers who consider technical alternatives one by one, in an order determined by parametric characteristics of the environment. In this model, the producer adopts the first satisfactory practice that he meets in his search (*satisficing behaviour*). The other type of technical search involves producers who, in any given 'state of nature', rank all the practices in $K(s)$ and then adopt the practice having the top position in that ranking (*optimizing behaviour*). Technical adoption is defined as optimizing, rather than satisficing, if it is based on the prior ranking of all feasible options rather than on the pairwise comparison of alternatives.

Satisficing technical behaviour may or may not be properly described as technical choice, since the producer's action may or may not be the consequence of deliberation. On the other hand, there is certainly technical choice when, as in the second model, the actual technical practice derives from a prior ranking of all practices known to be feasible.

7.2. SCALE AND TECHNICAL PRACTICE: THE SEQUENTIAL SCRUTINY OF ALTERNATIVES

7.2.1. *Sequential scrutiny and the technical adoption function*

If technical adoption is based on the sequential scrutiny of the practices known to be feasible for scale s, the actual technical practice may be determined in the following way:

(1) The scale s of the production process (here taken as exogenous) determines the set $\Phi(s)$ of feasible technical practices. This set non-strictly includes a set $K(s)$ of practices known to be feasible for s.

(2) The producer examines in turn the elements of $K(s)$, in some given order.

(3) The producer operates the first technical practice that appears to be satisfactory to him.[4]

This model allows a producer to respond to a change in his parametric scale in a great variety of ways. In particular, the specifications (1)–(3) allow him to follow a sequence of scrutiny which involves a very long search before a satisfactory solution is found. However, it is plausible that a producer conforming to the 'sequential scrutiny' model of technical adoption generally restricts his problem-space to a few alternative technical practices determined by the technological and economic environment. If this is so, the sequence of scrutiny will depend on the following factors: (i) the technical practices that are in fact feasible in the given state of nature and knowledge; (ii) the producer's 'perception' of the production process at the time when the alternative courses of action are being considered. The producer's perception of the production process often depends on the past history of the same process. If so, the outcome of technical adoption may well depend on habitual technical practice rather than on the producer's deliberate action. A practice that is like the one he is used to is more likely to be considered than a practice that looks strange to him. In these circumstances, most observed regularities in the behaviour of producers who face a changing set of scale-feasible technical practices could be explained by uncertainty about which practices are in fact feasible in the given state of nature and knowledge and by a 'selective' freedom of action in producers' behaviour.[5]

To sum up, the producer adopts or does not adopt a certain technical practice, depending on (i) the order of scrutiny, and (ii) the value of a *technical-adoption function* $V(s)$. The latter is a real-valued function defined for all the technical practices belonging to $K(s)$ which takes the value 0 for alternatives that are excluded and 1 for alternatives that are adopted.

The concept of technical adoption permits us to study the determination of the technical practice without assuming that the producer's behaviour is the result of deliberation and intentional action. A producer may follow a certain practice simply because he has not excluded it yet, for the technical-adoption function takes

[4] This method of selection was originally considered by Simon (1955).
[5] The connection between uncertainty about the environment and behavioural rules that restrict the flexibility to choose potential actions has recently been emphasized by Heiner (1983) and North (1991).

value 1 both when the technical practice is deliberately chosen and when it is followed as a result of custom or past history. In other words, either intentional action or lack of deliberation may account for the operation of a certain technical practice. The technical-adoption function allows us to treat both cases. It does not reduce all of technical behaviour either to deliberate choice or to 'technical inertia'.

7.2.2. *Scale and technical adoption*

The assumption of sequential scrutiny provides a simple framework for studying various cases of technical adoption. We shall consider the following two cases in turn: (a) for any given scale, the producer knows only a single feasible practice; (b) for any given scale, the producer knows $n > 1$ feasible practices. In case (a), for any two scales s and s', both $K(s)$ and $K(s')$ are unit sets. If $K(s) \neq K(s')$, a scale variation from s to s' is possible only if the producer learns the technical practice which makes s' feasible. In case (b), any process scale can be obtained by following a number of alternative practices. The practice actually adopted in a productive establishment depends upon (i) the set $K(s)$ of technical practices known to be feasible for s; (ii) the sequence of scrutiny that the producer follows in considering the elements of $K(s)$; (iii) the value that the technical-adoption function associates with each practice for each sequence of scrutiny.

In case (b), though changes in process scale may bring about changes of $K(s)$, there is no longer a one-to-one correspondence between changes in scale and changes in the technical practice, for any scale can be obtained with more than one practice and, in general, any practice is feasible at more than one scale.[6] However, a change of $K(s)$ may induce the producer to revise his practice, since the domain of the technical-adoption function has changed. Assuming that the set $K(s)$ has n elements, the possible sequences of scrutiny are $n!$ in number.

---

[6] Consider the following example. At scale s, the feasible practices are θ and θ'. At scale s' (such that $s' > s$), only θ' is feasible. A change in scale from s to s' would involve a change in technical practice only if, at s, practice θ was used. If, on the other hand, scale s was obtained using θ', the change in scale would leave the technical practice unaffected.

7.2.3. *The scale–practice relation*

The cases considered in section 7.2.2 lead to different types of relation between the scale of the production process and the technical practice. However, there is a common structure underlying such relationships. This can be seen as follows:

Let S be the set of process scales, T the set of *observed* technical practices, and $\Phi(s)$ the set of practices feasible at scale s.

A *scale–practice relation* $\phi(s)$ is a relationship between S and T, such that, for each scale s in S, the two following conditions hold: (i) $\phi(s)$ contains at least one technical practice; (ii) every practice associated with s under the relation $\phi(s)$ belongs to the set of feasible practices $\Phi(s)$.[7]

The existence of a non trivial scale–practice relation (such that $\phi(s)$ is not constant with respect to s) reflects the characteristics of feasible technology and does not imply that changes of scale are necessarily associated with changes of technical practice. However, changes of scale may only explain changes of practice, provided that a non-trivial scale–practice relation exists. The existence of a relation of this kind is thus a necessary condition for scale-dependent technical change.

If there is a non-trivial scale–practice relation, certain changes of process scale require a change in the technical practice (since not all the technical practices are feasible at all scales). In the particular case in which each set $\Phi(s)$ contains just one technical practice and each practice is feasible only at a particular scale (so that every technical practice is *scale-specific*), the scale–practice relation implies that there will be a change of technical practice whenever there is a change in process scale. In general, however, each set $\Phi(s)$ contains more than one element. In this latter case, a non-trivial scale–practice relation implies that a continuous change of process scale may be compatible with discontinuous change in the technical practice.

The actual pattern of scale-dependent changes in technical practice depends on: (i) the characteristics of each set $K(s)$; (ii) the particular sequence of scrutiny followed by the producer in considering the elements of each set $K(s)$; (iii) the characteristics of the technical-adoption function $V(s)$. If $K(s)$ is a unit set for every s, and

---

[7] In formal notation, $\exists$ a set $\phi(s)$ of observed practices from T, and $\exists$ a set $\Phi(s)$ of feasible practices; the 2 following conditions are satisfied: (i) $\phi(s) \neq \varnothing$; (ii) $\phi(s) \subseteq \Phi(s)$.

if $K(s) \neq K(s')$, then a change of scale from s to s' implies a change in the actual technical practice. In this case, any change of desired scale implies technical learning and the operation of previously unknown practices. Technical learning takes the form of a 'compulsive' sequence of discoveries, in which each discovery is made possible by the corresponding change of scale, for any such change makes the existing practice no longer feasible and brings new technical problems to the fore.

If $K(s)$ is a unit set for all s, and if $K(s) = K(s')$, then changes of scale leave the technical practice unaffected.

If every set $K(s)$ contains two or more practices, a change in the domain of the technical adoption function is not necessarily associated with a change of technical practice. Some practices may be known to be feasible at many different scales, so that a change in $K(s)$ may leave the technical practice unaffected, provided that: (i) the practice under consideration is known to be feasible at both scales; (ii) the sequence of scrutiny and the technical adoption function allow the same practice to be adopted by the producer. On the other hand, the technical practice may change, even if $K(s) = K(s')$, provided that there is a change in the sequence of scrutiny or in the technical-adoption function.

The sequence of scrutiny may plausibly change, independently of changes in process scale. The recurrence of the same sequence of scrutiny at different scales cannot be excluded. If the set $K(s)$ is the same at all scales and the technical-adoption function is unchanged, a recurrent sequence of scrutiny implies the adoption of the same technical practice at different scales. Similarly, if $K(s)$ and the sequence of scrutiny are constant, a recurrent technical-adoption function also implies the recurrence of the same technical practice at different scales.[8]

---

[8] We may note that such cases of recurrent practices are not the consequence of parametric change. This distinguishes the above instances of technical recurrence from the reswitching of technique considered in the literature (cf. esp. the papers by Bruno, Burmeister, and Sheshinski; Garegnani; Levhari and Samuelson; Morishima; Pasinetti; Samuelson; all published in 1966 by the *Quarterly Journal of Economics*; see also, for a recent evaluation of the debate, Pasinetti and Scazzieri, 1987; Scazzieri, 1987*b*; 1987*c*). The reason for this is that, in the reswitching case, the recurrence of a technical practice is the consequence of parametric changes in prices and income distribution.

7.3. SCALE AND TECHNICAL PRACTICE: RANKING OF
ALTERNATIVES AND THE SCALE–EFFICIENCY RELATION

7.3.1. *Global ranking of feasible practices and technical choice*

Let us now turn to the case in which 'technical exclusion' is based
on a producer's prior ranking of all the practices feasible at a given
scale (the second model of technical adoption mentioned in section 7.1.4). In this case, technical practice is determined as follows:
(i) the scale of the production process determines the set $K(s)$ of
the practices known to be feasible; (ii) the producer ranks all the
elements of $K(s)$ according to their relative 'desirability'; (iii) he
excludes all the feasible practices except one, by following a sequence of scrutiny in which each technical practice is considered
before all the practices having lower rank (in other words, the order
of scrutiny matches the rank-order mentioned under (ii), except in
the case of 'ties' in the rank-order).

In this way, the final outcome of a technical adoption process
depends *both* on the evolution of technological constraints, as
expressed in scale-technology expansion and contraction, and on
the producer's behaviour with respect to technical alternatives.
However, the assumption that the scrutiny sequence matches the
producer's ranking makes it possible to explain changes in technical
practice by changes in process scale without explicitly considering
the producer's problem-solving activity after any change of scale.
(It is as if a 'solution strategy' is already decided when the scrutiny
order is adopted.) The reason is that, in effect, given a change of
assigned scale, the ranking of all the feasible practices reduces the
domain of the technical adoption function to a unit set and only the
'top' feasible practice is considered for choice; given process scale,
the producer will either follow the 'top' practice feasible at that
scale, or he will abstain from production activity.

This a priori ranking of technical practices induces (in the absence
of 'ties') a one-to-one correspondence between the sets $K(s)$ of
practices known to be feasible for any scale s and the outcome of
technical adoption: once process scale has determined the set $K(s)$,
the technical practice is unambiguously determined by the ranking.
For, at each scale, the first technical practice to be considered is
always the practice that is 'top' in the ranking of feasible practices.
This is also the practice adopted by the producer at that scale.

At any given scale, the following two cases may be distinguished: (a) the producer knows only one feasible practice; (b) he knows $n > 1$ feasible practices.

Case (a) here reduces to case (a) of section 7.2.2: the domain of the technical adoption function has one element only, so that the producer, given process scale, may either adopt the feasible practice or abstain from production activity. The pattern of technical adoption is thus unaffected by our changed assumption about the 'rule' followed by the producer when scrutinizing technical alternatives.

In case (b), however, there is a difference. Suppose there is a change in process scale, determining a new set of feasible technical practices. Once this latter set is determined, the pattern of technical adoption is also determined. Thus when the 'rule' followed by the producer in scrutinizing technical alternatives is to follow the ranking of the feasible practices in the way described above, there is a functional relation between process scale and adopted practice, in spite of the fact that two or more practices are *feasible* at any scale.

The nature of the inquiry undertaken in the present study makes it pertinent to note a possible basis for a producer's preference ranking of technical practices. The position of any technical practice in this ranking may depend on certain 'scale dimensions' of the practice, such as the level of fund-input utilization and the unit cost of production. We define a *natural ranking* of practices as a ranking relation based on some such scale properties of the practices, and containing no expression of liking or preference otherwise based. We define a *preference ranking* as a ranking relation over technical practices, based upon a natural ranking in the sense that the producer ranks practice θ above practice θ' in the sense of the above model of scrutiny if and only if θ lies above θ' in the natural ranking.[9]

[9] The distinction between natural ranking and preference ranking is connected with a particular view of grading situations, according to which grading is always the result of 3 separate logical moves: '(a) the identification of the qualities associated with the attitude object; (b) placing the object on an ordered scale according to the qualities it possesses, and (c) expressing a liking or preference for the object' (Harré and Secord, 1972: 304). A similar view was expressed by Urmson, according to whom 'we must say firmly . . . that to describe is to describe, to grade is to grade, and to express one's feelings is to express one's feelings, and that none of those is reducible to either of the others; nor can any of them be reduced to, defined in terms of, anything else' (1950: 156). An important result is that 'where . . . the characteristics A B C are the relevant criteria [for the application of grading labels], to assert that something has the characteristics is never to take the same step as to judge it to be of a certain quality X. It is always possible that the same judgement might have

7.3.2. *The scale–efficiency relation*

When a producer adopts a practice by scrutinizing the known feasible practices in the order of his preference ranking of these practices (so that the 'top' practice is always the first to be considered), then the outcome of technical adoption is unambiguously determined at any scale (except in the case of 'ties' in the rank-order of technical practices).

Changes of process scale may bring about changes in the domain of the technical-adoption function. These latter may produce changes in the preference ranking of technical practices, since: (i) the set of practices known to be feasible may be different; (ii) whenever there is a change in this set, the relative position of any two technical practices in the producer's preference ranking may change (e.g. if practice θ is preferred to practice θ' when practice θ'' is absent, practice θ' might be preferred to θ if θ'' is available).[10] We assume that there will be a change of technical practice whenever a change of scale is associated with a change in the producer's preferences such that the 'top' feasible practice changes.

We shall now consider a special case of technical adoption, based on the 'global ranking' assumption, which is often considered in the economic literature (see also Chapter 8). This case has the following features: (i) there are certain practices that are feasible at all scales; (ii) technology contraction makes it impossible to follow the 'top' practices associated with any lower scale; (iii) technology expansion makes it possible to operate practices that are preferred to any practice that was feasible at any lower scale.

An interesting property of this case arises if there is some degree of *scale-neutrality* in the producer's preferences. This may be seen as follows. Assume that technical practices θ and θ' are both known at scales s and s' and that, if $\theta >_s \theta'$ then $\theta >_{s'} \theta'$ (where $>_s$ denotes preference at scale s). Also assume that an increase in scale makes it impossible to follow practice θ (the 'top' practice at the lower scale), and induces the producer to switch to practice θ' (the 'top' practice at the higher scale). In this case, the scale-neutrality of preferences permits us to say that the practice adopted at s' is 'worse' than the

---

been based upon a different set of characteristics—that the standard might have been different' (Britton, 1951: 526).

[10] In other words, the producer's preferences do not necessarily satisfy the property of independence of irrelevant alternatives.

practice adopted at s. Similarly, assume that producer's ranking of practices is as follows: $\theta' >_s \theta$ and $\theta' >_{s'} \theta$, and that an increase in scale, by making it possible to adopt θ' (which was not feasible at the lower scale), induces the producer to switch from θ (the 'top' feasible practice at the lower scale) to θ' (the 'top' feasible practice at the higher scale). In this case the scale-neutrality of preferences implies that the practice adopted at s' is 'better' than the practice adopted at s.

A formal treatment of this relationship between changes of scale and changes in the position of the actual technical practice in the producer's ranking of practices may be given as follows. Let S be the set of scales, T the set of observed technical practices, $\theta(s)$ the set of practices feasible for scale s, P_s the ranking of the producer over the practices known to be feasible for s.

A *scale–efficiency relation* is a mapping Ψ from S to T that satisfies the following conditions:

(1) there is a single adopted technical practice corresponding to each particular scale (so that Ψ is a function);
(2) there is a preference ranking P over T such that, for each s, P_s is a *subrelation* of P (that is, if $\theta, \theta' \in K(s)$, then $\theta P_s \theta'$ if and only if $\theta P \theta'$).

If conditions (1) and (2) are satisfied, changes in scale may determine a switch to a practice having higher (or lower) rank in the producer's preferences. (In particular, condition (2) permits *cross-scale comparability* of practices, which is an essential feature of the special sub-case of the ranking model of technical adoption in which there is a scale–efficiency relation.) We shall consider any switch of this latter kind as a change in *productive efficiency* (the 'efficiency' of any technical practice would emerge from the position of this practice in the producer's preference ranking).

The scale–efficiency relation reflects both the producer's behaviour (the producer's search for the 'best' technical alternative) and technological constraints (scale-technology expansion or contraction). It can be considered as the description of a virtual process in which hypothetical scale variations are associated with corresponding changes in technical practice through the action of a producer who ranks all the practices known to be feasible and then chooses, at any scale, the 'top' practice according to his ranking.

To say that the scale variation from s to s' is associated in the scale–efficiency relation with a switch to a practice having higher (or lower) rank in the producer's global preference relation P, is to say that, were the scale to be changed from s to s', there would also be a change of the 'top' feasible practice such that the 'top' practice feasible at s' would be superior (or inferior) with respect to the 'top' practice feasible at s.

The scale–efficiency relation may be considered as a static representation of the virtual sequence of technical choices the producer would make, assuming there is a sequence of scale-dependent changes of the technical practices known to be feasible.[11]

[11] In the present model, a scale–efficiency relation is an instance of the relationship between 'free choice' and 'determinism' (see Hicks, 1979) if *historical* processes of choice are considered. (See also Meacci, 1986; O'Sullivan, 1987.)

8

Scale and Productive Efficiency

8.1. INTRODUCTORY REMARKS

A theory of the scale–efficiency relation is best formulated by distinguishing between two broad categories of such relations: those associated with technology expansion and those associated with technology contraction.

One reason for making this distinction is that the sequence of changes in technical practice that may come about with a sequence of scale-technology contractions is compulsive, in the sense that no scale increase is possible unless the technical practice is also changed. On the other hand, this is obviously not the case with scale-technology expansion, in which scale increases make 'better' technical practices feasible, but the old ('worse') practices could still be used. A further reason for the distinction is that technology contraction brings about a (non-trivial) scale–efficiency relation only if the order in which the producer ranks the technical practices is the opposite of the order of the maximum scales at which they are no longer feasible. (If a practice θ is strictly preferred to a practice θ', a scale–efficiency relation Ψ can be defined only if the scale s at which θ is no longer feasible is lower than the scale s' at which θ' is no longer feasible.) The condition for a (non-trivial) scale–efficiency relation is different in the case of technology expansion. In this case, the producer must rank the technical practices in his preferences in the same order as they are ranked according to the criterion of the minimum feasible scale. (If a technical practice θ is strictly preferred to a practice θ', a non-trivial scale–efficiency relation Ψ can be defined only if the scale s at which θ becomes feasible is higher than the (lowest) scale s' at which θ' becomes feasible).

We shall call a scale–efficiency relation an *increasing efficiency relation* if the following condition holds: a technical practice θ is preferred to a practice θ' if the least scale at which θ becomes feasible is greater than the least scale at which θ' becomes feasible. We shall call a scale–efficiency relation a *decreasing-efficiency relation* if the following condition holds: a technical practice θ is preferred to a practice θ' if the least scale at which θ is not feasible is less than the least scale at which θ' is not feasible. More complex scale–efficiency relations will also be considered, in which both increasing and decreasing efficiency are possible over different intervals of scale.

In this chapter, we shall outline a theory of the scale–efficiency relation for the two cases of scale-technology expansion (section 8.2) and scale-technology contraction (section 8.3). We shall then consider the received theories of how scale variations may be related to changes of productive efficiency. We shall find that: (i) only one particular type of relationship between scale and efficiency considered in the economic literature conforms to our requirements for a scale–efficiency relation (section 8.4); (ii) the 'true' scale–efficiency relations examined in the literature are special cases of the theory outlined in this study (section 8.5).

8.2. SCALE–EFFICIENCY RELATIONS AND TECHNOLOGY EXPANSION

8.2.1. *Capacity utilization, technical adoption, and 'optimizing' search*

Scale-technology expansion leads to a change of technical practice only if the producer makes use of the new technical opportunities feasible at the higher scale. That is, a scale-dependent change of practice depends on both the pattern of technology expansion and the producer's behaviour in the face of technical alternatives.

Given a technology expansion, the technical practice varies according to the producer's adoption criterion (unless only one practice is feasible at each scale). If n practices are feasible at a certain scale and the producer follows the criterion of sequential scrutiny in his search, $n!$ different sequences of scrutiny are possible, at that scale. In this case, the sequence of scrutiny is likely to change with any change in the set of technical practices known to be feasible, provided we assume that n is fairly big. As a result, it would be impossible to determine a priori which practice will be followed at any particular scale. If, on the other hand, the producer ranks all practices known to be feasible on a preference scale, and then follows this ranking in selecting the 'top' practice, there is a single sequence of scrutiny at each scale. This sequence of scrutiny may change as a result of the scale-technology expansion, but the change is limited to the consideration of the extra practices that have become feasible at the higher scale.

Given two process scales s and s', and assuming that there is the required type of inter-scale consistency in producer's preference ranking of technical practices (see section 7.3.3), the consideration of a new practice does not bring about any inversion of the sequence of scrutiny. Thus in the case of preference-based scrutiny it is possible to determine a priori which practice will be followed at any given scale. In this section, we shall examine a set of scale–efficiency relations that can be derived on the assumption that increasing process scale determines an expanding set of technical practices that are feasible and known to be feasible, and two further assumptions. The producer is assumed to tackle the technical-adoption problem by following the optimizing search procedure discussed in section 7.3.1. And the specific assumption is made that the producer ranks the technical practices he knows to be feasible according to the extent to which each practice makes use of the task-performing capabilities embodied in the productive establishment. In this particular case, the position of each technical practice in the producer's preference ranking depends on the degree to which such capacities are being used, and the 'top' practice is the one that would permit the greatest 'capacities utilization' at the given scale, in the sense that the largest possible number of tasks would be performed at any given time, and that the longest possible times of fund-input utilization would be achieved. This third assumption makes the producer's behaviour satisfy the necessary conditions for an 'increasing efficiency relation' just described (see section 8.1). The assumption may also be considered to be empirically plausible.

8.2.2. *Scale, full utilization, and productive efficiency*

Scale-technology expansion, as we noted in section 5.3, derives from two different kinds of 'technological disequilibrium': (i) the existence of differences in the maximum levels of utilization of the various inputs per unit of time; (ii) the discontinuous utilization of certain fund inputs in any particular elementary process (e.p.). In the former case, scale-technology expansion makes it possible to increase the number of e.p.s that can be simultaneously operated using the same input, thus permitting a fuller utilization of productive capacity. In the latter case, scale-technology expansion makes it possible to increase the number of e.p.s using the same fund input during a working day (even if they are not all using it at the same time), thus permitting a more continuous utilization of productive capacity.

If technology expansion results from the possibility of increasing, by producing at a higher scale, the levels of utilization of certain inputs per unit of time, it is generally not possible for there to be a continuous scale increase without these levels falling over certain scale intervals (see section 5.3). Hence in this case, assuming that his behaviour conforms to the model of 'optimizing' choice, at any given scale the producer determines his technical practice by first ranking the practices he knows to be feasible at that scale according to their degree of capacity utilization per unit of time, and by then adopting the 'top' practice in that ranking.

As we have seen above, with certain scale increases goes a switch to 'better' technical practices (practices permitting higher utilization of productive capacity per unit of time), whereas with other scale increases goes the introduction of 'worse' technical practices (practices permitting lower capacity utilization per unit of time).

A relationship between process scale and capacity utilization is represented in Fig. 8.1, in which we assume that at most three technical practices are feasible and that each practice is associated with a different degree of capacity utilization per unit of time.

Proposition 5.1 (see Chapter 5) implies that, if the producer

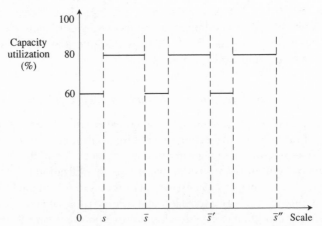

Fig. 8.1. *A relationship between process scale and capacity utilization*

adopts, at any given scale, the 'top' practice known to be feasible at that scale, a continuous increase in scale is associated here with a discontinuous change of technical practice. In the scale interval $(0, s)$ practice θ'' is used, so that capacity is utilized at 60%. In the interval $[s, \bar{s})$, practice θ' is used, so that capacity is utilized at 80%. At the precise scale $\bar{s}$ (a point in the continuum of scales) practice θ is used and capacity is utilized at 100%. The same pattern of changes of technical practice is repeated as process scale rises above $\bar{s}$.

This relationship between changes of scale and changes in the level of capacity utilization is the outcome of two distinct (though related) causes: a certain pattern of scale-technology expansion; and a preference ranking such that, at any given scale, the producer prefers and adopts the technical practice permitting fuller capacity utilization.

8.2.3. *Scale, continuous utilization, and productive efficiency: the job-shop case*

If scale-technology expansion is due to the possibility of increasing fund-input utilization over time as the scale grows, the sequence of changes of technical practice that is likely to come about with an increasing scale depends on whether the known-to-be-feasible technical practices consist of elementary processes whose 'internal' task-organization is of the job-shop or straight-line models (see section 4.2.3). But it will emerge that, if the efficiency of a technical practice depends on the degree of capacity utilization over time, the general form of the scale–efficiency relation is independent of the particular mode of organization—job-shop or straight-line—adopted in the establishment.

In the job-shop case, we have seen that there is a minimum scale at which continuous utilization of all the fund inputs is possible (see section 5.4.2). Fund inputs can be kept continuously active, provided that the scale of the process is increased by integer multiples of that minimum scale. Assuming that, at each scale, the producer ranks the technical practices known to be feasible by degree of capacity utilization over time, and then adopts the practice highest in this ranking, a continuous increase of process scale generally brings about a sequence of changes in technical practice. Assuming a certain degree of inter-scale consistency in producer's preferences (see section 7.3.3), a non-trivial scale–efficiency relation obtains. Productive efficiency is less than maximum at all scales that are not integer multiples of the minimum scale referred to above (see section 8.2.2). Fig. 8.1 may also be taken as an illustration of this scale–efficiency relation.

The job-shop organization enables the producer to change the output levels of certain commodities without varying the scale of the global production process and the 'use-times' of the fund inputs. As a result, it is possible for there to be a steady increase in the output levels of such commodities without variation in the efficiency of the technical practice, for a change in the output level of a commodity is compatible with constant 'use-times' of the fund inputs as long as the following two conditions hold: (i) the scale of the global process is unchanged; (ii) the output level of the commodity in question is varied by substituting certain elementary processes for others producing a different commodity but having the same precedence pattern of tasks.

If we consider as an example the tailor's shop case outlined in section 5.4, we see that it is possible to increase the output of commodity I without varying the scale of the process, as long as we can substitute some e.p.s of type I for e.p.s producing different commodities but having the same precedence pattern. In our example, the producer may increase the output of commodity I, while leaving the scale of the whole process unchanged, if the output of commodity II is simultaneously halved. A further increase in the output of commodity I is, however, impossible, unless either the technical practice or the scale of the process is changed. A change of technical practice that would allow the producer to increase the output of commodity I would be to substitute one e.p. of type I for one e.p. of type III (but note that e.p.s I and III have different precedence patterns, so that it would be impossible to maintain continuous utilization of the fund inputs). A change in process scale, on the other hand, may allow the producer both to increase the output level of commodity I and to maintain continuous utilization of all the fund inputs. A necessary condition for this would be to expand the global production process by integer multiples of the minimum scale permitting continuous utilization.

The output of commodity I can be increased, without changing either the process scale or the position of the technical practice in the producer's preference ranking, as long as the allocation of fund inputs to the various e.p.s can be changed in such a way as to expand the production of commodity I without varying the degree of capacity utilization over time. But note that this condition requires that a fixed proportion between e.p. types (each e.p. type being identified by a certain precedence pattern of tasks) be maintained at all scales (see section 5.4.2). In the example under consideration, if more than two e.p.s of type I have to be operated at the same time, the producer will either switch to an 'inferior' technical practice (a practice involving, at the given scale, the discontinuous utilization of certain fund inputs) or else will increase the scale of the whole process. In this latter case, a larger output of commodity I is compatible with continuous fund input utilization, provided that there is a stepwise increase in process scale (in this case, the output of commodity I will also increase stepwise). A continuous increase in the output of this commodity, by contrast, would be associated with scale intervals over which the degree of capacity utilization is lower.

We may conclude that the job-shop mode of organization allows the producer to change the output of certain commodities without varying the degree of capacity utilization, thus leaving productive efficiency unchanged. This is possible as long as the output of such commodities is varied within a relatively narrow range, for large fluctuations in output make it difficult to maintain the particular balance of e.p. types compatible with the continuous utilization of fund inputs.

8.2.4. *Scale, continuous utilization, and productive efficiency: the straight-line case*

In the straight-line mode of organization, scale-technology expansion can be explained by the fact that, at sufficiently high scales, the producer is able to transfer a given fund input from one e.p. to another (having the same precedence pattern among tasks), as soon as its task in the first e.p. is completed. This can be achieved in either of two ways: (i) by having the e.p.s arranged in line, in which case a fund input can be moved from one task to another regardless of the total number of tasks involved in each e.p.; (ii) by increasing the degree of task-specialization of the e.p.s (i.e. by reducing the number of tasks in each e.p.).

Both possibilities are specific to the straight-line mode of organization. In both cases, continuous fund-input utilization requires that a given number of tasks be performed in the course of a day in the establishment (see section 5.5.2). The smallest number of tasks needed for continuous utilization is partly determined by the number of different tasks that a particular fund input is able to perform. It so happens that, in the case of special-purpose fund inputs, the required number of tasks is the same, either with large-scale production (and an in-line arrangement of e.p.s) or with e.p. specialization (see section 5.5.4). On the other hand, the required number of tasks decreases as a fund input becomes more and more versatile (less specialized), by taking on more tasks in the same e.p. This property may or may not give rise to a condition on the minimum output of certain commodities, or on the minimum scale of the production process. For, in the case of e.p. specialization, the requirement that a minimum number of e.p.s be performed, one after the other, in the same establishment (a condition which entails a minimum output of the commodities produced in the establishment), may be satisfied by operating a single e.p. per unit of time. However, the in-line arrangement of e.p.s makes continuous utilization depend on a particular pattern of expansion in process scale and in commodity outputs, for, with both special-purpose and general-purpose fund inputs, a necessary condition for continuous utilization is that the scale of the global process (and the levels of the commodity outputs) be expanded by integer multiples of the minimum scale (and minimum outputs) that permit continuous utilization (see section 5.5.4).

In the straight-line case, the 'top' practice that will be adopted at each scale is the practice permitting the greatest 'use time' compatible with the given scale, provided at each scale the producer ranks the known-to-be-feasible practices according to their degree of capacity utilization. A continuous expansion of process scale would thus imply a sequence of changes in technical practice. Assuming inter-scale consistency in the producer's preferences, these changes in technical practice may involve changes of productive efficiency. In particular, the producer will switch to a 'better' technical practice whenever scale reaches a level which allows increased 'use-times' for the fund inputs on hand in the establishment. On the other hand, the producer will have to adopt a 'worse' practice, if the higher scale necessitates lower 'use-times' for such fund inputs. The position of the adopted practice in the producer's ranking stays constant only if scale gets expanded in integer multiples of the minimum scale compatible with continuous utilization. Fig. 8.1 illustrates a special case of this scale–efficiency relation. (Note that, if the efficiency of a technical practice depends on the degree of capacity utilization over time, the general form of the scale–efficiency relation is independent of the particular mode of organization—job-shop or straight-line. However, in the straight-line case the 'lower-efficiency' scale intervals are smaller when it is possible to use general-purpose fund inputs; see section 5.5.4.)

8.2.5. *Scale, efficiency, and productive organization: some further remarks*

We already know that straight-line organization does not normally allow a producer to change the levels of output of individual commodities unless the scale of the whole process is also changed, if he wishes to maintain continuous utilization (see section 5.5). For, though it is true that different e.p. types may be operated in the same establishment, continuous utilization is bound to a 'tight' allocation of fund inputs to the various e.p.s. Hence it is generally impossible to maintain continuous utilization by simply changing the proportions between different e.p. types at a given scale. And so any change in the outputs of individual commodities means that process scale must change. In production processes following the straight-line model, a given degree of capacity utilization over time is normally associated with a single technical practice, and changes in the outputs of particular commodities are often associated with changes in productive efficiency (assuming that technical adoption is by preference ranking and that this ranking is according to degree of capacity utilization). This is an important difference between straight-line and job-shop production. Straight-line organization makes it possible to achieve continuous utilization by producing a sufficient amount of a single commodity or of a fixed commodity basket (different commodities in fixed proportions). The job-shop organization, on the other hand, normally allows continuous utilization only if a range of different commodities are produced in the same establishment. But each commodity can be produced in a relatively small quantity, and it is often possible to change the composition of the commodity basket without varying the 'use-times' of fund inputs.

If we assume that technical adoption is by preference ranking and that producer's ranking is according to the degree of capacity utilization, the difference between straight-line and job-shop may be put as follows. For any given technical practice, the straight-line mode of organization induces a one-to-one correspondence between the scale of the production process and the output of any single commodity produced by this process. Changes in commodity output levels may thus oblige the producer to vary the degree of capacity utilization (and thus productive efficiency) much more frequently than in job-shop production. On the other hand, the job-shop mode of organization makes it possible to change the commodity output levels without varying the scale of the process. For with this mode a given allocation of fund inputs among the various e.p. types allows the producer to change the composition of the commodity basket without changing the 'use-times' of fund inputs. Productive efficiency may thus be kept constant, provided either of the following two conditions hold: (i) commodity outputs are varied by relatively small amounts while the scale of the process is kept constant; (ii) commodity outputs are varied by relatively large amounts while the scale of the process is also varied, without changing the proportions between e.p. types that have different precedence patterns.

8.3. SCALE–EFFICIENCY RELATIONS AND TECHNOLOGY CONTRACTION

8.3.1. *Technology contraction, technical adoption, and 'optimizing' search*

Scale-technology contraction may or may not bring about a change of technical practice, according to the criterion used by the producer in determining the actual practice out of the set of practices he knows to be feasible at the given scale.

If the producer uses the criterion of sequential scrutiny, and n practices are known to be feasible at the given scale, there are $n!$ different possible sequences of scrutiny, even if some sequences are more likely than others. (In particular, we may expect the producer to begin with the technical practice currently in use.) In this case, any change in scale that makes a technical practice no longer feasible may result in a change of the actual practice in use. However, technology contraction might also change the sequence of scrutiny if we assume that the technical practice that is scrutinized at any point of time may vary depending on which practice is scrutinized immediately before that one. In this case it is impossible to determine, given a sequence of changes in process scale, which particular practice would be adopted at a particular scale in this sequence without some hypothesis about the order of scrutiny. Consider, by contrast, the hypothesis that the producer ranks in preference all the practices he knows to be feasible, and then adopts the 'top' one in that ranking. A given sequence of changes in process scale may, in this case, determine a unique sequence of changes of practice—though only if we assume, in addition, that there is some degree of inter-scale consistency in the producer's preferences. For, in this case, scale-technology contractions do not involve radical changes in the order of scrutiny: at any given scale, the producer simply 'misses out' the infeasible technical practices, without changing the order of scrutiny of the known-to-be-feasible practices.

In the case, then, of scrutiny based on consistent preferences, it is possible to determine a priori which technical practice the producer will follow at each different scale. There are, therefore, changes in scale which give a technology contraction and also determine the adopted technical practice. The latter is the outcome of an enforced sequence of scrutiny based on the producer's preference ranking of practices. The notion of a scale–efficiency relation introduced in section 7.3.3 entails that, in these circumstances, any change in technical practice is generally associated with a change of 'productive efficiency' (the only exception being when the producer's preference ranking is incomplete).

In this section, we examine a set of decreasing-efficiency relations that follow from the assumption that an increasing process scale is associated with a contracting set of technical practices known to be feasible. Two sources of technology contraction will be considered: (i) when there is an upper bound on the 'productive capacity' of the productive unit under consideration; (ii) when it is necessary to use exhaustible inputs. The producer is assumed to follow the 'optimizing' model of technical adoption: at any given scale he adopts the 'top' technical practice he knows to be feasible.

8.3.2. *Scale, productive capacity, and decreasing efficiency*

The existence of indivisible inputs may generate scale-technology contraction because only discrete, stepwise changes in process scale allow full and continuous utilization of all inputs (see section 6.3.2).

This implies that the 'productive capacity' of a productive unit (the maximum number of e.p.s which may simultaneously be operated in it) may be taken as given with respect to small variations of process scale. It is because productive capacity may be neither increased nor reduced that changes in process scale may be associated with technology contraction.

Consider a productive establishment that is using machinery and/or land. Such an establishment is subject to technology contraction whenever an increase in process scale cannot be matched by an increase in the amount of machines or land available. Similarly, there is scale-technology contraction if, with a given technical practice, a downward variation of scale is not matched by a downward variation in the availability of such inputs. This type of technology contraction comes from inputs being in some degree indivisible, and is independent of whether the inputs in question are or are not produced. One special case is that of land and obsolete machinery: both types of input being in fixed supply, any increase in process scale is accompanied by technology contraction as soon as an upper bound on capacity utilization is reached.

Assuming that the producer follows the 'optimizing' mode of technical adoption, and that there is a sufficient degree of inter-scale consistency in the producer's ranking of technical practices, scale-technology contractions give rise to a decreasing-efficiency relation.

If a technology contraction is due to there being a fixed productive capacity, an increase in process scale brings about a 'worse' practice if the 'top' practice feasible at the lower scale cannot be operated at the higher scale.

In the case of certain inputs (such as machinery and workers), increasing scale is often associated first with technology expansion, then with technology contraction. If, at each of a sequence of scales, the change in the set of feasible technical practices (whenever it takes place) brings about a change in the 'top' practice known to be feasible, we may have a scale–efficiency relation of the form shown in Fig. 8.2. (We assume in this figure that at most three technical practices are known to be feasible at each scale, that the producer ranks the practices according to the unit cost of production, and that unit cost varies continuously and linearly between one scale and another.)

In the case of land the situation is different, for it is reasonable to assume that, for most uses, the range of scales over which increases

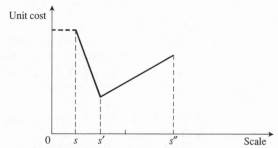

Fig. 8.2. *Increasing and decreasing efficiency in machine-using and worker-using processes*

in scale are associated with technology expansion is non-existent or negligible. Assuming that any change in the set of feasible technical practices changes the 'top' practice known to be feasible, an increasing scale is associated with the (monotonically) decreasing-efficiency relation represented in Fig. 8.3. (As in the previous case, at most three technical practices are known to be feasible at any given scale, and the producer ranks the practices according to unit cost of production.)

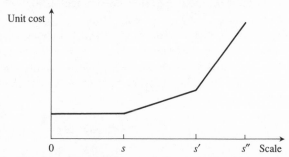

Fig. 8.3. *The decreasing-efficiency relation in land-using processes*

There is, lastly, a special case, associated with the use of workers or machines, in which technology contraction is combined with technology expansion, and decreasing-efficiency can be avoided in spite of the enforced abandonment of the 'current' top technical practice. This situation may arise in establishments in which machinery and/or workers are *fully* utilized (no more e.p.s can be operated per unit of time), but not *continuously*, so that machinery and/or workers are idle during certain intervals of the working day. In this case, a higher scale is possible without changing the e.p. type, if the e.p.s are arranged in line rather than in parallel. This scale increase can be achieved by reducing the periods of idleness of machinery, and the new technical practice, because it makes possible higher capacity utilization, is 'better' than the practice that was being operated at the lower scale. However, this opportunity for improving productive efficiency is limited to production processes using certain types of fund input (such as machinery and workers). Land is, in general, continuously utilized in the single e.p., so that a higher scale cannot be achieved by rearranging the e.p.s so as to increase its 'use time'. In short, the full utilization of land implies that any further scale increase can only be achieved by changing the characteristics of the individual e.p.s.

8.3.3. *Scale, exhaustible inputs, and decreasing efficiency*

Exhaustible inputs cause technology contraction, if the product of the unit input requirement and the process scale becomes strictly greater than the stock of that input available in the productive unit (see section 6.4). This kind of technology contraction is due to input depletion, and it is impossible to operate any technical practice for which that particular input is essential. If the producer follows the 'optimizing' mode of technical adoption and if any change in the set of feasible practices changes the 'top' practice known to be feasible, a sequence of technology contractions of this kind is associated with a decreasing-efficiency relation of the kind represented in Fig. 8.3.

8.4. SCALE–EFFICIENCY RELATIONS IN ECONOMIC THEORY: A DISCUSSION

8.4.1. *Genuine and spurious scale–efficiency relations*

A change in the position of the actual technical practice in the producer's preference ranking resulting from a change in process scale is generally explained in economic theory in terms of one of two models, which we may call model A and model B respectively. In economic literature, model A is mainly associated with the work of the classical economists, who derived scale–efficiency relations from the consideration of producer's choices in a situation in which changes of scale determine changes in the set of technical practices known to be feasible (see sections 3.2, 3.3, 8.4.2.) Model B, on the other hand, is mainly associated with the work of economists studying production relationships from the point of view of how the output of a production process reacts to differential changes in input quantities (a characteristic example of this approach is the law of variable proportions[1]). The distinction between models A and B may also be related to Wicksteed's distinction between descriptive curves and functional curves (see Wicksteed, 1933: 790–1; originally published as Wicksteed, 1914; see also section 3.3.2 and Scazzieri, 1982).

In model A, the change in position of the actual technical practice is a consequence of the behaviour of a producer who adopts the 'top' practice known to be feasible at any given scale. In model B, a single practice is assumed to be feasible at each scale. This means that producer's preferences can play no part in explaining which practice the producer adopts, given that scale. In the former case, the relationship between changes in scale and changes in productive efficiency reflects assumptions about the producer's preferences that are also used to explain his behaviour in technical-adoption. In the latter case, the solution of the technical-adoption problem is trivial for the producer; indeed, changes in technical practice can be derived from scale changes directly, without explicitly considering the producer. Any hypothetical sequence of scale changes uniquely determines a sequence of changes in technical practice. But these practices may none the less be ranked from the 'best' to the 'worst' by virtue of the preferences that the producer (or the economist, or any other individual) might express with respect to the technical practices feasible at the various hypothetical scales. Any change of practice may thus be associated with a change in 'productive

---

[1] The law of variable proportions is based on the consideration of an input–output space X^{m+1} (the first m elements of any vector of this space are input quantities, the last element is a quantity of output). The law examines which technical practices are generated by variations in x_i ($i = 1, \ldots, m$), under the condition $x_j = $ constant for all $j \neq i$ ($j = 1, \ldots, m$). A special hypothesis about the way in which the output level q varies as one goes through the sequence of practices so generated (it is assumed that q increases first at an increasing, then at a decreasing rate), permits the introduction of a preference ranking over the set of technical practices. This ranking is based on the different 'returns' associated with each particular practice. Early formulations of the law of variable proportions are due to Turgot (1808) and Edgeworth (1911) (see ss. 3.3 and 3.5). This law also provides the 'technological' foundations for the modern 'neoclassical' theory of production (see Shephard, 1953; 1970).

efficiency' (defined in section 7.3.3) and the sequence of scale changes gives a sequence of changes in productive efficiency. However, efficiency changes result from an *ex post* expression of preference, and do not depend on the producer's choices in the course of technical adoption.

The distinctive features of models A and B may be illustrated by the following example. Consider three technical practices θ, θ', θ'', such that the producer strictly prefers θ to θ', and θ' to θ'' (and assume that the ranking is transitive). In model A, a change in scale determines a change in the set of practices known to be feasible. In general, the producer knows two or more feasible practices at any scale, so that the solution of the technical-adoption problem is not trivial. Consider process scales s, s', s'', such that $s < s' < s''$. Suppose that at scale s practices θ' and θ'' are known to be feasible; at scale s' practices θ and θ'; and at scale s'' practices θ' and θ''. Assuming that the producer follows the 'optimizing' model of technical adoption, scale s is obtained by operating practice θ'. An increasing scale brings about a sequence of changes in technical practice; first θ is substituted for θ', then θ' is substituted for θ. Assuming that the producer's ranking of technical practices is based on the unit costs of production, we have the scale–efficiency relation shown in Fig. 8.4 below.

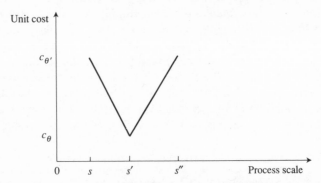

Fig. 8.4. *Unit cost and 'multi-scale' practices*

In model B, on the other hand, the technical practices are *scale-specific* (a given scale can be achieved only by operating one particular practice and no practice is feasible at more than one scale). At any scale the solution of the technical-adoption problem is therefore trivial. Assume that only θ is feasible at s, that only θ' is feasible at s', and that only θ'' is feasible at s''. Suppose the producer ranks technical practices according to unit cost; then there is a relation between process scale and unit cost of production of the form shown in Fig. 8.5. The relationship between scale and unit cost shown in Fig. 8.5 is independent of the producer's behaviour. The producer's preferences may be relevant in determining which *scale* is adopted, but they are completely irrelevant in determining which practice is chosen at any given scale.

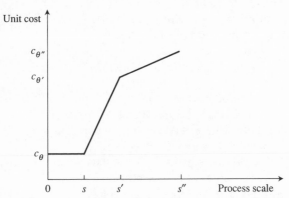

Fig. 8.5. *Unit cost and scale-specific practices*

From the point of view of our analysis, in which the producer is taken to be facing a 'parametric' scale (so that scale is never a matter of choice), model B is redundant, for the information it provides on the process of technical-practice determination is already contained in the theories of scale-technology expansion and contraction. Model B enables us to derive a relationship between changes of scale and changes in the position of the actual technical practice in a producer's ranking. However, the producer's technical-adoption behaviour plays no role in explaining this relationship. It is a spurious scale–efficiency relation from the point of view of the model of 'optimizing' choice outlined in section 7.3.

Some of the more important formulations of model A in the economic literature are briefly examined in the next two sections.

8.4.2. *Scale, continuous fund-input utilization, and the division of labour: the classical theory of increasing efficiency*

Smith regarded an expanding process scale as a necessary condition for increasing productive efficiency (Smith, 1976 [1776]). Gioja,

Babbage, von Hermann, and Marx considered this problem further (Gioja, 1815–17; Babbage, 1835; von Hermann, 1870 [1832]; Marx, 1983 [1867]. These latter writers (Babbage and Marx most fully) described a scale–efficiency relation in which changes of technical practice have the following features:

(i) The technical practice is changed discontinuously, although the expansion of process scale is continuous.

(ii) Changes of technical practice involve either bringing into operation more specialized practices or the substitution of special-purpose for general-purpose fund inputs.[2]

(iii) A higher process scale brings about a 'better' technical practice if, at that scale, the 'use-times' of workers and tools are higher.

(iv) The technical practice allowing continuous utilization is compatible with increasing scale only if scale is expanded by integer multiples of the least scale that allows continuous fund-input utilization (this condition is known as Babbage's Law).

(v) If the producer fails to meet Babbage's Law, a higher scale requires the operation of a 'worse' technical practice.[3]

(vi) Each production process consists of a single technical practice if Babbage's Law is satisfied; it consists of a 'mixed' technical practice if it is not.

(vii) There is a one-to-one correspondence between process scales and commodity outputs.

A characteristic feature of this theory is the relationship between higher efficiency and greater specialization of technical practices and/or fund inputs. This can be seen by considering the two ways in which a higher scale brings about higher efficiency: (i) specialized technical practices and special-purpose fund inputs are substituted for multi-task technical practices and general-purpose fund inputs; (ii) the 'in-line' arrangement of e.p.s is substituted for an arrangement of them 'in parallel' or 'in series', so that a fund input goes on

---

[2] This idea was clearly expressed by Babbage in his analysis of the division of labour in a productive establishment (see s. 3.2.3).

[3] 'When the number of processes into which it is most advantageous to divide it [the work to be executed]; and the number of individuals to be employed in it, are ascertained, then all factories which do not employ a direct multiple of this latter number, will produce the article at a greater cost' (Babbage, 1835: 212). The same idea was also expressed by Marx: 'When once the most fitting proportion has been experimentally established for the numbers of the detail labourers in the various groups when producing on a given scale, that scale can be extended only by employing a multiple of each particular group' (1983 [1867]: 327).

performing the same task (or set of tasks) as it is shifted from one e.p. to another e.p. of the same type in the same establishment.

Pattern (i) is characteristic of Smith's and Babbage's analysis of the division of labour, as well as of Marx's analysis of 'heterogeneous manufacturing'.[4] Pattern (ii) is characteristic of Marx's analysis of 'serial manufacturing'.[5]

The classical theory of the increasing-efficiency relation is thus based on special assumptions about the technical practices known to be feasible at different scales, for, in it, an expanding scale makes possible the use of 'better' technical practices, provided only that using more specialized practices permits an increase in the 'use-times' of fund inputs. However, this sort of increasing efficiency is possible only in productive establishments that are organized on the straight-line pattern and that use special-purpose fund inputs. In job-shop establishments, multi-task e.p.s and general-purpose fund inputs may be necessary conditions for the continuous utilization of fund inputs. In this case, specialized e.p.s and special-purpose fund inputs may be associated with 'worse' technical practices in which the 'use-times' of fund inputs are lower. Similarly, the in-line arrangement of e.p.s permits greater productive efficiency with growing scale only if the productive establishment follows the straight-line pattern. In a job-shop establishment, the in-line arrangement of e.p.s is incompatible with continuous fund-input utilization, because of the differences in the precedence patterns of the various e.p.s (such differences are, it will be recalled, an essential characteristic of the job-shop organization). Finally, there is a one-to-one correspondence between process scales and commodity outputs only in the case of a straight-line establishment.

---

[4] In this type of manufacturing, each article 'results from the mere mechanical fitting together of partial products made independently' (ibid. 323). As a result, a higher scale of the process makes it possible to operate better technical practices simply by increasing the degree of specialization of the individual practices.

[5] In this type of manufacturing, each article goes 'through connected phases of development, through a series of processes step by step' (ibid. 325). Under such conditions, 'the result of the labour of the one is the starting point for the labour of the other . . . It is clear that this direct dependence of the operations, and therefore, of the labourers, on each other, compels each one of them to spend on his work no more than the necessary time, and thus a continuity, uniformity, regularity, order, and even intensity of labour, of quite a different kind is begotten than is to be found in an independent handicraft or even in simple co-operation . . . Here we have again the principle of co-operation in its simplest form, the simultaneous employment of many doing the same thing; only now, this principle is the expression of an organic relation' (ibid. 326–7).

We may conclude that the increasing-efficiency relation considered in the classical version of model A presupposes a particular type of productive organization, such that the productive establishment follows the straight-line model and fund inputs are special-purpose, or *de facto* specialized in a particular task.

Another important characteristic of the classical increasing-efficiency relation is that production processes are assumed to consist either of a single technical practice or of a combination of practices, depending upon whether Babbage's Law is satisfied or not. Each combination of practices is such that the share of production delivered by the 'most preferred' practice is the maximum permitted by the required scale.

This situation may be illustrated by the following example. Let θ, θ', θ'' be three distinct technical practices (and such that none can be further subdivided into simpler practices). Suppose that the producer strictly prefers θ to θ', and θ' to θ'' (and that his ranking is transitive). At any given scale, the producer adopts either a single technical practice or a combination of practices according to the pattern shown in Table 8.1. (We suppose that $\bar{s}$ is the least scale at which θ can be operated, $\mu\bar{s}$ the lowest integer multiple of $\bar{s}$ with $\mu > 1$ at which it can be, and γ and γ' the shares of total production delivered by θ and θ' respectively).

Table 8.1. *Single and combined technical practices in a classical increasing-efficiency relation*

Scale	Share of technical practice θ	Share of technical practice θ'
$\bar{s}$	1	0
$\bar{s} \langle \bar{s} \langle \mu\,\bar{s}$	$0 \langle \gamma \langle 1$	$0 \langle \gamma' \langle 1$
$\mu\,\bar{s}$	1	0

As is shown in the table, scale $\bar{s}$ is obtained by operating practice θ alone. At any scale between $\bar{s}$ and $\mu\bar{s}$, the producer operates a combination of technical practices, which is obtained by combining practices θ and θ' (in this case, the whole production process is less specialized than practice θ alone, since practice θ' is less specialized than practice θ). Finally, at scale $\mu\bar{s}$, the producer goes back to the technical practice that was followed at $\bar{s}$.

This sequence of changes in the technical practices that get used reflects not only the sequence of changes in the practices that are feasible which may be derived from Babbage's Law, but also a special rule of technical adoption. In particular, the producer is assumed to choose, at every scale, that combination of practices which used the 'most preferred' practice at its maximum feasible share.

8.4.3. *Scale, non-produced resources, and industry-specific inputs: the classical theory of decreasing efficiency*

The English classical economists (in particular, Malthus, Ricardo, and West) considered a decreasing-efficiency relation due to upper bounds on the availability of certain non-produced inputs, of which land is the most important example.[6] The characteristic elements of this relation are set forth below.

First, in certain production processes, particularly in agriculture and mining, a continuous increase in process scale is associated with a sequence of changes in technical practice. These changes may follow one of two patterns: (a) a sequence of different non-produced inputs are used as scale is expanded (for example, increasingly 'inferior' land is cultivated as agricultural output is expanded); (b) a technical practice using a given non-produced input (such as a given plot of land) is substituted for another technical practice using the same input. We may call pattern (a) an *extensive decreasing-efficiency relation*, and pattern (b) an *intensive decreasing-efficiency relation*. Second, in the case of intensive decreasing efficiency, at most two technical practices can be used at the same time in the same productive establishment.[7] Finally, for each output x produced, there is

[6] Cf. Malthus (1815*a*; 1815*b*), Ricardo (1817), and West (1815). Ch. 3 of Ricardo's *Principles* deals with decreasing efficiency in mining, but the particular decreasing efficiency relation derived for this case is based on the fact that any given mine is a limited resource (in general, there is no 'abundance of equally fertile mines') rather than on the explicit consideration of exhaustible inputs. Decreasing efficiency in mining could thus be treated as a special case of agricultural decreasing efficiency. A modern formulation of the classical theory of decreasing efficiency is presented in Quadrio-Curzio (1967; 1980; 1990).

[7] Given 3 technical practices θ, θ', θ'', such that θ is strictly preferred to θ' and θ'', θ' is strictly preferred to θ'', a continuous increase in process scale is initially obtained by substituting θ' for θ on the given plot. When all this plot is cultivated by θ', a further increase in process scale is obtained by substituting θ'' for θ'. As a result, the production process is carried out by using either a single technical practice or a combination of practices consisting of at most 2 practices (This feature of intensive decreasing efficiency is considered in Sraffa (1960: ch. 11, 'Land'.)

a one-to-one correspondence between the scale of the process and the output of x.

The decreasing-efficiency relation considered by the classical economists derives from special assumptions about which technical practices are feasible at each scale and about the criterion the producer follows in technical adoption. The classical economists took for granted a particular structure of the requirements for non-produced inputs. They implicitly assumed that there is a non-produced input that is required in the production of one commodity only. That is, there is a pair of commodities, i and j say, for which the following three conditions are satisfied: (i) the amount of i needed to produce one unit of j is positive; (ii) the quantity of i needed to produce one unit of j' is zero if $j' \neq j$; (iii) commodity i is a non-produced input.

The classical economists implicitly made these assumptions in writing about decreasing efficiency in agriculture and considering the agricultural processes not one by one, but in terms of an integrated complex. But the same assumption would also make decreasing efficiency a possibility in any industry, as long as the non-produced input specific to that industry cannot be augmented as process scale is increased[8]. For in any structure of input requirements of the form of (i)–(iii), there is at least one production process in which the scarcity of one of the inputs cannot be made good by transferring quantities of that input from other sectors of the economy.

In this case, the matrix of upper bounds on the absorption of non-produced inputs into the various production processes has a special structure, of which an example is shown below:

$$
Z = \begin{bmatrix}
z_{11} & z_{12} & \cdots & 0 \\
0 & z_{22} & \cdots & 0 \\
\cdot & & & \\
\cdot & & & \\
\cdot & & & \\
0 & 0 & \cdots & z_{nk}
\end{bmatrix}
$$

Matrix Z is of dimension $n \times k$, where n are the non-produced inputs and k the produced commodities. Each element z_{ij} denotes

[8] This relationship between industry classification, input requirements, and decreasing efficiency was pointed out by Sraffa: 'The wider the definition which we assume for "an industry"—that is, the more nearly it includes all the undertakings which employ a given *factor* of production, as for example agriculture or the iron industry—the more probable will be that the forces which make for diminishing returns will play an important part in it' (1926: 583).

the upper bound on the absorption of non-produced input i into the process delivering commodity j. In our example, two non-produced inputs are process-specific. The corresponding upper bounds are respectively z_{22} and z_{nk}.

We may note that a decreasing-efficiency relation of the classical type is still possible, even if no non-produced input is commodity-specific, provided that at least one non-produced input is *process-specific*. In this case, however, there is no longer a one-to-one correspondence between process scales and commodity outputs. An increasing process scale might lead to the operation of a 'worse' technical practice, both when the product-mix is fixed and when it changes from one process scale to another, for a given relationship between resource endowments and upper bounds on process scales is in general compatible with a number of different output vectors (see section 6.5).

Another technological assumption behind the decreasing-efficiency relation considered by the classical economists is that no production process requires the use of more than one commodity-specific, non-produced input. If this assumption is dropped, it is no longer possible to maintain that a sequence of scale-technology contractions is associated with changes of technical practice such that, at any step of the sequence, the producer switches from one practice to the next lowest practice in his preference ranking. This 'continuity' of the changes of practice with respect to the producer's ranking is not always possible if the production process requires two or more process-specific, non-produced inputs. This can be seen by considering the three cases below.

(i) A different type of non-produced input u_i ($i = 1, \ldots, k$) and of non-produced input v_j ($j = 1, \ldots, m$) is needed in each technical practice. (We may interpret the u_i and v_j as different types of land and water respectively.) In this case, increasing scale produces changes of technical practice that follow the producer's ranking without 'jumping' over practices of intermediate rank.

(ii) A different u_i ($i = 1, \ldots, k$) but the same v_j is needed in each technical practice. In this case, increasing scale produces changes of practice that may or may not follow the producer's ranking without 'jumps'. The former is the case if, by switching from the existing practice to the next lowest practice in producer's ranking, the higher scale can be achieved with the quantity of v_j (the input of uniform quality) that is available. The latter is the case if one or more of the 'intermediate' practices are not feasible given the amount of v_j available. We may note that a sufficient condition for the continuous case is that the unit requirement of v_j is lower and lower as increasingly 'worse' practices are considered.

(iii) The same inputs u_i and v_j are needed in all the technical practices. In this case, the continuity of changes in technical practice requires that all the practices in the sequence are permitted by the given quantities of u_i and v_j. A sufficient condition for this is that the unit requirements of both u_i and v_j are lower and lower as increasingly 'worse' practices are considered.

The foregoing analysis shows that the decreasing-efficiency relations considered by the classical economists depend on a specific structure of input requirements. In general, however, the combination of scale-technology contraction and 'optimizing' technical adoption determines decreasing-efficiency relations that differ from the classical ones.

Another important feature of the classical model of decreasing efficiency is that input endowments and process scale determine whether production processes consist of either a single technical practice or of a combination of practices. Each combination of practices is such that, at any given scale, the share of production delivered by the 'most preferred' practices is at the maximum permitted by that scale. This situation is illustrated by the example below.

Let θ, θ', and θ'' be three distinct technical practices. Suppose that the producer strictly prefers θ to θ' and θ' to θ'', and that his preferences are transitive. As the given scale varies, the technical practice, or combination of practices, adopted by the producer changes according to one of the two patterns in Tables 8.2 and 8.3.

In the intensive case of decreasing efficiency, only θ is used as long as the process scale is below s_1. At scales between s_1 and s_2 the producer uses a combination of practices θ and θ' such that the share of production delivered by practice θ is always the maximum that the resource endowment permits. At scale s_2, practice θ' is used. At scales between s_2 and s_3, the producer uses a combination of practices θ' and θ'' such that the share of production delivered by θ' is the maximum permitted by resource endowment. At scale s_3, only θ'' is used.

In the extensive case of decreasing efficiency, θ is the only practice in use as long as the process scale is below s_1. At scales between s_1 and s_2, the producer uses a combination of practices θ

Table 8.2. *Classical decreasing efficiency: the intensive case*

Scale	Share of θ	Share of θ'	Share of θ''
$s \leqslant s_1$	1	0	0
$s_1 \langle s \langle s_2$	$0 \langle \gamma \langle 1$	$0 \langle \gamma' \langle 1$	0
$s = s_2$	0	1	0
$s_2 \langle s \langle s_3$	0	$0 \langle \gamma' \langle 1$	$0 \langle \gamma'' \langle 1$
$s = s_3$	0	0	1

Table 8.3. *Classical decreasing efficiency: the extensive case*

Scale	Share of θ	Share of θ'	Share of θ''
$s \leqslant s_1$	1	0	0
$s_1 \langle s \langle s_2$	$0 \langle \gamma \langle 1$	$0 \langle \gamma' \langle 1$	0
$s \rangle s_2$	$0 \langle \gamma \langle 1$	$0 \langle \gamma' \langle 1$	$0 \langle \gamma'' \langle 1$

and θ', such that the share of production delivered by θ is the maximum that the resource endowment permits. Above the scale s_2, the producer uses a combination of practices θ, θ', and θ'' such that the shares of production delivered by θ and θ' respectively are the maximum that available resources permit.

In both the intensive and extensive cases, decreasing efficiency derives from the existence of upper bounds on land's productive capacity. In addition, the producer's selection of technical practices reflects a particular attitude towards the combinations of practices, for he is assumed always to choose that particular mix of practices that allots the greatest possible share of production to a 'most preferred' practice.

8.5. CONCLUDING REMARKS

Scale-technology expansion and contraction do not always lead respectively to a more *efficient* and to a less *efficient* technical practice. Indeed, a scale–*efficiency* relation can only be defined if the producer satisfies what we have called the 'optimizing' model of technical adoption. If he does, only the 'top' feasible practice is considered for choice at the given scale, and thus scale-induced changes in the set of feasible practices may cause a change of practice—for a change in the 'top' feasible practice implies, on this model of adoption, the choice of a different technical practice. The latter practice may generally be considered more or less 'efficient' than the practice it replaces as scale rises, as long as there is some degree of inter-scale consistency in the producer's preferences.

If, on the other hand, technical adoption conforms to the model of sequential search, the same patterns of scale-technology expansion and contraction might leave the technical practice unaffected. This would be the outcome if, at the assigned scale, the 'satisficing' technical practice is unaffected by the change in the set of feasible practices.

The idea that there is a regular relationship between changes in scale and changes of technical practice, and that these latter changes tend to show increasing or decreasing efficiency, is the result of a particular way of modelling the producer's behaviour—namely, according to the 'optimizing' model of technical adoption. If the producer follows the criterion of sequential search, whether or not a change of scale produces a change of technical practice depends on the particular sequences of scrutiny which the producer follows at different scales. Moreover, a change of scale may in this case produce a change of technical practice quite independently of the occurrence of technology expansion and contraction. For a different scale may be associated with a different sequence of scrutiny, and a change of technical practice may simply be the consequence of a difference in the search path; there need be no change in the set of feasible practices.

The analysis of this chapter also shows that scale–efficiency relations may take a form quite different from that which is taken for granted by most of the economic literature. In particular, an increase in scale which brings about a switch to a 'better' or to a 'worse' technical practice does not always imply increases in the outputs of commodities, for there are cases in which, as the scale of the production process is changed, so is the commodity-mix. In such cases, scale-technology expansion and contraction may be the consequence of expanding the outputs of certain commodities, while contracting or holding constant those of the other commodities produced in the same productive unit. Increasing or decreasing efficiency of the actual technical practice is thus possible (as an outcome of scale-technology expansion or contraction respectively) even though certain commodity outputs are decreasing or constant. This latter case suggests in particular that the basic explanatory relationship of all scale–efficiency phenomena is the relationship between the number of technical practices simultaneously using a given stock of productive resources and this stock of resources. A certain variability in commodity outputs is presupposed by any scale–efficiency relation, but this variability can hardly explain the direction of such a relationship. For certain commodity outputs may be decreasing when an increasing scale of the global production process brings about technology contraction and decreasing efficiency. Similarly, other commodity outputs may be increasing when a decreasing process scale brings about technology expansion and increasing efficiency.

The importance of the link between the scale of a production process, its 'structure' (i.e. the mix of e.p. types characteristic of any given technical practice), and the amount of productive resources available in the establishment at a given time also suggests that the scale–efficiency relation is essentially a static concept. Given the producer's technical knowledge (a universal listing of the sets of technical practices he knows to be feasible at different scales), his preferences over technical practices, and available resources, determine a particular scale–efficiency relation. The evolution of preferences over time and changes in the stock of resources available will normally upset this relationship. However, with given preferences and resources, the 'optimizing' producer can be described as choosing his (θ, s) pair as if a particular scale–efficiency relation held.

PART III

The Analysis of Scale and Productive Size

9

The Relation of Scale and Size and its Historical Development

9.1. HISTORY AND THEORY

9.1.1. *'Weak' and 'strong' theories*

In the previous chapters we considered the relationship between scale and technical practice from a theoretical point of view. After presenting a rational reconstruction of the economists' views about this issue (Chapter 3), we introduced a new model of the production process (Chapter 4). This model, which is based on viewing productive activity as a network of tasks performed in real time, was then used in order to analyse two different 'scenarios' in which a change of process scale brings about a change in the set of technical alternatives available to the producer: scale-technology expansion and scale-technology contraction (Chapters 5 and 6). In both 'scenarios' the change of scale brings about a change in the range of possible outcomes (feasible technical practices). The actual outcome (the technical practice actually adopted) depends on the pattern followed by the producer in searching for a 'suitable' technical practice (Chapters 7 and 8). This search is based on 'optimizing' or 'satisficing' behaviour.

A model of technical adoption based on the Simon-type sequential scrutiny of alternatives does not generally lead to a determinate outcome, for any given technical practice may be adopted or not, all other things being equal, depending on the particular scanning sequence followed. Any given technical practice is either 'satisfactory' or 'not satisfactory', and there is no ranking of 'satisfactory' practices in terms of their degree of 'satisfactoriness'. This makes technical adoption in Simon-type framework independent of search time, except in the special case in which the scanning process is so short that no satisfactory technical practice is found. (This result contrasts with the dependence of the outcome of search on search duration in models of the optimizing kind, such as the one considered in Kohn and Shavell, 1974.)

Only in the special case in which technical adoption is based on the global ranking of feasible technical practices may we 'ignore history' by considering choice in a timeless framework. (Note that choice may be based on global ranking even if scanning is of the sequential type. For the producer who knows that the choice set is of a certain size can consider each option in turn, then choose the best at the end of the scanning process.)

Theories based on a satisficing and sequential view of technical adoption appear to be 'weak' from the point of view of the determinacy of theory, but they deal with historical time better than 'strong' theories in which determinacy is taken for granted. The reason for this is that 'strong' theories derive their determinate results from a conception of 'choice', in which choosing is independent of the scanning sequence. On the other hand, 'weak' theories introduce the consideration of real time in the definition of 'choice', which appears to be a process rather than an isolated event. However, theories of this type consider only subsets of the space of possible options rather than individual options. This is the price that must be paid for their greater realism. (An early recognition of the duality between rational-choice models and historical processes may be found in Åkerman, 1936; 1940; 1942; 1944; see also Hicks, 1976; Meacci, 1986.)

In this chapter, we shall discuss a number of historical episodes that can be better understood in the light of the present theoretical framework. As a preliminary, the following section considers various methodological issues connected with the use of our theory.

9.1.2. *Scale-practice relations and technological history*

The knowledge of the technical practice–scale pairs (θ, s) that are observed in history is not enough to tell us which practices are feasible at any given scale. It can only provide us with the information that certain pairs (θ, s) were feasible and that they were adopted by some producer at a given historical time. If pair (θ, s) is never observed, we do not know whether this is because that pair was never feasible or because it was never adopted, though it was feasible. However, if we observe n pairs (θ, s), in which the first element is the same for all pairs and the second element varies from one pair to another, we may conclude that technical practice θ is feasible at the n different scales. Similarly, if we observe n pairs (θ, s), in which the second element is the same and the first element varies from one pair to another, we may conclude that the n different technical practices are feasible at the given scale.

We have evidence for scale-technology contraction if:

(i) we observe a set Ω of (θ, s) pairs;

(ii) there is a partition of Ω into subsets $\Omega_i s$ $(i = 1, \ldots, m)$, such that a pair (θ, s) belongs to Ω_i when $s \leqslant \bar{s}_i$ $(i = m)$ and θ is never observed at $s > s_i$. ($\bar{s}_i$ is thus an upper bound on the process scales that are permissible in Ω_i.)

If (ii) is satisfied, our evidence supports the hypothesis that any technical practice in Ω_i is not feasible at scales higher than $\bar{s}_i$.

Evidence for scale-technology expansion may be obtained if the following conditions are satisfied:

(i*) we observe a set Ω of (θ, s) pairs;

(ii*) there is a partition of Ω into subsets Ω_i's $(i = 1, \ldots, m)$ such that a pair (θ, s) belongs to Ω_i when $s \geqslant \bar{s}_i$ $(i = m)$ and θ is never observed at $s < \bar{s}_i$. ($\bar{s}_i$ is thus a lower bound on the process scales permissible in Ω_i.)

If condition (ii*) is satisfied, our evidence supports the hypothesis that any technical practice in Ω_i is not feasible at scales higher than $\bar{s}_i$.

Conditions (ii) and (ii*) are necessary for scale-technology contraction and expansion respectively. If our information is limited to a number of (θ, s) pairs, we may be justified in a presumption that certain scale–practice relations do exist, but we cannot give sufficient reasons for the adoption of a certain technical practice at any given scale. Given n pairs (θ, s) belonging to Ω_i and such that $s \leqslant \bar{s}_i$ or $s \geqslant \bar{s}_i$, we may say that no technical practice in Ω_i is used at scales higher (lower) than $\bar{s}_i$, because of certain scale–practice relations. However, we cannot say why scale $\bar{s}$ is associated with technical practice θ and not with θ', where both θ and θ' belong to Ω_i. In order to give sufficient reasons for the adoption of a certain technical practice at a given scale, it is necessary to consider actual historical episodes in which a movement from one scale to another is associated with the substitution of one practice for another. Any such episode can be considered to be a case of scale-dependent change of technical practice if and only if the following additional condition is also satisfied.

(iii)/(iii*) the substitution of pair (θ', s') for pair (θ, s) coincides with the switch from Ω_i to Ω_j $(i, j = 1, \ldots, m;$ and $i \neq j)$.

Thus, unless every technical practice is scale-specific, a change of scale cannot be a sufficient reason by itself for the associated change of practice. In particular, the change of practice cannot be considered to be a result of the change of scale as long as the scale–practice change occurs within a single Ω_i region. It also follows that, when technical practices are not scale-specific, we may have a range of scale–practice variations in which no scale variation is a sufficient reason for the associated variation in technical practice.

We shall now devote a few words to the role of the producer's behaviour in determining scale–practice variations. The pattern of technical adoption (satisficing behaviour versus optimization) is relevant in so far as we are interested in determining a priori which technical practice would be associated with a particular scale, for the technical practice adopted by a producer at any given scale may differ according to whether the producer follows the 'satisficing' model or the 'global optimization' model for technical adoption. (See Chapter 7.) The pattern of technical adoption may be unimportant, on the other hand, if the economist is interested in giving *sufficient* reasons for particular historical episodes of 'scale-dependent' technical change. If technical practice θ' is substituted for θ, when scale s' is substituted for scale s, the change of practice can be considered a result of the change of scale—provided that condition (iii)/(iii*) above is satisfied—regardless of whether technical adoption is of the optimizing or the satisficing kind. In such case, feasibility logically precedes mode of adoption, and the actual episodes of technological history can be 'reconstructed' without knowing the technical-adoption criterion. Indeed, the indeterminacy of the 'weak' theory (the satisficing model) with respect to a producer's behaviour makes this theory 'open' to history, for it allows for—indeed, requires—consideration of the contingent and/or institutional influences that affect behaviour in an uncertain environment.

The theory outlined in the previous chapters also identifies a number of influences of a more regular character, which affect technical behaviour on the 'objective' side, i.e. regardless of the mode of adoption of technical practices.

9.1.3. *Intentions, objective conditions, and technical practice*

Any given episode of technological history results from two distinct sets of causes: (i) the producer's intentions (these may be defined as rules of action on which technical adoption depends); (ii) the 'objective conditions' under which technical adoption takes place. Intentions and objective conditions may, of course, interact with each other. (For example, a change of intention may bring about a change in feasible technical practices, and this latter may influence the technical adoption criterion.) Interaction takes time, however, and the possibility of it does not alter the fact that intentions and objective conditions are logically independent factors.

Standard economic theory takes technical adoption to be the result of intentional behaviour (such as optimizing choice) under conditions of 'accommodating' technology. (This means that the producer's intentions determine adoption behaviour, and that technical practice cannot vary as a result of technological factors alone.) Technical behaviour is examined by assuming that the producer follows a well-defined adoption rule and that the organization of the production process is adjusted accordingly.[1] Standard theory is unable to deal with two important features of productive activity: (i) the producer's intentions can seldom be described in terms of a single and stable objective function (they are often the result of interaction between different 'interests', and may change as the producer's perception of his own environment changes); (ii) the set of feasible practices is seldom as 'accommodating' as standard economic theory portrays it to be. (For example, the introduction of a technical parameter, such as a speed or strength requirement, might oblige the producer to 'switch' to a different set of feasible technical practices. A similar outcome may result from the change of process scale.)

Standard economic theory takes the view that a producer's intentions are given, and that productive organization, though essentially exogenous, is also 'accommodating'. We have followed an alternative strategy, by assuming that a producer's intentions cannot be reduced to any fixed-choice criterion, and that technology can provide sufficient reasons for switching from one technical practice to another, as certain parameters are varied. How this can happen may become clearer in the following sections. In them, we shall consider a number of technical episodes in which the adoption of a technical

---

[1] This assumption is independent of the degree of substitutability between inputs. In the case of limited substitutability (or of fixed input proportions), the producer is assumed to choose the technical practice from among a narrower set of feasible practices (a point-set in the case of fixed proportions). Here, however, technical adoption depends on producer's intentions rather than on some 'transformation law' internal to the current practice.

practice reflects certain characteristics of feasible technology regardless of producer's choice criterion.

9.2. SCALE, SIZE, AND FUND-INPUT UTILIZATION

9.2.1. *Process scale and size of the productive unit*

It will be recalled from the previous chapters that we considered an abstract production process, and that we defined scale as a property of the process rather than of the place in which that process is carried out. In fact, scale was defined as the number of elementary processes (e.p.s) simultaneously operated in a conventional productive unit, even if in various places this unit was taken to be a productive establishment. On the other hand, a productive unit was taken to be a conventional 'batch' of e.p.s, and no effort was made to describe its size. As a matter of fact, alternative notions of 'productive unit' may be used, such as the establishment, the enterprise, or the industrial district.

The problem of size is not a new one in economics. However, economists have not generally distinguished the size of a productive unit from process scale. This is partly a result of the fact that economists did not take up Adam Smith's suggestion that division of labour can be studied independently of establishment size. (This opinion led Smith to concentrate on 'trifling manufactures' such as pin-making, disregarding the production processes that require large-size productive units.) By the time Dugald Stewart was considering the organization of production, division of labour was associated with the idea that special advantages are to be derived from an increase of size: 'By carrying on all the different processes at once, which an individual must have executed separately, it becomes possible to produce a multitude of pins completely finished in the same time as a single pin might have been either cut or pointed' (1855–6: viii. 319). This identification of scale with size was examined in greater detail by Gioja, Babbage, and Mill (see Chapter 3), and remained common among economists even after certain advantages of small-sized establishments had been recognized (by Marshall and others). An early criticism of such an identification is to be found in Luigi Valeriani's comments on Gioja: 'I am really concerned that we might be discussing words, not real things. In fact, as everyone knows, greatness and smallness are relative, rather than absolute properties. Additionally, if we consider this problem from the point of view of division of labour . . . *a small factory occupied with one or few things could be large, whereas a large factory occupied with many operations could be small* (1817: 42; my translation and italics). Valeriani's view is a development of the position originally expounded by Adam Smith, and suggests a distinction between size of factory and scale of production (in so far as scale is a matter of the division of labour). The spread of the large-sized machinery that accompanied the first Industrial Revolution led economists to concentrate on the special case in which large size coincides with large scale, thus abandoning a conceptual distinction that might have been useful in developing a general theory of the production process. Initially, the size of the productive unit, which was identified with the size of the productive establishment, was taken to be large or small, depending upon whether the advantages of large-scale production are a significant element in technical adoption or not (see Gioja, Babbage, and Mill). Later on, a number of economists recognized that the technological advantages of large-scale production may sometimes also be had within a network of small-sized establishments (see e.g. Marshall's theory of the 'industrial district' considered in section 3.4.2). This left establishment size to be explained in terms of non-technological factors (financial constraints, managerial abilities, and so on).

The relationship between size and scale is often blurred by the lack of a clear distinction between the production process (the network of tasks delivering a certain output) and the productive unit (the place in which one or more tasks are performed). Scale, as defined in Chapter 4, is a characteristic of the production process that is independent of the amounts of the inputs needed for its various tasks. On the other hand, the size of a productive unit, as usually understood, is independent of the complexity of the task network, and reflects the input quantities assembled in a given place in order to carry out the production process.

The distinction between scale of process and size of productive unit may be put in terms of changes. Process scale is increased or decreased whenever there is an increase or decrease in the number of e.p.s carried out side by side in the same productive unit. The size of a productive unit gets larger or smaller whenever there is an increase or decrease in the input quantities assembled in the same place for the purpose of production. An important implication of this distinction is that, in general, 'the optimum size of an economic organization is not a technical problem like that of the optimum size of a plant' (Georgescu-Roegen, 1976 [1964]: 296). In particular, determination of the optimum size of organization involves comparisons of quality' (ibid.), and institutional factors often play a critical role in establishing the size distribution of productive units under given historical conditions (see following section).

A change in the size of a productive unit is usually associated with a change in its maximum process scale (the maximum number of e.p.s that can be simultaneously operated in it). On the other hand, a change in process scale is often possible without any change in the size of the productive unit. This may happen if the existing resources are more effectively used, or if the number of e.p.s is increased by 'splitting' each e.p. into constituent tasks and having these performed in separate establishments.

The above argument implies that inventive activity may perform a critical role in changing the relationship between scale and size, for this relationship depends upon the way in which a production process is identified, in terms of technical recipe and output specification(s). (The technical and commodity structure of a process determines which pools of active factors are capable of executing it in an efficient way.) In this connection, recent empirical studies suggest that large organizations are more inclined to undertake in-house research, without necessarily being very innovative themselves. On the other hand, small- and medium-sized firms tend to introduce innovations at a higher speed even if they do not easily undertake major research efforts (see e.g. Soete, 1979; Kaplinsky, 1981; Rothwell and Zegveld, 1982; Rothwell, 1984; Oakey, Rothwell, and Cooper, 1988; see also Scherer, 1965).

A general explanation of the behaviour of large organizations with respect to invention and innovation may be that large capacity is often associated with economies of scale and internal specialization, which make it feasible to operate an independent research and development (R. and D.) department. On the other hand, our analysis suggests that large size is often associated with the utilization of a straight-line practice, which in turn makes it difficult to innovate (except through e.p. specialization).[2] Small-sized establishments

---

[2] According to Beckett, 'if many of the operations are sequential . . . it may not be possible to employ the managerial principles postulated by Schumacher', i.e. small-size production (see Beckett, 1977, quoted in Eilon, 1979: 6; see also Schumacher, 1973).

may be associated either with specialized e.p.s or with job-shop practices. In both cases, an independent inventive activity may be difficult, since it would be inconsistent either with the existing pattern of specialization or with the stop-and-go character of specific activities within the job-shop framework. Innovation could be easily accepted, on the other hand, especially if it reinforces the effectiveness of small and specialized units, or that of small-batch establishments using a job-shop practice, in producing according to customer's requirements (see Oakey, Rothwell, and Cooper, 1988; see also Amsden, 1983; 1985).[3]

To sum up, inventive activity seems to be differently related to size and to the propensity to innovate depending upon the internal structure of the productive unit. The straight-line organization is associated with a type of research activity aimed at standard solutions for relatively large classes of problems. This makes invention easier (provided there is a concentrated effort) but its successful application to specific cases more difficult. The job-shop organization is associated with a type of research activity aimed at *ad hoc* solutions for relatively narrow classes of problems. This makes inventive activity rather informal and not so clearly distinct from other tasks, such as production engineering. Its application is much easier, however, owing to the problem-specific character of invention.

9.2.2. Fund-input 'period of circulation' and measures of establishment size

In the two previous sections we discussed the relationship of scale to size without committing ourselves to any particular notion of productive unit. We shall now take the productive unit to be a productive establishment. It will be recalled that there are different notions of size of a productive unit. The determination of which size variable is relevant in measuring establishment size depends on the

---

[3] A relationship between an 'informal' pattern of R. and D., a high propensity to innovate, and production within small-sized units has been identified by A. H. Amsden in the case of commodities that are 'typically produced with little capital but with large amounts of skilled labor (non electrical machinery, ships)' (1983: 336; see also Rothwell and Zegveld, 1982). With particular reference to newly industrialized countries (NICs), it has been noted that 'there is . . . an interconnection or virtuous circle between production engineering and project execution in the capital goods sector that is absent or less pronounced elsewhere: project execution with (per force) local involvement leads to greater adaptive engineering; and adaptive engineering and learning-by-doing lead to a greater ability to design' (ibid.; see also Amsden, 1977; 1985).

physical and economic characteristics of the various fund inputs and, in particular, on fund input natural units, on the ratio between circulating or 'working' capital and the amount of capital that is 'sunk' in fund inputs, and on the relative lengths of the 'capital immobilizations' in the various fund-input categories. In general, the fund input that has the largest natural units (in terms of output capacity) is likely to set a lower bound on the size of the productive unit in which it is used (the maximum feasible number of e.p.s in the productive unit cannot be lower than the output capacity of one unit of that fund input). However, the fund input that has the largest natural units does not necessarily coincide with the relevant size variable. For example, a technical practice requiring skilled workers and tools of an elementary kind may be associated with a lower bound on the size of the establishment due to the tools' natural units, even if the relevant size variable is the number of workers forming that unit.

Considering now the ratio between circulating or 'working' capital and the amount of capital sunk in the various fund inputs, we may argue that, if this ratio is high enough, raw materials and semi-finished products are the main prerequisites for productive activity, so that working capital is the relevant size variable, and actual establishment size will be large or small, depending on the concentration of wealth among owners of capital. On the other hand, if that ratio is low enough, technological considerations become over-riding. In this case, two distinct rankings of fund-input categories must be considered. One is the ranking according to the *amount of capital* sunk in each category. The other is the ranking according to the *length of time* that capital is sunk in each fund input. The time needed by any fund input to transfer its value to the product (its *period of circulation*) is inversely related to the scale of the production process at any point of time. In other words, the greater the number of e.p.s that are simultaneously operated on a given fund input at each point of time, the shorter will be the period needed to transfer the value of that fund input to the product.

Large-sized establishments are likely, for purely technical reasons, when the amount of capital sunk in the fund inputs is sufficiently large in comparison with the working capital. In this case, the fund-input period of circulation would be too long, unless process scale at the establishment level is large enough. If the amount of capital sunk in the fund inputs is large enough, compared with the working capital, the fund input having the longest period of circulation determines the dimension in which size is measured. Thus the size of a farm is measured by the land it occupies, not by the number of peasants or by the stock of tools and machines. Similarly, the size of a modern factory is measured by its physical capital stock, not by the number of workers or by the land on which the factory is built. The size of an artisan workshop is measured by its stock of skilled workmen, not by its stock of tools or by the workshop area. The reason for this convention is that the provision and maintenance of any fund input requires the advance of a certain capital. The fund input having the longest period of circulation is also the one requiring the longest 'capital immobilization'. As a result, the standard way of reckoning establishment size reflects the relative importance of capital immobilization for the various fund inputs.

Economic history provides many examples of this general pattern. In traditional economies, the size of non-agricultural establishments is generally small, if it is measured conventionally by workshop area or perhaps by the stock of tools. But the same establishment might be 'large' if it were measured by the number of skills available in the workshop, or by the human capital embodied in it. We might measure it thus, moreover, if skilled labour were the fund input requiring the longest (and perhaps also the largest) capital immobilization, while relatively minor capital advances were required for the provision of tools and workplace.

The transition from a traditional to an industrial economy is marked by the growing importance of tools and machinery, while labour-skills lose their former pre-eminent position (see also Benvenuti, 1988). This phase is associated with the spread of 'large-sized production', which had remained relatively inconspicuous before the first Industrial Revolution.[4] The size of a manufacturing establishment has been measured by its stock of machines ever since. This suggests that, by this stage of industrial development, machinery required the longest capital advances.

[4] Nef, in his classic paper, maintains that '[t]he industrial plant owned by private capitalists, who employed in it dozens and sometimes scores or even hundreds of workmen, was not the novelty it was once believed to be . . . [L]arge-scale industry, in this sense, was common in mining and many branches of manufacture long before the middle of the eighteenth century' (1934: 3). However, it was later pointed out that '[m]any a large plant or massive concentration of workers in this pre-Industrial Revolution era owed its existence, directly or indirectly, to state support' and that '[m]any a big enterprise or would-be factory owed its life to the nourishment of boom conditions and perished with the cold winds of a slump' (Coleman, 1959: 510).

9.2.3. *Scale and size in technological history*

The volatile character of large-sized production before the first Industrial Revolution suggests that in this period the existence of large productive establishments was due (in most cases) to short-run advantages rather than to a permanent requirement of technical practice. In the textile industry, for example, early factory production involved water-driven machinery (such as the silk-mills *alla bolognese*, which John Lombe brought to England around 1716–17). This made factory production a better way of organizing the production process in the presence of large and expanding demand for a particular commodity (Poni, 1972). However, no task in the corresponding production process made a large establishment necessary, because of complementary relations with indivisible inputs. (Water-power was equally available to small and large establishments, a feature not to be found in the later steam-engine technology.)

The first Industrial Revolution is marked by an increase in the average size of manufacturing establishments, mainly as a result of steam-engine technology.[5] The second Industrial Revolution, with its discovery of additional sources of energy, seemed to halt this tendency.[6] This brought about a revision of the widespread view that large size is inherent in modern industrial development. As Jewkes put it:

as a matter of historical event it seems far from clear that the big equipment is everywhere replacing the smaller. Indeed, the use of electric power has opened up a new field for small, independently operated machines. The aeroplane, the road lorry, the passenger bus are smaller technical units than the ship or the railway train. The jet engine is a smaller, cheaper mechanism

---

[5] See e.g. Derry and Williams (1982: 311–42, 585, 643–6).

[6] At the very beginning of the technical upheavals of the 2nd Industrial Revolution, the technologist Franz Reuleaux noted that the discovery of 'small and economical motive machines' would possibly provide the basis for a reduction in the average size of manufacturing establishments (see Reuleaux, 1876: 482; see also s. 3.4.5 above). A few years later, the French economist Paul Leroy-Beaulieu wrote that 'concentrated production might one day give way to dispersed production once again. Thanks to the invention of small and cheap motors, or to the distribution of inexpensive motive-power in small quantities, the putting-out system will possibly be reintroduced into a number of industries' (1896: 462). A different view about historical changes in the average size of productive units around the end of the 19th c. is expressed by Chandler (1977), who argues that average size increased over that period (see s. 9.3.3 and my comment there). The relationship between the co-ordination *advantages* of large size (high speed) and the range (variety) of commodities produced has recently been considered in Chandler (1990).

than the traditional type piston engine . . . It is often argued that factories grow big because they must be organised around some large central piece of equipment which must be kept running full time if it is to operate economically. The rest of the equipment of the factory must then be provided on a scale large enough to consume the product of the dominating central machine. But there is another way of organising in such circumstances. Factories may specialise in operating the central machine and provide materials for other, much smaller, factories engaged in prior or subsequent operations . . . And the British motor vehicle industry, particularly in the Birmingham area, consists of a small number of large assembly plants surrounded by a mass of very small engineering factories specialised to an almost inconceivable degree in the making of parts for the final assembly. (1952: 247–9)

The organizational features noted by Jewkes are consistent with the requirements of large-scale production when straight-line practices are operated (see section 5.5). More recently, a combination of volatile demand for mass-produced commodities and of innovations permitting 'flexible' arrangements of tasks (information technology) has brought about the decline of assembly-line practices.[7] As a result, production processes traditionally associated with large equipment are now increasingly carried out in establishments that appear to be small or medium-sized, if size is measured by the stock of material equipment in each technical unit (see also Pratten, 1991). However, certain features of production processes based on numerical-control practices may call into question the conventional way of measuring size. This issue deserves to be considered in greater detail.

Numerical-control practices often bring about a separation between the arrangement of tasks in the process and the physical organization of the establishment. The establishment is transformed into a multi-purpose organism, whose structure consists of a network of 'general' functions related to each other in a way that is independent of the particular tasks carried out on any given occasion. The linking of tasks belonging to the same elementary process is achieved by well-defined 'codes of behaviour', which cause a given task to be performed when a certain signal is received. As a result, the structure of the establishment is fixed in 'functional' but not in 'operational' terms, and a variety of different sequences of tasks can be performed without changing the establishment's basic identity.

---

[7] See e.g. Skinner (1983).

The establishment takes shape around a well-defined body of 'abstract' skills, in a way that reminds us of the craft organization of production.[8]

This change in the nature of the establishment might significantly change the relative importance of the measures of capital immobilization for the various fund inputs. In particular, capital 'locked up' in the material equipment might become negligible compared to capital embodied in the establishment's abstract 'ability to operate'. In this case, the critical factor in determining establishment size will be the range of mutually compatible tasks and the possibility of 'classifying' tasks under relatively distinct skills. The establishment would thus be 'large' or 'small' depending on the number of (potential) tasks that can be performed in it, rather than on the size of its material equipment.

9.2.4. *Scale, size, and production theory*

Size and scale are features of the production process quite independent of each other in the long run, but they may influence each other significantly in the short run. No abstract treatment of production is able to give necessary and sufficient conditions for a given process to be performed at a certain *scale* within a productive unit of given *size*. In particular, theories that consider the production process as a combination of inputs (rather than as a network of tasks) can determine size (the amount of productive resources pooled together) but not scale (the number of e.p.s operated together using that pool of resources). On the other hand, theories, like ours, that consider the production process as a network of tasks can determine scale but not size. For scale is determined, in general, by the need to organize the network of tasks so that the idle times of fund inputs are kept to a minimum. Hence, given the pool of fund inputs in the establishment, it is possible to determine the scale that permits continuous

---

[8] In craft production, '[c]raft institutions . . . are more than craft trade unions; they are also a method of administering work. They include special devices of legitimate communications to workers, special authority relations, and special principles of division of work' (Stinchcombe, 1959: 170). The production process is governed by the worker 'in accordance with the empirical lore that makes up craft principles' (ibid.). Such organizational features may be traced back to the fact that '[t]he central requirement on the system as a whole is that it be capable of adjusting its activities quickly and responsively, according to the plans for the particular project that [craft-production workshops] are making' (Stinchcombe, 1983: 114).

fund-input utilization (see sections 5.4 and 5.5). However, we still have to explain the existence of relatively stable pools of certain amounts of fund inputs, and thus of establishments of given size.

Scale can be related to technical practice regardless of the particular way in which productive resources are lumped together in the establishment. Establishment size, however, is often a constraint on the practices feasible for any given scale. This provides an important connection between the abstract theory of production of the previous chapters and the institutional characteristics of the economy in which production takes place.

9.3. SCALE, SPEED OF 'THROUGHPUT', AND LARGE-CAPACITY PRODUCTION

9.3.1. *Large scale and large capacity*

In the previous section we considered the relationship of scale to size without explicitly asking under what circumstances big equipment is a necessary condition for large-scale production. In this section, we shall analyse what may be called *large-capacity production*— large-scale production carried out with big equipment. We shall treat this phenomenon here as a purely technical issue.

This treatment of large-capacity production is based on our definition of establishment size. In our definition, establishment size is independent of the size of the individual fund-input elements, for a large establishment may consist either of many small fund inputs or of fewer fund inputs of large size; and a small establishment might consist of a limited number of large fund-input elements. This approach will allow us to explain certain apparent paradoxes in technological history.

It will be recalled from the previous analysis that large-scale production is the result of factors that are logically independent of whether productive equipment is big or small. However, there are cases in which big equipment is a necessary condition for large-scale production. Concentration on such cases has often led economists to identify *large scale* with *large capacity*. In our view, this identification involves a serious fallacy, both because it suggests a wrong causal relationship (from larger plants to higher productive efficiency) and also because it overlooks important technical episodes in which higher efficiency can be explained by larger process scale, even if the capacity of individual productive installations remained small.

9.3.2. *Speed, capacity, and mechanized practices*

Large process scale is not an advantage in itself, but the operation of many e.p.s together is often an advantage, because of the economies of time it makes possible.

Beccaria stressed that the fundamental criterion for 'economical operation' is 'to make small gains each time, but as often as possible' (1804 [1771–2]: 397). The reason he gave was that, by reducing the time needed for producing and selling a commodity, the 'circulation period' of capital advances would also be reduced. (The critical role of the economy of time in shaping the productive structure is also considered in Hicks, 1969: 141–52, and Chakravarty, 1987: 57.) Adam Smith, by connecting the extent of the market with the speed of production, called attention to the fact that the advantage of a high rate of 'throughput' (a large quantity of materials processed per unit of time) comes from the speed at which each batch of work is finished rather than from the quantity of work carried out in each period of time.

Speed rather than large capacity gives the clue to the advantage of division of labour in Smith's treatment, as is shown by his belief that no further insights into its workings are to be gained if we consider 'great manufactures' instead of 'trifling manufactures' (Smith, 1976 [1776]: 14).

Economies of time associated with division of labour can be found in their 'pure' form (i.e. independently of large capacity) when the elementary process consists of a sequence of tasks and each task is performed by an individual worker (or workers' group) operating a specialized tool (or set of specialized tools).[9] Mechanization of the technical practice often brought about imbalances between the speeds at which the different tasks of a given process

---

[9] This situation seems to have been characteristic of Smith's times: '[before the Industrial Revolution] the sequence of activities [tasks] was associated with a single skilled worker and tools were specialized, though not ordered with the activities of the worker . . . [T]oday the sequence of activities is associated with a single machine, and workers are specialized, though not ordered with the activities of the machine. Adam Smith's case of division of labour is a special one: workers and machines can be put into a sequence of pairs of which the production line is an example' (Ames and Rosenberg, 1967: 353).

could be performed. The substitution of complex machines for the simple, hand-powered tools of pre-industrial technology had the result of making speed co-ordination difficult when tools had to be operated at different speeds by distinct moving mechanisms. The problem of speed co-ordination is already present when production is carried out by a team of individuals using hand-powered tools, but it became more serious when tasks were taken up by a number of disconnected mechanisms. This is partly because the quantity of work processed by any single mechanism is generally much larger than that performed by any worker–tool pair in the same period. In addition, speed differences between mechanical tools are normally much larger than speed differences between hand-powered tools (see Usher, 1954; see also Gille, 1966; Gimpel, 1977; Faler, 1981).

The introduction of mechanical methods made the problem of speed more urgent than it had ever been. This development provided a critical stimulus for the creation of large productive units (see also Graziani, 1891; Jannaccone, 1904). A. D. Chandler has described this feature of technological history as follows:

Mass production industries can . . . be defined as those in which technological and organizational innovation created a high rate of throughput and therefore permitted a small working force to produce a massive output. Mass production differed from existing factory production in that machinery and equipment did more than merely replace manual operation. They made possible a much greater output at each stage in the overall process of production. Machinery was placed and operated so that the several stages were integrated and synchronized technologically and organizationally within a single industrial establishment. As a result, the speed of throughput was faster at each stage than if each stage had been carried on in separate establishments.   (1977: 241)

Speed co-ordination was often achieved by integrating mechanisms operating at different speeds within a complex mechanism in which the shortest tasks could be performed side by side with tasks requiring more time.

As shown in Chapter 5, the time co-ordination of tasks involves certain conditions on process scale (see sections 5.4 and 5.5). In addition, the tools that have to be combined often cannot work below a certain minimum capacity. This implies that large-capacity production is often a *necessary condition* for the time co-ordination of tasks (see section 5.3.1).

The economies of time associated with advanced tools and

machinery are sometimes possible only if many different e.p.s can be carried out side by side in the same large productive installation. However, '[i]ncreases in productivity and decreases in unit costs (often identified with economies of scale) resulted far more from the increase in the volume and velocity of throughput than from a growth in the size of the factory or plant' (Chandler, 1977: 281).

9.3.3. *Large capacity in proto-industrial and modern economies*

Historical evidence shows that large-scale production (the simultaneous operation of a great number of e.p.s in the same network of tasks) is often the factor that brings about high-speed production and continuous fund-input utilization. (An abstract argument supporting this statement is given in Chapter 5.) By contrast, large *capacity* is seldom the critical element in achieving a more efficient organization of production. Indeed, there have been cases in which the introduction of big equipment, induced by soaring demand, but unnecessary for the time co-ordination of tasks, weakened the resilience of the productive establishment by making it more vulnerable to demand fluctuation and unused capacity (see Coleman, 1959; Poni, 1972).[10] In such cases, high demand brought about large-scale production, and this latter 'degenerated' into large capacity. Big equipment was associated with the operation in parallel of many identical e.p.s, thus increasing the likelihood of fund-input idleness. (If *n* e.p.s are arranged in parallel, fund inputs are needed in a quantity *n* times greater than in the individual e.p.)

A different case is that in which large capacity is needed to allow a certain amount of work to be performed in a shorter time (see section 9.3.2). This possibility arises both in job-shop and straight-line production (see Chapter 5). However, large capacity was traditionally considered a prerequisite for high speed when the production process followed the straight-line pattern. This reflects the need for

---

[10] Coleman, in particular, pointed out that, in proto-industrial Europe, 'even in those industries where techniques demanded some concentration of work, the slowness of processes, the low productivity, the notorious unreliability of water- or wind-power, and the difficulty of securing capital combined to provide the maximum inducement to keep the plant small rather than large . . . In industry as in trade, many a monopolistic, joint-stock giant in seventeenth-century England or France had to give way to smaller and more realistic competitors' (Coleman, 1959: 509–10). The overproduction crises afflicting factories using water-driven silk-mills in the 17th c. are described in Poni (1972: 1487–8).

time co-ordination of tasks of fixed length in this type of production. Chandler has examined this issue in some detail in describing the rise of modern factory management in the United States:

The creation of a continuous-process or automatic factory was more complex than the invention of a single machine. It involved a number of inventions, each of which had to be synchronized with the others; it also required perfection in plant design . . . Modern factory management was first fully worked out in the metal-making and metal-working industries. In metal-making, it came in response to the need to integrate (that is to internalize) within a single works several major processes of production previously carried on in different locations. In metal-working, it arose from the challenges of co-ordinating and controlling the flow of materials within a plant where several processes of production had been subdivided and were carried on in specialized departments.   (Chandler, 1977: 258)

In Chandler's case, large capacity permitted better time co-ordination of tasks and thus also a higher general tempo for the production process as a whole. This shows that certain economies of time often underlie the advantages of large-capacity production. Large capacity might, in certain cases, be a necessary condition for high-speed production, but it is never a sufficient condition for it. This may be a reason why Chandler considers the end of the nine-teenth century a period in which the average size of the productive units did increase, whereas a number of writers of that time thought that there was a remarkable resilience of small units (see Reuleaux, 1876: 482; Leroy-Beaulieu, 1896: 462). As a matter of fact, if the present interpretation of Chandler's view is adopted, his opinion is not really at odds with that of Reuleaux and Leroy-Beaulieu. For the latter writers' argument might explain the resilience of small-sized establishments in situations in which the co-ordination among tasks may be achieved by means other than the 'visible hand' of the large corporation, as in the industrial district case.[11]

---

[11] The distinction between size and the advantages associated with greater scale has recently been stressed by Lioukas and Xerokostas (1982) in considering the restructuring of organizational divisions: 'The benefits of larger size . . . are seldom readily available for taking. Firstly, grouping of existing divisions or functions would require re-allocation of tasks and adjustments in the administrative machinery. The economies would have to come from *functional synergy*, i.e., by re-designing the larger bureaucracy so as to utilize the idle capacity of individuals and to make more use of labor-saving means such as formal rules, specialization and standardization in support services' (p. 867).

9.4. SCALE, SIZE AND DIVISIONS OF
THE PRODUCTION PROCESS

9.4.1. *Division of labour in straight-line and job-shop practices: some historical evidence*

The relation between scale and size is also closely linked to the pattern of division of labour adopted in the productive unit. (Division of labour is defined as a function from the set of tasks to the set of skills, so that any skill may be associated with one or more tasks and any task with only a single skill.) As shown in section 4.3.3, the pattern of division of labour reflects the general organizational pattern adopted in an establishment (i.e. whether it is organized according to the job-shop or straight-line model). It follows that the relation between scale and size generally differs according to which pattern of organization is adopted.

In a job-shop establishment, continuous fund-input utilization presupposes the introduction of a suitable division of labour regardless of the number and types of tasks executed by the various fund inputs (see section 5.4). In a straight-line establishment, continuous utilization presupposes that a suitable division of labour is introduced, and that each fund input executes a fixed number of tasks in each working day (see section 5.5). Even in this case, continuous utilization is independent of the output level of single commodities, unless certain fund inputs are task-specific *and* product-specific.

The introduction of task-specific fund inputs has a different impact on fund-input utilization, depending upon whether the production process is job-shop or straight-line. In the former case, the introduction of task-specific fund inputs may lead to longer, rather than shorter, periods of fund-input idleness. In the latter case, task-specific fund inputs are generally an advantage, provided that certain conditions on process scale are satisfied (see sections 5.5.3 and 5.5.4).

The relationship between task-specialization, e.p. specialization, and straight-line practices is illustrated by various historical cases. An early example is provided by the production of woollen textiles in fourteenth-century Italy:

This branch of industrial production acquires an altogether special character because of the great number and variety of technical processes that the raw material and the semi-finished output have to go through before the finished product is obtained . . . Such a great number of operations . . . is ill-suited to the more common characteristics of artisan production; i.e. a type of production that completes its whole cycle in the workshop of the individual artisan working with the help of some member of his family or few assistants. This type of production, perhaps, is also possible in the wool industry; but only in very small towns, in which there is a restricted body of customers providing a safe market, based on modest and uniform needs . . . But as soon as demand increases and the body of customers becomes less uniform, more demanding, and more subject to fluctuation, such a concentration of all activities . . . in a single concern is no longer possible, as a result of the high cost of tools and the most valuable raw materials. The main obstacle, however, is that the making of a product of good quality requires the operations to be performed by specialized workers, thus accomplishing a division of labour not to be found in any other industry of the Middle Ages.   (Luzzatto, 1963: 199–200; my translation)

This passage shows that the great number of tasks needed to complete the making of woollen cloth made 'permanent' division of labour (characterized by the introduction of task-specific fund inputs and e.p. specialization) a common type of productive arrangement in this branch of industry. For once the standard of quality was set sufficiently high, the various tasks became so numerous, different from one another, and 'product-specific' that the job-shop organization could not allow continuous fund-input utilization.[12] This might explain why the production process had to be organized on the straight-line pattern, even when the whole production cycle was carried out in the same establishment.

The straight-line model is the most natural way of organizing production when the manufacture of a commodity is split into a large number of tasks, and each task is distinct from all others not only in terms of the physical operations performed but also in terms of the skill used. Once the straight-line pattern is adopted, the allocation of tasks to fund inputs is determined once and for all and becomes a basic principle of operation of the production process. Each task is precisely identified and is clearly distinguishable from all the other tasks in the same process. This feature of straight-line organization

[12] In a job-shop establishment, continuous fund-input utilization is possible on condition that different tasks be carried out by relatively unspecialized fund inputs and be arranged according to sequences that are independent of one another (see s. 5.4). This is often the case in an establishment producing a range of different commodities, where tasks have low 'product-specificity' and certain groups of tasks make use of the same general skill. Neither condition above is satisfied if each commodity requires a great variety of product-specific tasks.

makes a whole series of 'divisions' of the production process possible, from the separate production of commodities that can be independently sold to the separate performance of tasks that can be independently carried out. The scale of each specialized part of the process would depend on its length, whereas the size of each establishment would depend on the amount of capital required by each installation, and on the relative importance of the capital advances for the various categories of inputs (see section 9.2).

9.4.2. *Size, technology, and division of labour*

The medieval textile industry illustrates the wide dispersion of establishment sizes possible with straight-line production:

While [textile production] was late in becoming a stronghold of factory enterprise, it lent itself from medieval times to another capitalistic form of organization. This has been frequently called the 'putting-out system', because the workers labored in their own homes—in cellars, garrets, or cottages—and sometimes, when water power was used, as in fulling, at little mills built along the streams. In the rooms where they cooked and slept and lived with their wives and children, these men worked on raw materials and partly finished cloths, which were 'put-out' to them by merchants.   (Nef, 1950: 72)

On the other hand,

semifactory conditions in connection with the finishing processes—dyeing, fulling, and calendering—were much less exceptional even in medieval times than was once believed. It is not possible to estimate the extent to which such conditions existed in England before the Reformation. But a number of developments during the next century encouraged their spread. The growth in the demand for cloth of all kinds, and especially for worsteds, cottons, and linens, which were being extensively produced in England for the first time, was accompanied by a notable increase in the proportion of all cloth dyed and dressed at home. It was the finishing processes, most readily suited to semifactory conditions, that expanded most rapidly in importance. With the great increase in the market for cloth in London, as a result of both the rapid growth in population and the increase in the quantity of clothing, bedding, and hangings used by the rising middle class and by domestic servants, the advantages of concentration in the finishing processes grew. Before the middle of the seventeenth century, some London dyers were buying coal in as large quantities as the chief brewers and soap boilers. This suggests that their equipment in furnaces and metal boilers may have been equally extensive.   (ibid. 139–40)

Small and large establishments existed side by side in other productive branches as well:

The drawing of metal wire, which is said to have been carried on exclusively by hand labor until the 1560's, changed its character during the next few decades. Water-driven machinery was adopted both for hammering the metal bars into the proper form and for the actual drawing of the wire from the metal. The new processes involved an extensive outlay in buildings and machinery, for there were two mills, one for the small and another for the large wire, besides the furnaces in which the metal was annealed. The celebrated wireworks at Tintern apparently employed about a hundred workers as early as 1581. So, except in the finishing processes, the considerable plant, consisting usually of a group of small buildings and based on water-driven machinery and furnaces much larger than those common in medieval England, made its way into one branch of the metallurgical industry after another. (ibid. 131–2)

[Shipbuilding] had long been organized in some cases in large enterprises, for while smiths and carpenters, sail- and rope-makers might prepare the materials in their own households, the shipyards where these materials were assembled were often costly establishments in which many workers labored for wages. These in seventeenth-century Holland were fitted with wind-driven sawmills and large cranes for moving heavy timbers; and it seems probable that similar machinery was set up in some English yards before the civil war. (ibid. 138–9)

All these historical cases illustrate a typical feature of straight-line production: the tendency to the strict identification of tasks and to the allocation of tasks to specialized fund inputs, for this tendency often involves elementary-process specialization on the basis of fund inputs' 'natural' skills. This, in turn, involves a wide dispersion of establishment sizes, depending upon the criterion followed in allocating tasks to fund inputs when dividing the original e.p. into a certain number of specialized e.p.s. Here we may find a source of 'technological heterogeneity' in manufacturing processes characterized by a sequential arrangement of fabrication stages (see e.g. Carr, 1981; Harper, 1981; Bruch, 1983; Cortes, 1987). The characteristics of tasks and their sequencing over time would determine whether small or large establishments execute the early stages (or, respectively, the final stages) of each type of industrial production. (Note that, in general, large establishments may be found in the final stages of the cloth industry and in the initial or intermediate stages of the metallurgical and shipbuilding industries.)

In job-shop production, the relationship of size to division of labour is entirely different. In fact, the set of tasks executed in each establishment is generally partitioned into subsets, each requiring a given general skill. The establishment itself is 'built around' a collection of skills and, since any skill could be used for a variety of tasks in different e.p.s, task-specific fund inputs are generally absent. The scale of the overall process is determined according to establishment size (capacity), and the scale at which any given commodity is produced depends on the length of its particular e.p. Establishment size is determined by the need to organize 'coherent' pools of general skills, so that enough e.p.s can be carried out to avoid fund-input waste. The size of each establishment would thus depend on how many general skills are needed in order to set up a 'coherent' pattern of productive abilities. It would also depend on the minimum capacity of the fund inputs associated with the various subsets of tasks.[13]

The minimum size of the establishment is determined, in job-shop production, by the smallest 'coherent' pool of general skills rather than by the smallest coherent sequence of tasks permitting continuous fund-input utilization (as is the case with straight-line production). Minimum establishment size can vary a great deal from one pool of skills to another. However, any given establishment is large or small, depending upon the size of the smallest pool of fund inputs in which skills and tasks can be so combined to minimize (or eliminate) fund-input idleness and under-utilization. On the other hand, minimum size would not depend on the length of any particular task or set of tasks (indeed, no task has fixed duration with job-shop practices).

Agricultural practices are a clear example of how minimum efficient size is determined in the job-shop case. It has long been recognized that division of labour in agriculture is not as important as it is in manufacturing.[14] In such conditions, minimum efficient size requires that 'no family who have any land, should have less than they could cultivate, or than will fully employ their cattle and tools' (Mill, 1965 [1848]: 143). But the size requirement for continuous and full fund-input utilization varies greatly from one type of crop to

---

[13] Establishment size derives not only from the relative cost of the various categories of inputs (as was the case with straight-line practices) but also from the way in which the 'general' skills are interrelated. This reflects the higher degree of interdependence between tasks in the case of job-shop practices.

[14] See Smith, (1976 [1776]: bk. i, ch. 1).

another (see also Hazlewood and Livingstone, 1978; Polidori and Romagnoli, 1987; Romagnoli, 1992). This may be one reason why it is generally found that large farming is suitable to corn and forage, whereas small farming allows highest productive efficiency in the cultivation of vine and olive, roots, and leguminous plants (see Mill, 1965 [1848]: 151). In fact, agricultural practices consist, in the former case, of relatively few and simple tasks, which seldom permit continuous and full utilization of all necessary fund inputs in the same farm. In this situation, large crops, by increasing the degree of capacity utilization of workers and machines at certain intervals, allow a degree of fund-input idleness over time that small farms could not afford. On the other hand, agricultural practices consist, in the latter case, of more numerous and complex tasks, thus permitting a more continuous pattern of fund-input utilization at any given size. (A high degree of fund-input utilization over time can be achieved by switching multi-skilled fund inputs from one task to another.) The fact that the mechanization of agricultural practices was faster in the 'simple' processes than in the complex ones might be an additional reason for the resilience of small farming in the latter type of production. (Mechanical fund inputs are generally economical in farms above a certain 'threshold size').[15]

9.4.3. *Tasks, skills, and work-in-process: an introduction to the theory of industrial districts*

The analysis of industrial districts traditionally considers concepts of size and the manifold relationship between size and economies of scale. As pointed out by Marshall, 'the advantages of production on a large scale can in general be as well attained by the aggregation of a large number of small masters into one district as by the erection of a few large works' (1930 [1879]: 7; see also section 3.4.2 for a more detailed discussion of Marshall's argument).

The co-operation between large and small plants within the same productive sector may be related to any one of the three fundamental dimensions of the productive process: the organizational pattern of tasks, the capabilities of agents, or the structure of the work-in-process. The operational features of a process imply that, in certain

---

[15] As David (1975: 6) has pointed out, below 'threshold size' the farm would normally avoid switching from hand to machine methods of harvesting. (See also Sturrock, 1977.)

cases, 'the simultaneous, or nearly simultaneous, combination of a number of different *acts* is required' (Sidgwick, 1883: 112; my italics), whereas in other cases a complex process consists of clearly differentiated tasks that are operationally independent of each other. On the other hand, the possibility of identifying sophisticated and specific skills distinct from the general set of capabilities required to the execution of a certain process, may sometimes lead to the formation of specialized productive units. Their size may be large or small depending, in practice, on the number of elementary transformation processes that may simultaneously be executed within a particular unit. In general, the size of a specialized productive unit will be small or large according to the speed of the fabrication stage executed within it. A stage lasting only a minor fraction of the duration of the complete process is likely to be executed by a relatively small-sized unit, since not many transformation processes have to be simultaneously operated when one batch of raw material may quickly be substituted for another at that stage. On the other hand, a slow fabrication stage is, *ceteris paribus*, a condition favouring the formation of a large-sized unit. For, in this case, that unit is likely to require the simultaneous operation of a relatively high number of distinct transformation processes, if co-ordination requirements with the units executing 'quick' stages are to be met.

A similar argument holds when we consider the skills and specialization pattern of workers and machines to be given, but we want to examine how size may be affected by the structure and scale of the material in process. In this case, the full and continuous utilization of the different agents (fund inputs) is likely to require (see Part II) rather strict conditions upon the overall number of simultaneous e.p.s (with a straight-line practice) or upon the composition of the product-mix (with a job-shop practice). However, the actual level of finished output may be such that the corresponding quantities of work-in-process materials do not allow a sufficient degree of utilization of the agents executing intermediate fabrication stages (see, in this connection, the analysis by Jannaccone discussed in section 3.4.3).

This situation may be one in which a 'networking' of materials-in-process takes place, so that a given specialized unit executes the same fabrication stage upon materials belonging to different sequences of stages and leading to different batches of finished product. The resulting materials network is such that small and large productive units may exist side by side. The former may execute many times a day the same fabrication stage upon different batches of semi-finished output in a sequence; the latter may also complete a given fabrication stage by transforming different batches of materials, but these will have to be processed at the same time within the establishment. To sum up, industrial districts may be analysed by alternatively considering the organizational networks of tasks, agents, or materials-in-process. In each case, specific features of scale and size may emerge. The consideration of the task–process network highlights the fact that, in some cases, task execution requires the simultaneous performance of a certain number of actions (as in glass-making), whereas in other cases a one-to-one correspondence between actions (or types of motion) and tasks may be established. The consideration of the agents network leads one to distinguish between 'slow' stages, to be executed within a relatively large establishment, and 'quick' stages which may be executed by small-sized units. Finally, the consideration of the materials network brings to the fore the number of batches of semi-finished output that have to be processed at any given time in order to achieve the full and continuous utilization of fund inputs.

Different types of co-ordination problem have to be solved depending on which features of an industrial district are considered. Thus, the co-ordination of tasks primarily requires the co-ordination of information flows within each establishment and across different establishments. The co-ordination of agents' activities is primarily associated with the co-ordination of set-up times and agents' capabilities. Finally, the existence of a materials' network requires the co-ordination of work-in-process flows among different fabrication stages.

In industrial districts of a traditional type, such as the early cases of the 'putting-out' system (see e.g. the case of Florentine medieval textile production considered in section 9.4.1), task co-ordination is achieved by means of customary technical practices, agents' capabilities (essentially, agents' *capacities*) cannot be stretched beyond a certain range, and the burden of co-ordination falls primarily upon the processes of stock accumulation or decumulation that ensure the medium- and long-run consistency of work-in-process flows.

More recent cases of district networking based upon subcontracting achieve co-ordination by setting up new capabilities (again, essentially new capacities) when they are needed in order to expand the overall capacity of the district. Finally, industrial networks using flexible manufacturing techniques trying to achieve a zero-inventories goal (just-in-time production) would require a rather sophisticated combination of co-ordination devices. At the task level, a trend has been noted away from Taylorist differentiation and towards a 're-integration' of simple tasks into more complex units (see e.g. Bessant and Haywood, 1986: 472). More generally, it has been stressed that recent manufacturing developments have deeply affected the task–process structure of production, which is often built upon an explicit recognition of task complexity, for which 'an ideal representation has an intermediate rather than an extreme degree of precision' (Kochen, 1980: 16; see also, on the general issue of task complexity, Leplat, 1988). At the level of agents' capabilities, the above trend is associated with an emphasis upon 'multiple-skilling and the ability to switch rapidly between tasks' (Bessant and Haywood, 1986: 472). Finally, at the level of work-in-process flows, one finds at the same time an attempt to detach the sequence of fabrication stages from particular product specifications, another attempt to mould materials according to producers' needs (this is a relevant feature of so-called 'new materials'), and a tendency to 'work when needed' upon the materials-in-process (this is an essential property of the 'pull system' ensuring the just-in-time transfer of work-in-process from one fabrication stage to another). (See Deleersnyder *et al.*, 1989.)

It is important to realize that developments within one sphere may be closely related to developments elsewhere. For example, the new, relatively 'loose' way of identifying tasks reflects the need of the 'pull system' of materials transformation, while the introduction of multi-skilled workers or machines generally requires 'piecemeal automation and robotics, which is *problem-pull* rather than *technology-push* automation' (Schonberger, 1987 [1984]: 6).[16]

The industrial district is a network of distinct but technologically interrelated establishments. The task–process framework suggests that the whole district may be considered as a single productive unit. The set of active factors supporting the network of tasks and processes identifies the potential *size* of the district, which may vary according to the technical recipes and the product(s) specification. Actual size, as measured by the number of elementary transformation processes executed at any given time, is related to the quantities of work-in-process materials existing within the district during the

---

[16] A classical anticipation of the distinction between the 'pull system' and the 'push system' of manufacturing may be found in Smith's distinction between 'work to be done' and 'work done'. An application of Smith's distinction in the analysis of the restructuring of the car industry in the 1980s is proposed in Bianchi (1984).

time-interval under consideration. Finally, the *scale* of the district is a measure of its organizational complexity, for it is identified by the number of parallel e.p.s. executed at any given time but is not necessarily associated with the quantities of work-in-process. (There may be cases in which economies of large *process scale* may be achieved even with small amounts of materials, particularly if production requires a considerable 'immaterial' support in terms of technical or commercial services.)

Any given industrial district may consist of establishments organized according to the job-shop or straight-line pattern. In general, both types of establishments may exist within the same district. Indeed, the decentralization of production associated with district networking makes it feasible to identify *subsets* of compatible production programmes to which a distinct organizational logic may be applied.

Industrial districts of the early 'putting-out' type characteristically exploit the periods of idleness of the peasant economy in order to allocate tasks to workers in the countryside who are operating within the framework of agricultural job-shop production (see Chayanov, 1966 [1925]; Mendels, 1972; see also Cazzola, 1988). On the other hand, other fabrication stages (such as dyeing) may be allocated to establishments following the straight-line pattern.

Traditional industrial districts could also follow an urban, rather than rural, pattern. An example is provided by the silk district in early modern Bologna (see in particular Poni, 1990). Here, the strength of urban guilds makes rural industry impossible, and the existence of concentrated demand for the output of a particular stage (the silk thread) determines the introduction of big equipment (the water-driven silk-mill) in which straight-line principles are followed. At the same time, other fabrication stages are allocated to relatively marginal sectors of the urban population (women, children), in which work rules are presumably nearer to the informal logic of a job-shop.

More recently, industrial districts have shown a combination of straight-line establishments, executing relatively slow stages in the transformation of the work-in-process, and job-shop units, executing either sophisticated complementary stages (such as the fabrication of machine tools) or relatively easy and quick stages belonging to the main sequence (such as certain finishing stages in textile production). A characteristic feature of production networking is, in this case, the adjustment to a higher scale by means of process-splitting. Scale increases that would not be compatible with the law of multiples for an integrated process may thus be achieved by introducing specialized e.p.s (a theoretical argument relative to this pattern of scale expansion may be found in sections 5.5.3 and 5.5.4).

Industrial districts depending upon a relatively tight and permanent division of labour among co-operating establishments require that demand for finished products be easily predictable in scale and composition. In fact, industrial networks of the above type may easily accommodate demand expansion but not demand contraction: '[a] crisis in final demand, even of a transitory character, may be sustained, within certain limits, by the subcontracting firm but not by the system of subcontractors, whose technical, economical, and balance-sheet structure is not compatible with an effective management of plant under-utilization' (Barbiroli, 1991: 190; my translation).

The introduction of new management techniques and technical recipes has led, in most recent years, to the formation of industrial networks of a new type (see also Bessant and Senker, 1986). Their most distinctive feature is the application of certain job-shop principles to the organization of the whole network. This means that the production process is considered as a continuous flow from the point of view of the working unit(s), even if the individual batches of work-in-process may actually be stopped at certain fabrication stages until they are 'pulled' by the subsequent stage:[17] 'the succeeding stage demands and withdraws items from the preceding stage, according to the rate at which the succeeding stage consumes items' (Deleersnyder *et al.*, 1989: 1079). Just-in-time manufacturing, which is partly associated with the traditional job-shop as well (see section 4.3.2), provides the unifying framework for a variety of technical and organizational innovations by means of which some disadvantages of the old job-shop may be overcome. We may mention in particular: (i) group technology or cellular manufacturing, 'in which similar parts are identified and grouped together to take advantage of their similarities in manufacturing and design' (Groover, 1987: 433); (ii) the 'random-order' flexible manufacturing system, which is especially

---

[17] As Prof. Michio Morishima has recently pointed out in private conversation and invited lectures at Bologna University, the 'stoppability' of production is a most important feature of productive activity, especially if an effective and flexible organization of manufacturing is to be achieved (see Morishima, 1991).

suitable when 'the part family is large, there are substantial variations in the part configurations, there will be new part designs produced on the system and engineering changes in parts currently made
on the system, and the production schedule is subject to change
from day to day' (ibid. 465). The random-order-FMS requires multi-
skilled machines and is capable of processing parts in different
sequences (see ibid. 464–5);[18] (iii) the consideration of line-balancing
(the assignment of jobs to work stations) as a dynamic rather than a
static issue (see Sculli, 1979); (iv) the attempt to introduce 'produc-
tion-smoothing' devices in job-shop processes characterized by no
back-orders and no uncommitted inventories. (A possible solution
here would be to introduce some staggering of production times
with the formation of an inventory of finished goods committed to
orders; see Cruickshanks, Drescher, and Graves, 1984).

In principle, just-in-time co-ordination may be introduced in
industrial networks in which job-shop and straight-line establishments exist side by side. However, both types of establishment
would have to undergo a considerable rearrangement. In particular,
the job-shop units would have to allow for greater flexibility in
coping with variations of the *scale* rather than the structure of
output, whereas straight-line units should adjust to the processing
of a highly differentiated and changing product flow.

9.5. JOB-SHOP AND STRAIGHT-LINE FORMS OF PRODUCTION ORGANIZATION

9.5.1. *Scale–practice relations in job-shop and straight-line production*

We know from Chapter 7 that any non-trivial scale–practice relation
is such that certain changes of process scale require a change of
technical practice. We also know that the existence of a non-trivial
scale–practice relation is a necessary condition for scale-dependent
technical change (see section 7.2.3). Now, the adoption of any

---

[18] One should not overlook the 'smoothing' influence of just-in-time and the
resulting effect upon automation: 'Once [just-in-time] is embedded, the resulting
production system is much more simple and stable. These conditions are ideal for
automation, and many Japanese and Western companies are using [just-in-time] as a
necessary precursor of automation' (Voss and Clutterbuck, 1989: 157).

particular scale has very different implications depending upon whether the production process is of the job-shop or straight-line type (see section 4.3.5). Consequently, any given scale–practice relation would entail different patterns of scale-dependent technical change in the two cases.

In the job-shop establishment, 'scale' is related to the stock of fund inputs and general skills existing in the establishment, regardless of the production levels of individual commodities. Scale-technology expansion (and contraction) would thus be associated with the change of establishment size, and the outputs of some commodities might actually vary in the opposite direction. (That is, the output of a commodity x might shrink with technology expansion and expand with technology contraction.[19])

In the straight-line establishment, we have an altogether different pattern, for in this case there is a one-to-one relationship between the scale of the process and the number of tasks of any given type performed in the establishment. If each task is commodity-specific, any given scale is associated with a single vector of commodity outputs. If all tasks are commodity-indifferent, any given scale is compatible with different output vectors. (But even in this latter case, no more than a finite number of output vectors would permit continuous fund-input utilization at the given scale.) Scale-technology expansion and contraction are associated with the proportional expansion in the output levels of all groups of technologically homogeneous commodities. (Different commodities produced with the same sequence of tasks belong to the same technological group.) A scale increase is not necessarily associated with an increase of establishment size. Indeed, scale is determined independently of size. This is an important feature of straight-line production, which may account for the great variety of establishment sizes, for any given scale, under different historical circumstances.[20]

---

[19] However, continuous fund-input utilization would become impossible if the change in the number and type of commodities produced made the continuous utilization of all the available skills impossible (see also s. 5.4.3).

[20] Given a straight-line organization, the same number of simultaneous e.p.s can often be obtained by many independent small producers or by a few large establishments. An example of this is the resilience of the 'domestic system', based on the hand-loom, when confronted with competition from the factory system based on the power-loom, in the cotton textile industry of 19th-c. Britain (see Habakkuk, 1962: 147–50). In such cases, the average size of the establishment can sometimes be explained by the relative costs of the different inputs. The relative prices of machinery and labour may thus have had a considerable influence in determining the

The different character of scale–practice relations in job-shop and straight-line production is reflected in the scale–efficiency relations that can be derived from them. In particular, job-shop production is associated with scale–efficiency relations in which higher (lower) scale is not necessarily accompanied by higher (lower) commodity outputs. As a result, changes in efficiency are related to changes in market conditions only in a loose and indirect way. (For example, the degree of fund-input utilization would not normally be affected by a decline in the demand for one of the items produced, except in the special case in which the fall in demand makes it necessary to discontinue a certain precedence pattern of tasks.) Straight-line production is associated with scale–efficiency relations in which a higher (lower) scale is necessarily associated with higher (lower) levels of commodity outputs (though, in certain cases, we might consider groups of technologically homogeneous commodities rather than individual items). In this case, therefore, changes in efficiency would be directly related to changes in market conditions, and the degree of fund-input utilization would be directly influenced by the fall in the demand for certain commodities or commodity groups.

9.5.2. *Scale, versatility, and innovative potential*

Job-shop and straight-line production may be seen as two ways of dealing with a changing environment. Both types of organization offer ways of dealing with the fact that production takes time, and that the production process needs to be set up today in order to bring about an output at some future period.

It has long been recognized that production is associated with 'the risk arising from the immobility of invested resources' (Lavington, 1921: 25). The need to allocate resources in the present with only imperfect knowledge of the future leads to a relationship between uncertainty (of future outcomes) and flexibility (of productive organizations) (see Marschak and Nelson, 1962).

relative success of small- and large-sized establishments when labour-intensive and machinery-intensive techniques prevailed in one or the other category of size (Habakkuk, 1962). Standardization of components and 'interchangeable manufacturing' may be considered as factors leading to a multiplicity of output vectors and establishment sizes for any given process scale (see Woodworth (1905), esp. ch. 1 on Eli Whitney's manufacture of muskets; and Rosenberg, 1969*b*).

Jones and Ostroy (1984) have developed a formal analysis of this relationship. They argue:

The more variable are a decision maker's beliefs, the more flexible is the position he will choose. This principle potentially applies whenever (i) there will be opportunities to act after further information is received, and (ii) current actions influence either the attractiveness or availability of different future actions.   (p. 13).

It could also be argued that the adoption of a flexible practice expresses the 'latent choice' of postponing a decision (see Indelli, 1989).[21]

Our analysis raises doubts as to the possibility of defining 'flexibility' of production in an unambiguous way. In fact, both job-shop and straight-line organizations leave a certain number of future options available, but such options concern: (i) the proportions between e.p.s having different precedence patterns in the job-shop case; (ii) the proportions between e.p.s having the same precedence patterns in the straight-line case. An establishment cannot be 'flexible' in both ways. In the job-shop establishment, it is impossible to change the product-mix by varying the sequence in which the fund inputs are employed in the different e.p.s. In the straight-line establishment, it is impossible to change the product-mix in ways that would demand the introduction of different precedence patterns between tasks. It follows that it is generally impossible to rank technical practices on a single flexibility scale. As a result, the degree to which an establishment adjusts to unforeseen circumstances depends on the two following factors: (i) the types of change that would be required; (ii) the organizational pattern that makes these types of change feasible.

The pattern of division of labour (as defined in section 4.3.3) associated with straight-line practices may sometimes be a serious obstacle to the adjustment, if this adjustment requires a radical change in the number and type of fund inputs' skills. H. J. Habakkuk has noted that a major cause of the slow rate of technical progress of British industry in the last decades of the nineteenth century is the 'complex division of labour between processes and industries which had developed during the long period of British industrial supremacy'

---

[21] I am pleased to acknowledge my debt to Paola Indelli, from the University of Padua, for stimulating conversations on this issue. This acknowledgement is also a sad recollection of her early departure.

(1962: 218). In Habakkuk's view, the British entrepreneur was severely constrained, in his adoption of a technical practice, 'by history and by the need to shape his investments "to fit the inherited structure of complementary assets" ' (p. 218).[22] In such conditions, the number of technical improvements that could be introduced was limited by '[t]he fact that division of labour had been carried out so far in English industry, and that the structure of inherited assets was so complicated' (ibid.).

The drawback of division of labour when the economic system is confronting change in skills and specializations required has also been noted by Cipolla (1952), Hicks (1959), and Ames and Rosenberg (1967) in their analyses of economic decline in old industrial countries.

An outdated division of labour is the most serious danger facing a production system based on straight-line practices. In fact, any given pattern of specialization 'closes up' a certain number of future positions, thus reducing the flexibility of the system with respect to alternative arrangements of tasks (see also section 7.1.3 above). Straight-line production may still prove to be considerably 'flexible', however, as there may be many product specifications compatible with a given precedence pattern between tasks.[23]

Job-shop practices also appear to be either 'flexible' or 'rigid', depending upon how flexibility is defined. Flexibility is most prominent when a change in market conditions calls for an alternative specification of fund inputs' 'general' skills, regardless of the particular skills employed in the current practice. Another feature of flexibility with a job-shop practice is that alternative ways of sequencing a given set of tasks are normally feasible in the same establishment (see section 4.3.2). Both reasons might explain the resilience of apparently backward practices, when confronted by competition from more advanced practices, in a number of historical cases. For example, they might explain why the Swiss rural workshop, which combined textile-making and agricultural tasks, was more successful than the more advanced textile industries of other countries of Continental Europe in meeting British competition during the first Industrial Revolution. (In the Swiss rural workshop,

[22] Habakkuk's quotation is from Richardson (1960: 114).

[23] This type of flexibility is demonstrated in many cases of industrial history. E.g., various 'mature' sectors of Italian industry were able to change the range of commodities produced, without disrupting the existing arrangement of tasks, in order to cope with changing demand conditions in the course of the 17th c. (see Sella, 1969: esp. 244–7).

labour could be shifted from spinning to weaving without disrupting the current pattern of fund-input utilization.[24]) The special flexibility that can be achieved with job-shop production also explains the substitution of job-shop for straight-line practices which has recently been carried out by a number of electronic data-processing firms in order to meet demand for quick changes in the product-mix, and to increase the number of goods delivered at any given time.[25] On the other hand, the job-shop practice proved to be rigid rather than flexible in cases of a sharp increase in demand for a particular commodity. The reason for this is that the job-shop establishment does not allow the steady increase in the supply of any given class of goods unless supply of the other classes of goods is also increased.[26] This lack of flexibility might explain why the expansion of demand for individual commodities (or for groups of technologically homo-geneous commodities) was often associated with the substitution of straight-line for job-shop practices. The rise of many early 'manu-factures' can be explained in this way, as can the spread of the 'putting-out' system of production (see sections 9.4.2 and 9.4.3). Both types of organization are possible in the framework of straight-line technology, and both reflected the need to meet an expanding demand (see Luzzatto, 1963; Nef, 1964).

A final point can be made about the alternative strategies the producer is likely to follow, when searching for a 'satisfactory' practice at a 'parametric' scale, in the straight-line and job-shop case respectively (see section 7.1.3 for the treatment of technical adoption as a problem-solving activity).

In both cases, the first stage of a producer's adoption behaviour can be described as a search through the set of technical practices known to be feasible for scale s. If this initial search reaches no solution, a change of problem-space normally takes place. At this stage, there is an important difference between the straight-line and the job-shop case. In the straight-line establishment, the producer is likely to search through the existing set of tasks (the primitive elements of any would-be satisfactory practice). The satisfactory practice that may eventually be discovered would result from a different arrangement of these existing tasks. This is what we have called a 'technical learning problem' (see section 7.1.3). Learning

---

[24] See Biucchi (1973: esp. 633–4).   [25] See Skinner (1983).
[26] Any 2 goods belong to the same class, or 'technological group', if they have a common precedence pattern of tasks (see ss. 5.4 and 5.5).

by doing and learning by using can be seen as special cases of this search strategy. In the job-shop establishment, the producer's behaviour is likely to be different, for the elementary components of the production process would now be general 'productive functions' (*skills*) rather than well-defined tasks. In such conditions, the satisfactory practice that may eventually be discovered would generally result from the discovery of new tasks on the basis of the existing stock of general skills, i.e. from the exertion of what we may call *inventive ability*. (The distinct problem-solving attitudes characterizing straight-line and job-shop practices may be related with the distinction between 'knowing-that' and 'knowing-how' in scientific research work. (See Funtowicz and Ravetz, 1990: esp. 65–8; see also Ravetz, 1971.)

10

Conclusion: Tasks, Processes, and the Economic System

10.1. ARRANGEMENT OF TASKS AND TECHNICAL PRACTICES

10.1.1. The 'task–process' description of productive activity

The foregoing analysis derives from a particular description of the production process. This process has been described as a network of tasks rather than as a combination of inputs. Tasks are performed in real time, and their repeated performance leads to certain productive procedures. This approach has a number of distinctive features which may be summarized as follows.

First, the 'arrangement' of tasks is independent of the inputs used in these tasks. A given task is often feasibile with alternative input combinations, and a given input combination generally permits more than one pattern of task co-ordination (see Chapter 5). Second, technical 'adoption' is a two-dimensional process: (a) a certain combination of inputs must be assembled and (b) a certain procedure must be followed. This dual and often sequential character of technical adoption leaves room for bottle-necks and disequilibria within each technical practice, for the input set and the pattern of task co-ordination may not match, if the former or the latter reflects past choices and procedures and cannot be instantaneously adjusted. The dual character of technical adoption makes it relevant to examine technical change as a process generated through a sequence of technological disequilibria (see section 5.1). Third, consideration of time is essential in the description of the production process: the pattern of task co-ordination must specify whether tasks are simultaneous or not (the precedence pattern). Fourth, emphasis on the procedural dimension of technology makes production conceptually distinct from exchange, particularly if the latter is described as an instance of 'discrete transaction' (see below). A procedural approach to the analysis of production directs attention to features of productive activity that differ sharply from those allocational aspects considered by the economic theorists who attempted the analytical 'reduction' of production to exchange (see e.g. Pantaleoni, 1889: 155 *n*.; Pareto, 1906: 171–2; Wicksteed, 1933 [1910]: 367; see also Baranzini and Scazzieri, 1986: 29–47). Fifth, emphasis on procedures requires the explicit consideration of the institutions in which production takes place, for institutions are the relatively permanent sets of relationships between agents and tools that influence in an important way which pattern of task co-ordination is adopted (whether the job-shop or straight-line model). Finally, the description of production is process-oriented rather than product-oriented. As a result, the conditions for continuous and complete fund-input utilization can be formulated independently of the 'product specification' of each process.

An important consequence of the 'task–process' view is the special attention for the 'immaterial side' of production, i.e. for the 'body of ideas which express the goals of the work, its functional importance, and the rationale of the methods employed' (Woodward, 1982: 36). The 'material side', i.e. 'the tools, instruments, machines, and technical formulas basic to the performance of the work' (ibid.), is not overlooked, but it is integrated into a more comprehensive notion of technology. The basic idea is that a technical practice is not adequately determined by technical knowledge alone. On the other hand, the institutional framework of productive activity does itself depend on the development of material technology: 'Elaboration of technology leads to increasing complexity of the enterprise using it, and the type of technology available for productive purposes sets limits to the types of structures appropriate for organizations' (Thompson and Bates, 1957: 325).

To summarize, the 'task–process' description of productive activity is associated with the idea that production is an outcome of the interaction between operations and material objects. A complete description of productive activity is impossible, unless the pattern of this interaction is explicitly considered. This involves a stress on the procedural dimension of production and has one important corresponding implication, for in it decisions influencing the production process are not uniquely and unambiguously associated with the state of demand and supply in factor markets, as is often assumed when production phenomena are taken to be instances of discrete transaction.[1] The production process is regarded as having a complex

---

[1] A characteristic example of the 'discrete transaction' approach may be found in Wicksteed: 'by hypothesis [the entrepreneur, or 'undertaker', in Wicksteed's

structure of its own, which is based on relationships between task-lengths and fund-input capabilities, and is relatively independent of demand and supply in factor markets (see also Leijonhufvud, 1986).[2]

10.1.2. *The scale of the production process and the size of the productive unit*

Confusion between process scale and size of productive unit has led to apparently contradictory statements in the economic literature. On the one hand, a number of authors have stressed the association between modern technology and 'large' productive units:

Large-scale organizations have evolved to achieve goals which are beyond the capacities of the individuals or the small group. They make possible the application of many and diverse skills and resources to complex systems of producing goods and services. Large-scale organizations, therefore, are particularly adapted to complicated *technologies*, that is, to those sets of man-machine activities which together produce a desired good or service. (Thompson and Bates, 1957: 325)

On the other hand, it has also been argued that too narrow a concentration on the economies of size may divert attention from more important sources of productivity gain:

Economists have . . . often failed to relate administrative coordination to the theory of the firm. For example, far more economies result from the careful coordination of flow through the processes of production and

terminology] is dealing with limited resources, and in applying these resources he must draw commodities, services, and privileges out of the circle of exchange, and so combine and direct them as to produce a result, that can itself be returned into the circle of exchange with value higher than that of the factors or ingredients that were drawn out' (1933 [1910]: 367). The treatment of production within the 'discrete transaction' or 'exchange' framework is considered in Hennings (1986).

[2] The relationship between the 'task–process' view of production and standard production analysis is similar to the relationship between the 'relational' and the 'classical' systems of law recently examined by a number of American legal scholars. In the classical law system, contracts are based on the 'discrete transaction' assumption of the exchange paradigm. In the relational system of law, an adjustment mechanism internal to the contract is substituted for the adjustment mechanism of the classical law system, based on 'what happens in some kind of a market external to the contract' (MacNeil, 1978: 901). In the former case, adjustment is based on 'what can be achieved through the political and social processes of the relation internal and external. This includes internal and external dispute-resolution structures. At this point, the relation has become a minisociety with a vast array of norms beyond the norm centered on exchange and its immediate processes' (ibid.).

distribution than from increasing the size of producing or distributing units in terms of capital facilities or number of workers. (Chandler, 1977: 490)

The 'task–process' view permits us to reconcile these apparent contradictions, for both economies of scale and 'economies of speed', which include many of the economies arising from specialization, may be related to the same basic principles governing continuous and full fund-input utilization. (See in particular Chapter 5.)

Given the pattern of task co-ordination (whether 'job-shop' or 'straight-line'), necessary and sufficient conditions for continuous and full fund-input utilization can be formulated independently of the size of the productive unit. (Note that 'size' generally sets an upper bound upon the number of e.p.s that can normally be operated at the same time in any given place for a fixed composition of output.) Process scale has to be sufficiently high and must vary according to a given criterion if continuous and full fund-input utilization is to be achieved (see sections 5.4 and 5.5). Now, process scale has been defined independently of the size of the productive unit, and the condition on process scale may be satisfied with alternative sizes of the productive units. For example, section 5.5.3 considered the case in which continuous fund-input utilization is possible either by arranging in line a sufficient number of e.p.s or by arranging 'in series' (that is, one following the other) a sufficient number of task-specific e.p.s. The former alternative generally entails that the productive unit be of a certain minimum capacity. The latter alternative entails no condition on capacity (apart from the conditions arising from indivisibilities in fund-input natural units).[3]

The 'task–process' approach to production permits us to establish the relationships between process scale and fund-input utilization in terms of the system of tasks rather than in terms of the productive unit. In this way, the conditions under which technical practice may be influenced by a variation of process scale can be examined independently of the productive capacity of individual establishments. This allows the study of cases in which technical practice is influenced by scale but the production process involves the co-operation of

[3] Continuous fund-input utilization requires, in the former case, the simultaneous operation of a certain number of interconnected e.p.s, and this condition normally entails a certain minimum capacity of the productive unit. In the latter case, continuous utilization is possible, regardless of the number of e.p.s simultaneously carried out in the same productive unit. As a result, process specialization makes continuous fund-input utilization possible, even if capacity is so small that only a single e.p. per unit of time may be operated.

different establishments. In particular, Marshall's 'industrial district' may be defined as a set of interrelated tasks in which continuous fund-input utilization is achieved, or approximated, by the operation of elementary processes consisting of a single task or of a limited range of tasks (see section 5.5.3). The characteristic feature of the industrial district is that e.p. specialization is based on co-operation among establishment types each performing a distinct range of tasks. The complete production process calls for division of labour among establishments, and the tasks carried out in the various establishments are made mutually compatible by a system which is based on technological co-ordination, even if its operation may depend upon the market mechanism. The industrial district case shows that, in particular, scale factors may affect the technical practice through interaction between distinct and different productive units.

The 'task–process' approach concentrates attention on this technological co-ordination between establishments by considering the productive activities of the whole district as a single process. It may be of interest to note that this result is obtained by adopting an apparently abstract description of productive activities, which stresses the interdependence of tasks in a district rather than the identity of establishments operating task-specific e.p.s.

Production processes that are subject to availability upper bounds on certain fund inputs, such as land, provide another important example of a scale–practice relation that must be examined by considering a productive unit other than the establishment. Availability upper bounds on a certain fund input are better examined by considering all the activities using that input as parts of a single process, independently both of the commodities produced and of the establishments in which the several activities are carried out. In fact, an increase in the scale of this aggregate process may bring about 'scale-technology contraction' (see Chapter 6). This means—by the definition of scale-technology contraction—that certain technical practices that were feasible at a lower scale cannot be operated at the higher scale. It would be impossible, however, to determine which practices are used at the higher scale, unless the allocation of the fund input among establishments and processes were explicitly considered (see sections 6.5 and 6.6).

The distinction between process scale and size of productive unit brings to the fore an important aspect of productive activities. This is the fact that there is no simple relationship between the direction of scale effects and the capacity of individual establishments. For example, continuous fund-input utilization may involve a *reduction* in establishment size, if continuous utilization is achieved by e.p. specialization. (In this case, individual establishments operate specialized e.p.s, and the complete production process requires the operation of various independent establishments. Continuous utilization would generally involve an increase in the scale of the complete process, but this scale is obtained through the operation of many independent establishments, which may be small-sized.) (See section 5.5.3.) On the other hand, if the e.p. consists of different types of task, and continuous utilization is obtained by an in-line arrangement of e.p.s, a reduction in establishment size below the minimum capacity compatible with continuous utilization would make continuous utilization impossible (see sections 5.5.3 and 5.5.4). A similar condition on establishment size has been shown to hold in the case of job-shop production (see section 5.4.3). It is worth considering again this issue in some detail.

In the 'task–process' approach, the production process is conceived as a set of simultaneous e.p.s (see Chapter 4). More precisely, it is described as a network of tasks arranged according to sequences interrupted by 'terminal nodes'. Each terminal node completes a particular e.p. and permits a certain task-sequence to be repeated once again. Under certain conditions, the arrangement of e.p.s permits the establishment to achieve, or to approximate, continuous fund-input utilization. This result may be obtained in two different ways, depending upon whether the task network is organized according to the job-shop or the straight-line pattern. In the former case, continuous utilization may be achieved by taking advantage of the difference between the precedence patterns of the various e.p.s operated in a given establishment (see section 5.4.2). In this case, the number of fund inputs available in the establishment and their types of skill are essential to determine the arrangement of tasks, since the type and length of tasks would be adjusted to the available skills. In the straight-line case, on the other hand, continuous utilization may be achieved by taking advantage of the minute subdivision of work that is possible when task-lengths are known a priori and independently of the fund-input types available in the establishment (see section 5.5.2). For this case, the necessary and sufficient condition for continuous utilization was formulated in terms of task-lengths and the length of the working day, and independently of process scale and establishment size. Another condition on process scale must be satisfied, however, if continuous utilization is to be achieved with the in-line arrangement of the e.p.s in the production process (see section 5.5.3). In this case, the arrangement of tasks is independent of the number and type of available fund inputs: the skills needed in the production process are adjusted to the type and length of tasks, thus establishing a skill–task relationship opposite to the one characteristic of the job-shop establishment.

The task-composition and the total duration of an e.p. are often determined by non-technological factors. For example, it is often immaterial, from the technological point of view, whether tanning and shoe-making are part of the same e.p. or of two different e.p.s. Indeed, it is only in the straight-line case that the task-composition and total length of the e.p. determine the process scale at which continuous fund-input utilization is possible. In the job-shop case, the condition on process scale reflects the task-composition and precedence pattern of the whole establishment rather than the characteristics of the individual e.p. In this particular case, the 'elementary process' may be considered as a theoretical concept imposed on the actual arrangement of tasks carried out in the establishment rather than a real feature causally determining the shape of the production process (see section 5.4).

Process scale is generally independent of the size of the productive unit, if tasks are arranged according to the straight-line pattern. In particular, large-scale production may be feasible by operating a network of small productive units, and, indeed, large productive units may be unable to take advantage of the economies associated with large process scale (see the discussion between Gioja and Valeriani considered in section 9.2.1).

In straight-line production, conditions for continuous utilization may be identified regardless of the size of the establishment. This makes the size of the establishment dependent on social institutions and wealth distribution rather than on production technology. Scale may be regarded as a purely technological dimension of productive activity independent of the capacity of productive units.

The job-shop pattern involves a completely different relationship of scale to size. Here, scale cannot be defined independently of size, for the length of tasks and e.p.s can only be determined once the size of the establishment is known, since task-lengths are variable and can be adjusted according to the needs (e.g. to achieve continuous utilization). The scale of the production process cannot be determined unless the lengths of the tasks and the e.p.s are known. Here, the production process takes a particular structure and scale after the size of the productive unit is determined. Once this size is known, continuous fund-input utilization may or may not be possible, depending upon whether the precedence pattern of tasks allows fund inputs to be switched from one task to another as soon as the first is completed. As a result, the size of the productive unit and the scale of the process carried out in that unit may only be increased by integer multiples of the minimum size and scale compatible with continuous utilization. Another characteristic feature of job-shop production is that continuous utilization is normally achieved by using multi-skilled fund inputs in a productive unit in which different precedence patterns of tasks are possible (see section 4.3.2). This implies that multi-commodity production is common, and that a continuous increase in the output level of any given commodity is possible only on condition that the variety of precedence patterns is preserved (see section 5.4.3). As a result, the job-shop establishment is generally small. (Mass production in large establishments is normally associated with the large-scale operation of a single e.p. type, or of e.p. types having the same precedence pattern. This pattern of task co-ordination would make continuous utilization impossible in a job-shop establishment.) The above feature of job-shop production is important in explaining certain aspects of the structural dynamics of medieval handicraft production: 'Whenever any one line of handicraft threatens to become too large, new handicrafts split off from it and appropriate part of its sphere of production. This is the medieval division of labour, which continually creates new and independent trades' (Bücher, 1968 [1893]: 171).[4]

The historical process described by Bücher may be interpreted in terms of the relationship between tasks, production processes, and fund-input utilization. A necessary condition for continuous utilization in the job-shop case is that the proportions among the sets of e.p.s having various different precedence patterns stay fixed when

---

[4] Bücher's explanation of this phenomenon is as follows: 'It is a principle that handicraft endeavoured to carry out whenever possible—an article should pass through all the stages of its preparation in the same workshop . . . The direct relationship between the handicraftsman and the consumer of his products, makes it necessary that the business remain small' (Bücher, 1968 [1893]: 170–1). A technological reason for this principle is given in the text below.

process scale is varied (see section 5.4.3). The need to satisfy this requirement as the demand for particular commodities is increased leads either to the 'splitting off' of new handicrafts that are also based on the job-shop pattern or to the introduction of the straight-line establishment.

10.1.3. *Scale-constrained technical adoption*

The 'task–process' view of production is associated with the description of the production process as a procedure governed by a relatively fixed relationship between inputs and tasks. An important outcome of this approach is that attention is drawn to the 'feasibility element' in technical 'adoption'. The producer takes the structure of the production process to be given in the short run, but a tendency to the transformation of this structure may be inherent to the process itself. For, in certain cases, a 'technological disequilibrium' may emerge as process scale is varied and a new 'technological equilibrium' may not be possible unless the structure of the process is changed (see Chapters 5 and 6). As a result, process scale emerges as a crucial element in the dynamics of productive structure. There are technical practices that are feasible at certain process scales but not at others. As a result, an increase in scale may involve the transition to a situation in which a previously feasible technical practice becomes no longer feasible (scale-technology contraction). If the technical practice adopted at the original scale is not feasible at the new scale, this scale cannot be achieved unless the practice is varied. In other cases, an increase in scale makes it possible to operate a previously unfeasible technical practice (scale-technology expansion). The possibility of scale-technology contraction and expansion suggests that the structure of the production process may change under the influence of factors unrelated to producers' choice and to the variation of input prices. Consideration of scale-technology contraction and expansion has led us to distinguish between the following two relationships: (i) the relationship between the set of process scales (S) and the set of observed technical practices (T), which merely reflects the *feasibility* of observed technical practices (this is the *scale–practice relation*); (ii) the relationship between S and T which reflects, in addition to the feasibility of technical practices, special assumptions concerning the way in which the producer ranks the feasible practices and chooses from among them (this is the *scale–efficiency relation*). A scale–efficiency relation is well defined as long as the technical practice that is 'top' in a producer's ranking is also the first to be considered by him in the process of technical adoption, so that the outcome of the technical-adoption process is unambiguously determined at any scale. We have also found that a certain degree of inter-scale consistency of a producer's ranking is necessary for an increase in scale that is associated with scale-technology contraction or expansion to determine a switch to a 'more efficient' or to a 'less efficient' technical practice (see section 7.3.3 and Chapter 8).

The scale–practice relation reflects objective characteristics of production technology, and is independent of the criterion followed by producers in technical adoption. The scale–efficiency relation, on the other hand, presupposes a certain scale–practice relation and a particular type of producer's behaviour. The existence of a non-trivial scale–practice relation (such that the set of technical practices feasible at scale s is not constant with respect to s) implies that a change of scale may require a change of technical practice. The scale–practice relation reflects the fact that certain practices are feasible only at certain scales. However, scale-constrained feasibility is in general not sufficient to determine the actual change of technical practice (see section 7.2.3.) However, a precise correspondence between scale and technical practice *is* brought about either if all technical practices are scale-specific or if a scale–efficiency relation applies (see sections 7.2.3 and 7.3). In these two cases, the relationship between scale and productive structure leads to a definite outcome: any change of scale is unambiguously associated with a change of technical practice. In all other cases, the scale–practice relation does not permit us to identify which particular practice would be associated with any particular scale; indeterminacy is therefore the only alternative to scale-specificity or to 'optimizing' technical adoption. In practice, however, freedom to choose will be constrained by current practices and the technological environment (see sections 7.1 and 7.2). In this case, the process of technical adoption may lead to a determinate outcome, even if the technical practices are not scale-specific and the producer considers alternative practices by following the 'sequential scrutiny' criterion rather than an optimizing criterion. A particular new practice may be adopted because it is 'similar' to the old practice, which has become unfeasible, or because it allows for the disappearance of 'technological disequilibria' unavoidable at the former scale. Determinacy of technical adoption can be obtained in this way if technical adoption is regarded as a historical process rather than as a timeless deliberation, for this perspective makes it natural to allow for linkages between different periods and to attribute to the productive unit an identity that is maintained from one period to another. As a result, current technical practices appear to be influenced in an important way by the practices adopted in the past.

Consideration of scale-constrained technical behaviour shows that indeterminate technical-adoption functions may be more suitable to the analysis of the historical dynamics of productive structure than models based on deterministic assumptions about human behaviour. It would generally be impossible to derive the actual technical practice from feasible practices on such assumptions, unless a producer's knowledge and the technical-adoption function were fixed (see Chapter 7). On the other hand, a 'flexible' adoption function, such as that provided by sequential scrutiny, would properly describe the variable adjustment procedure adopted by producers as the change of scale brings about a change of producer's knowledge through the change in the set of feasible technical practices (see section 7.1.2). In particular, a 'flexible' adoption function would permit us to consider phenomena such as technical learning and unlearning, technical invention and technical loss that cannot easily be accommodated within the framework of 'rational' behaviour and optimizing choice. This result depends on taking economic actions to be the outcome of both 'external' and 'internal' determination. (On this distinction, see von Wright, 1980.) In this case, a non-deterministic theory of human action (such as the one associated with the sequential-scrutiny hypothesis) may be combined with the idea that freedom of choice is restricted by factors independent of the agents' preferences and beliefs. This makes technical adoption more easily predictable on condition that economic theory is able to model the generation of the 'external' constraints.

10.1.4. *A process-based approach to technical change*

The 'task–process' view of production focuses on tasks and e.p.s rather than inputs. It is also characterized by the consideration of procedures and institutions rather than market transactions. As a result, productive activity is described as an ongoing process rather than as a matter of deliberate planning. Within this framework, changes in technical practice appear as the substitution of one 'commonly accepted' procedure for another, rather than as the outcome of deliberate choice. It follows that a producer's actions may often be described as elements of an 'objective world' external to human beliefs and other states of mind.

A change in technical practice is described, in this view of things, as a change in the organization of tasks rather than as a change in the input types or in quantitative input–output relationships (see also Morroni, 1992). Attention is thus concentrated on the actual process in which a given technical practice is transformed into a different practice, for it is at this level that most external constraints on a producer's behaviour actually operate. (An example is the influence of tradition in moulding the generation and diffusion of new technical practices.)

If the 'task–process' view is adopted, technical change is characterized by the following elements. First, it is a process through which current practices are transformed rather than a matter of the instantaneous substitution of one input combination for another. Second, its generation is often associated with the discovery of new ways of organizing existing tasks rather than with the invention of new tasks. Third, the rapidity of its diffusion reflects the degree of flexibility of the institutional framework within which the new technical practices are constructed. Fourth, the change of technical practice may be described at different 'institutional' levels, for the abstract notion of production process used in the 'task–process' view permits us to concentrate alternatively on the individual establishment, the 'subsystem' of interrelated activities (such as the set of all activities that are directly and indirectly necessary to deliver a certain final product, or the set of all activities that make direct or indirect use of a certain raw commodity), or the productive system as a whole, depending on which technical transformation is considered.

10.2. SCALE AND SIZE IN THE 'TASK–PROCESS' FRAMEWORK

10.2.1. *Co-operation, division of labour, and scale*

The theory of scale outlined in this study concerns the co-operative aspect of productive activity. The procedures adopted for task-organization, and thus for the co-operation of different agents, determine the scale of the production process and the size of the productive unit. *Scale*, as an abstract concept in task–process theory, may be defined as the number of elementary processes (e.p.s) simultaneously operated within a productive unit. *Size*, on the other hand, determines the *maximum* number of parallel e.p.s that can be operated at the same time in that unit. Our notion of scale may be applied to any productive unit, regardless of whether we take the latter to be a factory, an industry, or an economy. As a result, the concept of 'process scale' may be used at different levels of complexity, and the condition for continuous fund-input utilization may be identified independently of the non-operational elements determining the size of individual establishments.

The 'task–process' approach brings to the fore the operational linkages among co-operating inputs (human beings and machines), both in cases in which these inputs perform identical tasks and in those in which they perform different tasks (e.g. cases of division of labour). Division of labour is a special case of the 'association' or 'union' of labour (see section 3.2.4 and also Bücher, 1968 [1893]: 244 ff.); the conditions for continuous and full fund-input utilization may be found both in cases in which fund inputs are task specific and in cases in which they are not (see Chapter 5).[5]

The issue of fund-input specialization does not arise in the case of job-shop production, since here fund inputs are generally multi-skilled (see sections 4.3.2 and 5.4). In straight-line production, on the other hand, a general condition for continuous fund-input utilization may be formulated by considering the pattern of task co-ordination, regardless of whether fund inputs are task specific or not (see section 5.5.2).

In the straight-line case, continuous fund-input utilization may be achieved on condition that a sufficient number of tasks is performed by a fund input in a working day. If all fund inputs are task specific, this number of tasks is the same both with the in-line arrangement of e.p.s and with e.p. specialization (see section 5.5.4). In the former case, continuous utilization requires that a certain minimum scale be attained by the production process at the establishment level. In the latter case, continuous utilization involves no condition on the minimum process scale for the individual establishment: the required

---

[5] This result confirms the conjecture of Gioja (1815–17) and Wakefield (1835–43) that the 'association of works' is essential in fund-input utilization and that 'complex co-operation' (division of labour) is a special case of 'simple co-operation' (the association of agents performing identical tasks). (See s. 3.2.4.)

number of tasks can be performed even in a productive establishment operating a single e.p. at each point of time. But it is likely that highly specialized e.p.s would deliver an output that is not a 'finished commodity' (here defined as a commodity that can be traded on the market in the absence of 'technological co-ordination' with producers of other commodities). In this case, specialized e.p.s are likely to combine so as to bring about a larger 'productive unit' consisting of a number of distinct establishments such as in Marshall's 'industrial district' (see section 3.4.2). Here, continuous fund-input utilization requires a certain minimum scale of the whole district, even if continuous utilization in the individual establishments is independent of their respective scales. (If district scale is below the required minimum, specialized establishments would not be continuously operated throughout the working day.) Multi-purpose fund inputs make a considerable difference to the above results. If we consider an e.p. consisting of two or more tasks, the minimum scale permitting minimum fund-input idleness is generally lower with multi-purpose than with special-purpose fund inputs (see section 5.5.4). The minimum process scale permitting continuous utilization increases as fund inputs become increasingly specialized. In the case of a complete task-specialization of fund inputs, continuous utilization is possible if one or other of the two following conditions hold: (i) the in-line arrangement is adopted and the minimum process scale compatible with continuous utilization is operated (note that, in this case, minimum scale would often be large); (ii) the original e.p. is replaced by e.p.s which perform a narrower range of tasks and are co-ordinated with one another in the same industrial district.

It is worth noting that process scale needs to be large at the establishment level only if the way that continuous utilization is obtained is by operating special-purpose fund inputs and multi-task e.p.s. In all the other cases, continuous utilization may be achieved at relatively low scales, or even independently of constraints on the scale of the production process carried out in individual establishments. This result is useful in explaining the survival of small productive units even at a mature stage of industrial development. For an increasing division of labour, by reducing the range of tasks which may be performed by any given fund input, creates a situation in which continuous utilization can only be achieved either by the in-line arrangement of e.p.s or by the operation of e.p.s performing a narrower range of tasks.

As a result, economies of scale and economies of specialization emerge as alternative operational characteristics of the basic law governing continuous fund-input utilization in straight-line production.

10.2.2. *Co-operation, division of labour, and size of productive unit*

It will be recalled that there are alternative notions of size of a productive unit, and that the relevant size variable may change as a result of a change in the productive unit or in technical practice (see sections 2.3, 9.2.1, and 9.2.2). However, the size of a productive unit determines the maximum number of e.p.s that can be operated at one time in that unit. In this technical sense, size *is* the maximum feasible scale of the production process that may be operated in that unit in the sense of scale used in this study.

It will also be recalled that there are alternative notions of productive unit. A productive unit is a 'batch' of e.p.s that may be distinguished from the rest of the productive system on the basis of some conventional criterion. As a result, a productive unit may alternatively consist of a single establishment or of a number of various establishments, depending upon which convention is adopted.

A certain process scale is associated with a certain degree of 'capacity utilization' (given the size of the corresponding productive unit, scale may be any number up to the capacity associated with that particular size), but scale and size are both defined relatively to a certain 'productive unit', and this may consist of one or many productive establishments. As a result, a large-sized productive unit is compatible both with a large and a small process scale, and a large scale may be achieved either with a large-sized establishment or with a set of interrelated small-sized workshops, as in the industrial-district case.

In section 9.2.3 it was noted that, at the establishment level, the relevant size variable depends on the interplay of various technological and economic factors such as the circulating/fixed-capital ratio and the relative lengths of the periods during which capital is sunk in the various fund inputs. As a result, establishment size is not always related to the output capacity of fund-input natural units, and it is possible for there to be large establishments in which e.p.s need a small amount of capital sunk in the fund inputs or small establishments in which a large amount of fund-input capital is needed.

Establishment size will tend to be large if the output capacity of fund-input natural units is such that the minimum feasible scale of the e.p. is also large. In all the other cases, the proportion between circulating capital and the amount of capital sunk in the fund inputs is the critical factor. If that proportion is high enough, there is no characteristic of the technical practice that determines size, and the appearance of large-sized establishments generally reflects the existence of trade advantages associated with the transformation of large quantities of 'work-in-process'. Here, a relevant historical example is the formation of large manufactures that were using a relatively small 'fund' of fixed-capital items in the centuries that immediately preceded the first Industrial Revolution. In many cases, such manufactures could be considered as an extension to the fabrication stage of a firm whose structure was still rooted in the trading stage of business activity, so that capital was mainly 'working or circulating capital—capital that is *turned over*' (Hicks, 1969: 142), and the fixed-capital items could still be considered as 'no more than containers for the stock of goods', on which business activity was centred (ibid.). On the other hand, if the proportion of circulating to fixed capital is low enough, size will tend to depend on the relative amounts of capital sunk in the various categories of fund inputs. In this latter case, the relevant size variable is determined by the fund-input category requiring the largest and longest-lasting capital immobilization. Once this input is known, actual size will often reflect the concentration of property rights among owners of this input. This situation highlights a remarkable feature of the interaction between institutional and 'material' factors of productive organization (see also Georgescu-Roegen, 1988; Baranzini and Scazzieri, 1990; Scazzieri, 1992a).

10.2.3. *Scale, size, and the nature of the firm*

A productive unit defined in operational terms is a set of e.p. types identified in terms of relationships among tasks and e.p.s. A productive unit defined in terms of *capacity* is a set of e.p.s that forms a 'bunch' of activities, regardless of the difference among e.p. types. In this latter case, size is naturally measured by considering a synthetic index of the output level, such as maximum tons per day or maximum number of bushels per acre. We may note, however, that this measure of size has no absolute significance, since it depends on particular e.p. types and, in general, will vary with any change in the e.p. types forming the complete process of production.

To summarize, in the 'task–process' approach the productive unit is described as a set of e.p.s governed by a given network of precedence relationships. It is worth considering how this concept is related to the traditional concept of the firm. R. H. Coase defined the firm as 'the system of relationships which comes into existence when the direction of resources is dependent on an entrepreneur' (1937: 393). This definition has a family resemblance to the concept of the 'plant', which is generally identified with a given work station and a given stock of technical equipment, regardless of the pattern adopted for the coordination of tasks and e.p.s. Indeed, there is not necessarily a one-to-one correspondence between firms and task networks, for there are cases in which a single task network corresponds to a number of distinct productive establishments. There are also cases in which a single firm is associated with many different task networks, unrelated to one another from the operational point of view. (A firm consisting of a set of e.p.s that are connected only in that a single agent finances them all will not be a 'productive unit' from the point of view of 'task–process' theory.) This result brings out an important feature of the firm, for the existence of the firm is related to the formation and direction of resources rather than to the actual organization of tasks and e.p.s. A firm is a system of relationships *within which* human activities are co-ordinated directly through 'administration' rather than indirectly through exchange and the price mechanism. On the other hand, the firm is not necessarily the important unit of analysis, if attention is focused on the direct relationships between tasks. (Note that these relationships may also connect tasks carried out within distinct firms.) An important example is Marshall's 'industrial district', which is based on the direct co-operation among specialized establishments rather than on market transactions among these establishments. In this connection, it is worth noting that e.p. specialization is often based on non-market co-ordination, because the output of the specialized e.p. is often not marketable as an independent commodity, so that the activities of specialized establishments can only be made compatible through direct co-operation. In this case, an increase in fund-input specialization brings about greater complexity of the production process, and the latter is associated with the existence of relatively large 'regions' of the productive system in which co-ordination among individual e.p.s is achieved outside the market.

If the amount of capital 'tied up' in the various fund-input categories is negligible with respect to the circulating capital needed in the production process, the size of the productive unit is determined outside the production sphere (see section 10.2.2). In this case, the production process may therefore be examined at the firm level without any significant loss of generality, and production may be described by confining attention to the exchange sphere, as in Wicksteed's analysis of the entrepreneur (see also p. 243 n.).

by hypothesis he [the entrepreneur] is dealing with limited resources, and in applying these resources he must draw commodities, services and privileges out of the circle of exchange, and so combine and direct them as to produce a result, that can itself be returned into the circle of exchange with value higher than that of the factors or ingredients that were drawn out.   (Wicksteed, 1933 [1910]: 367)

On the other hand, if the amount of capital that is 'fixed' in the various fund inputs is large in relation to circulating capital, the size of the productive unit reflects the relative weight of the different fund-input categories and is determined by a combination of technological and institutional factors (see above). In this case, it is impossible to determine the range and variety of operations and the capacity of the productive unit at the level of markets and firms. For the range and variety of operations will in this case depend on the pattern of fund-input specialization and task-organization, whereas capacity will be influenced by the concentration of property rights among fund-input owners (see above).

10.2.4. *A comparison with other approaches*

Certain aspects of size-determination considered in task–process theory are also examined in other approaches. I will discuss some of these here, trying to bring out the similarities and the differences from the 'task–process' view.

Heinrich Storch long ago considered the concentration of property rights to be an important factor influencing the capacity of the productive unit:

It is not sufficient that the capital required for the subdivision of handicrafts should be in readiness in the society: it must also be accumulated in the hands of the employers in sufficiently large quantities to enable them to conduct operations on a large scale . . . The more the division increases, the more does the constant employment of a given number of labourers require a greater outlay of capital in tools, raw material, etc. (Storch, 1823: i. 250–1; quoted in Marx, 1983 [1867]: i. 340 n.)

Marx also stressed the connection between co-operation among workers and production in large-sized units. This led him to study the relationship between the concentration of productive activities and the concentration of capital:

As a general rule, labourers cannot co-operate without being brought together: their assemblage in one place is a necessary condition of their co-operation. Hence wage-labourers cannot co-operate, unless they are employed simultaneously by the same capital, the same capitalist, and unless therefore their labour-powers are bought simultaneously by him . . . Hence the number of the labourers that co-operate, or the scale of co-operation, depends, in the first instance, on the amount of capital that the individual capitalist can spare for the purchase of labour-power; in other words, on the extent to which a single capitalist has command over the means of subsistence of a number of labourers. (Marx, 1983 [1867]: i. 312)

The above passage shows that Marx recognized in the distribution of property rights an essential element in capacity determination. His argument implies that greater concentration of capital is associated with greater concentration of productive activities and thus with larger establishment capacity. Marx also considered the relationship between increasing concentration of capital, which he called 'centralization', and the increasing use of machinery and mechanical power:

Centralisation completes the work of accumulation by enabling industrial capitalists to extend the scale of their operations . . . Everywhere the increased scale of industrial establishments is the starting point for a more comprehensive organization of the collective work of many, for a wider development of their material motive forces—in other words, for the progressive transformation of isolated processes of production, carried on by customary methods, into processes of production socially combined and scientifically arranged. (Marx, 1983 [1867]: i. 588)

Marx regards increasing concentration of property rights as a necessary condition for the existence of large productive units. He also regards increasing capacity as historically prior to the growth of technical practices that require a high proportion of machinery to labour and raw materials; thus he explains large capacity ultimately in terms of non-technological factors.

The relationship between capacity and the amount of capital required to set up the establishment was also stressed by Karl Bücher, who examined the function of changes in the 'possession of wealth' in determining the average capacity of the productive establishment. If inequality in wealth distribution is low, as in the medieval craftsman class, increased demand for the output of a given commodity is satisfied by splitting the original e.p. into a certain number of specialized e.p.s carried out in independent workshops. This solution 'limited the demand for capital and kept the business small' (Bücher, 1968 [1893]: 331). On the other hand, this pattern of division of labour was generally confined to periods of exceptional demand expansion. In normal conditions, craftsmen operated on ordered piece-work, and the complete process of transforming the raw material into a finished product was generally carried out in a single workshop (see ibid.). This is because

[t]he longer the duration of the process of production the smaller the business capital that the single producer requires . . . In the Middle Ages, to cite a very familiar example, the shoemaker was frequently tanner as well. The whole process of industrial elaboration from the raw hide to the finished footwear thus lay in one hand. Assuming now that the tanning of the hide required half the time that was necessary to its transformation into shoeware, a shoemaker desiring to carry on tanning alone would have required three times as much business capital as the tanner who at the same time made shoes.   (ibid.)

In Bücher's account, the size of a medieval workshop is subject to two contrasting influences. The need to reduce the amount of 'business capital' (in Bücher's example, this is essentially the circulating capital required to maintain a certain amount of 'work-in-process') works against e.p. specialization and makes it difficult to operate small workshops performing one or a few tasks only. In fact, the amount of circulating capital (such as raw materials and semi-finished products) necessary to achieve continuous fund-input utilization in a workshop whose e.p. lasts one hour will normally be twice as much as the circulating capital required in a workshop whose e.p. lasts two hours, if, in this latter case, fund inputs are multi-purpose and can be switched from one task to another. (Note that this was generally the case in medieval craft production.) On the other hand, scarcity of capital funds makes complex e.p.s impossible as soon as an increase in the number and type of tasks is associated with an increase in the need for capital.[6] As a result, the number and type of tasks performed in the medieval workshop is ultimately determined by the constraint on business capital. If the available capital allows the existing workshop to take on a higher number of e.p.s, all the e.p.s necessary to deliver a greater amount of final output are performed in that workshop. If, on the other hand, the greater number of e.p.s creates a need for more capital, e.p. specialization takes place in order to keep business capital down to the level compatible with the small holdings of the craftsman class.

Bücher's argument applies to the type of task operated in a single workshop rather than to productive capacity (this is the maximum feasible scale of the production process operated in that workshop). However, the medieval workshop is also 'small' in terms of capacity. One reason for this was suggested in section 5.4.3, where we examined the conditions for continuous fund-input utilization in job-shop establishments. Fund inputs can be continuously used only if the process scale increases by integer multiples of the minimum scale compatible with continuous utilization. This condition also implies that capacity is increased according to the same pattern. On the other hand, as the analysis of section 5.4.3 made clear, the job-shop organization allows for changes in the proportion between e.p. types at a given scale and capacity, so that small variations in the output levels of individual commodities are possible without changing the capacity of the productive unit. Large-scale variations, however, cannot be accommodated with the existing task-organization at the given capacity. The pattern of e.p. fragmentation and labour specialization often followed by medieval craftsmen facing demand expansion is also a result of this constraint on 'efficient' capacity under conditions of limited capital availability.

Bücher and Marx draw attention to the relationship between size-determination and availability of capital, but each of them stresses a different aspect of the process. Bücher is mainly concerned with the influence exerted by the relative shortage of business capital on the number and type of tasks carried out in the individual workshop. Marx examines size-determination from the point of view of the

---

[6] There is, in this case, a definite relationship between the evolution of the technical structure and the dynamics of wealth distribution. (A comprehensive appraisal of the way in which the distribution of wealth is related with the growth of an economic system may be found in Baranzini, 1991.)

minimum capacity needed for the economic operation of one or more e.p. types. In both cases, however, size is related to distribution of wealth rather than primarily to technology and levels of demand. This view was taken up by Hicks when examining the distinctive features of 'modern industry' with respect to previous types of industrial organization. Hicks calls attention to the high proportion of working capital to fixed capital in handicraft production, in which 'the turnover of . . . materials was the centre of [the craftsman's] business' (1969: 142). In Hicks's view, the essential feature of the Industrial Revolution is that 'the range of fixed capital goods that were used in production, otherwise than in trade, began noticeably to increase' (ibid. 142–3). But the operation of technical practices requiring considerable investment in fixed capital is subject to a condition that was seldom satisfied before the Industrial Revolution of the late eighteenth century (see ibid. 142–5). This is the availability of capital funds sufficient to allow people to invest in a type of capital that 'is embodied in a particular form, from which it can only gradually, at the best, be released' (ibid. 144). The capital-availability condition for fixed capital investment derives from the special feature of fixed capital:

In order that people should be willing, in an uncertain world, to *sink* large amounts of capital, they must either themselves be in possession of other resources, which they hold in a more liquid form, so that they can be quickly realized to meet emergencies; or they must be confident of being able to borrow . . . In the end, it is the availability of liquid funds which is crucial. (ibid. 144–5)

Hicks's stress on liquidity is in line with Storch's and Marx's attention to the accumulation of financial capital as a prerequisite for the introduction of technical practices that require considerable fixed capital investment. It is also in line with Bücher's analysis of the way in which shortage of funds gives a distinctive character to medieval artisan production and to its pattern of structural change.[7]

---

[7] The analysis of Hicks had been anticipated by Lilley (1948), who emphasized that alternative capital structures are associated with different technologies, and used such a conceptual framework in order to explain the social transformation that accompanied the transition from the Bronze Age to the Iron Age in ancient Greece. (The relationship between capital accumulation and technical practices is also considered in Crouzet, 1972, and Anderson, 1974. The connection between different forms of capital and division of labour is examined in Perelman, 1981; 1983; see also Meacci, 1989. A recent development of the Hicksian suggestions about the relationship between liquidity and fixed capital may be found in Amendola and Gaffard, 1988.)

The 'task–process' view of production provides a comprehensive framework for studying the aspects of size-determination discussed by the above authors. In particular, it allows for a distinction between the 'versatility' of an establishment (measured by the number of e.p. types carried out in that establishment) and its size (the maximum number of e.p.s that may be simultaneously carried out within it). The number of e.p. types depends on the pattern of task-organization and fund-input specialization. In job-shop establishments, unspecialized fund inputs generally perform a considerable range and variety of e.p. types. Transactions are of finished products rather than parts. Straight-line establishments are generally associated with a certain degree of fund-input specialization and with a narrow variety of e.p. types. It has been shown above that in straight-line establishments lack of fund-input specialization would preclude efficient allocation of tasks to the various skills (the 'Gioja–Babbage' principle) and that all e.p. types must follow the same precedence pattern of tasks (see sections 4.3.2 and 4.3.3). This condition applied to the precedence pattern permits the existence of 'versatile' establishments, but restricts each establishment to a special category of e.p. types. Unlike the job-shop production model, continuous fund-input utilization in straight-line establishments does not require the use of the same fund inputs in e.p.s that have *different* precedence patterns. This makes e.p. specialization easier and allows for the exchange of parts, rather than finished products, among different establishments. In the 'task–process' view, productive capacity is related both to technology and to the distribution of wealth (see above). The former determines whether large-capacity production is feasible or not. As shown in section 5.4, it is impossible to increase the capacity of a job-shop establishment over certain ranges and patterns of e.p.s if continuous fund-input utilization is to be achieved. On the other hand, straight-line production is compatible both with small and large capacity, since continuous utilization may be achieved either with e.p. specialization or an in-line arrangement of e.p.s (see section 5.5). In this case, the actual capacity depends on the proportion of working capital to fixed capital and on the distribution of wealth and property rights among fund-input owners (see section 10.2.2).

Attention to firm size is also characteristic of a number of recent contributions in which the firm is considered from the organizational point of view. This literature takes up Coase's idea of the firm as a 'system of relationships', rather than as a mere combination of productive factors, and examines this system both in its internal structure and in its relation to the market. One important issue considered in the above framework is the existence of transaction cost and its bearing on the 'versatility' and capacity of the productive unit. Oliver Williamson has pointed out that '[i]n more numerous respects than are commonly appreciated, the substitution of internal organization for market exchange is attractive less on account of technological economies associated with production but because of what may be referred to broadly as transactional failures in the operation of markets for intermediate goods' (1971: 112; see also Williamson, 1985). However, it is also recognized that 'technology is an important factor in the evolution of the modern business enterprise' (Williamson, 1980: 187). In particular, a change of technology might be the crucial factor in inducing firms 'to shift transactions out of the markets' (ibid.), as is shown by the introduction of steam power and the associated incentive to move to large-sized engines and large-capacity establishments. It should not be assumed, however, that technological change always encourages non-market at the expense of market methods of co-ordination. Comparing the modern car industry with the carriage industry of the late nineteenth century, Williamson writes:

Although automobile firms are much larger and incur considerable expense in coordinating the manufacture and marketing of cars, it is not clear that the proportion of activity that is administratively coordinated by the automobile manufacturers is greater than that which characterized carriage manufacture. Rather, as the complexity of the product increased, the number of transactions that are processed through intermediate product markets and the number that are processed administratively both increased. (1980: 194)

The transactions-cost approach to size pertains primarily to the number of e.p. types carried out in a given firm. The factors determining the maximum number of e.p.s that can be simultaneously carried out in a given establishment (the capacity of that establishment) are external to the theory of transactions cost *stricto sensu*: the determination of capacity is associated by Williamson with technological lower bounds on the scale of certain technical practices, rather than with the organizational features of the production process.

A different approach is taken by Armen Alchian and Harold Demsetz in their attempt to explain 'the conditions that determine whether the gains from specialization and cooperative production can better be obtained within an organization like the firm, or across markets' and 'to explain the structure of the organization' (1972: 777). Alchian and Demsetz propose an approach that is 'contractualist' and 'relational' rather than immediately 'exchange-oriented'. Their answer to the question 'Wherein . . . is the relationship between a grocer and his employee different from that between a grocer and his customer?' (pp. 777–8) is found in the *'team* use of inputs and a centralized position of some party in the contractual arrangements of *all* other inputs' (p. 778).

The existence of the firm is explained in terms of a special category of contracts, structurally different from the kind of contract between partners in a classical exchange situation. In the latter case, 'contracts facilitate efficient specialization, according to comparative advantage' (p. 794), whereas the relationship between individuals in a firm is generally governed, not by a set of bilateral contracts between pairs of parties on the same 'level', but by a set of bilateral contracts between 'a central, common party' (the employer) and each other party (the different employees). In this case, it is essential to identify and explain the characteristics of the 'central party' (see p. 791). This party may be identified by considering that an essential feature of co-operative production (or *team production*) is that 'a union, or joint use, of inputs yields a larger output than the sum of the products of the separately used inputs' (p. 794). Presumably, not all fund-input owners will have the same 'withdrawal power', i.e. not all of them may affect the execution of the production process in the same degree by withdrawing the service of their input. For example, in a modern factory the owner of machinery will normally have a much greater 'withdrawal power' than any individual worker. The 'central party' will generally be the fund-input owner who has higher withdrawal power. This power will depend in turn on the evolution of technology. (The discovery of large steam-power engines, for instance, was an important prerequisite for the widespread introduction of the pattern of firm-ownership based on identification of the 'central party' with the owner of the engine and other types of physical equipment.) In Alchian and Demsetz's thesis, the changing pattern of firm-ownership reflects the changes in the contractual arrangements among individuals within the firm, which are in turn affected by the changes in the *technical* relationships among the various fund-input categories.

A similar attention to the evolution of technology may also be found in the theory of 'contestable markets' formulated by William Baumol and his school (see Baumol, Panzar, and Willig, 1982). Here, it is pointed out that 'asset specificity' is essential in determining whether a certain activity is 'contestable' or not—i.e. whether or not it is vulnerable to potential attack by 'competitors'. The greater the amount of 'sunk investment' in an activity, the greater will be the need for that activity to be 'sheltered' from market forces. In the absence of this 'protection', the amount of investment in that activity is likely to fall 'substantially short of its optimal level' (Baumol, 1986: 280). The degree of contestability of any given activity would be inversely related to the amount of fixed capital 'sunk' in the production process, unless fixed capital items can be easily switched from one use to another. If fixed capital is relatively untransferable, the degree of contestability would depend on the minimum investment needed for the operation of that activity. In this case, contestability reflects minimum capacity constraints which in turn reflect technological indivisibilities.

The 'task–process' approach shares the attention to technological and institutional constraints characteristic of the transactions-cost, contract-relational and contestability analyses, but its view of the production process is different. Technology is described as a 'technical practice', i.e. as a set of tasks carried out at a given time in a given productive unit. The description of each technical practice is in terms of tasks and task networks rather than inputs and their combinations. The availability of certain inputs is a *necessary* condition for the performance of tasks and e.p.s, but there is not, in general, a one-to-one correspondence between technical practices and input combinations. For example, a given tool may generally be used in more than one practice; furthermore, one and the same practice may often be performed with different tool types (see section 4.2).

Another characteristic feature of the 'task–process' approach is that it allows for the study of the general principles governing productive organization, regardless of the 'agents' by whom that process is carried out. As a result, the production process may be initially studied without explicitly considering productive institutions. This allows for the formulation of an analytical framework independent of the level of aggregation of productive units. The same general principles may be applied to the establishment, the 'industry' or 'group', and the economic system as a whole: in each case, a certain network of tasks and e.p.s may be identified and the 'task–process' framework may be used. (We may note that it is immaterial, in the 'task–process' account of production, whether a given physical transfer of a physical object is paid for or not.) Productive institutions may be considered at a second stage of analysis. They are essential to determine how 'task–process' principles are applied in particular cases.

Our approach has considered the time-structure of production as an essential feature of the arrangement of tasks and processes. In particular, the sequencing of tasks and e.p.s is a critical factor determining the utilization pattern of workers and machines. There is clearly a connection between task–process theory and certain features of Austrian production theory (see also Skousen, 1990).

For example, Menger's approach in terms of unidirectional time draws attention to the sequencing of *fabrication stages* (see C. Menger, 1871; see also Mayer, 1925), and this is clearly a feature closely connected with our attention for the sequencing of *tasks* by which fabrication stages are executed.[8]

Other features of the Austrian (or Neo-Austrian) approach are the consideration of causal linkages associated with uni-directional time, so that the explanation of an event is generally found in some other event, or action, which precedes it in time (see Hicks, 1979). One remarkable implication of the Austrian approach is its attention to processes of *morphogenesis*, in which the sequencing of events is associated with the transformation of existing structures over time (see Schumpeter, 1912). (The latter feature is also prominent in contributions from Swedish economists such as Johan Åkerman (1932; 1944) and Erik Dahmén (1950; 1955).

Finally, some recent work in the Neo-Austrian tradition stemming from Hicks's *Capital and Time* (1973) has considered 'capital liquidity' (i.e. the liquidity of some general productive fund) as a critical feature in determining the flexibility of existing structures, thus making structural change easier (see Leijonhufvud, 1986; Amendola and Gaffard, 1988; Hicks, 1989: 116–20).

---

[8] The distinction between Menger's and Böhm-Bawerk's approaches is worth mentioning. As pointed out by Hicks, 'in Menger time is uni-directional, Menger's theory is an economics *in* time but Böhm's is an economics *of* time, in which time is no more than a mathematical parameter—a parameter of what we should now call capital-intensity' (1976: 139).

In the task–process approach, time is real rather than logical (this is a feature in common with Menger's formulation of Austrian theory). On the other hand, such an approach focuses upon tasks rather than fabrication stages. This implies that the production process is primarily considered as an arrangement of operations consistent with some final goal, rather than as a transformation leading from raw materials to finished products. In this connection, the task–process framework emphasizes the need to integrate the analysis of sequential linkages with that of the *mutual dependence* between different elements of the productive structure (an instance of 'contemporaneous causality', as identified in Hicks, 1979). Finally, the task–process view brings to the fore a conception of 'technical liquidity' which is related to the capital liquidity mentioned above but is more explicitly based upon the consideration of flexible arrangements of tasks and e.p.s.

10.3. EPILOGUE AND LINES OF FURTHER RESEARCH

In the last paragraph in the section above, it was pointed out that the 'task–process' framework may be used to investigate the operating characteristics of the production process independently of productive institutions. Institutions are absent in the primitive terms and axioms of 'task–process' theory.

Task–process theory may be interpreted in a number of different ways, according to the level of aggregation of productive units. For example, there are alternative interpretations, depending upon whether the productive unit is the establishment, the 'industry' or 'group', or the whole economic system. In each case the same basic principles concerning the operating characteristics of the production process apply, but a number of special issues emerge. This suggests that task–process theory may be expanded in different directions, according to the kind of productive unit under consideration.

In the case in which the productive unit is the individual establishment, task–process theory may be expanded by considering the institutional arrangements governing the scope and capacity of the establishment, such as the relationship between fund-input owners, the distribution of property rights in the various fund-input categories, and the social conventions governing fund-input utilization. These factors influence the 'versatility' of the establishment and its capacity, by determining the pattern of fund-input utilization (job-shop and straight-line) and other features of the production process such as the length of the working day. They also have considerable influence on the relationship between establishments, thus determining whether establishments are connected with one another through market or non-market methods of co-ordination.

In the case in which the productive unit is the 'industry' or 'group', task–process theory may be expanded by considering alternative criteria ensuring the mutual consistency of e.p.s within each 'industry' or 'group'. The simplest route to consistency is having a set of establishments that do not depend technologically on each other. In this case, there is an analogy with the in-parallel arrangement of e.p.s (see section 4.3.3) and mutual consistency is a trivial matter, since no production process is based on direct technological interdependence between establishments. However, an 'industry' or 'group' in which different establishment types specialize in different tasks is also a possibility. In this case, the complete process of the whole 'industry' or 'group' is the outcome of co-ordination between different establishments. This co-ordination may take different forms, according to whether mutual consistency is achieved through the market or through a system of 'physical obligations' operating outside the market. Marshall's 'industrial district' is an example of the former co-ordination pattern. The 'system of arts' linking medieval guilds of the same trade is an example of the latter pattern. In this case, the activities of each trade make up a vertically integrated sector in which the tasks leading to the same final commodity are co-ordinated with one another by means of purely physical arrangements. Such arrangements reflect technological interdependence. They are generally independent of demand fluctuations. For example, skinners are obliged by the regulations of each trade to purchase all skins supplied by butchers, and shoemakers all hides supplied by skinners. The market would operate with respect to final consumer goods, but not within the network of technologically related tasks (see Poni, 1989; 1991).

Each 'industry' or 'group' is either a set of identical e.p.s or a set of interdependent e.p.s. In the latter case, the relationship between tasks reflects the tempo of each task and the conditions for continuous fund-input utilization in the various establishments. It is also possible, however, to consider the relationship between different e.p.s regardless of the pattern of task-organization. In this case, the set of e.p.s delivering a single commodity would be described as an 'industry', and interdependence between e.p.s would take the form of a relationship between different industries. Industries would be related to one another in terms of input requirement and output deliveries, regardless of the links between technologically inter-dependent tasks belonging to the same or to different e.p. types. For example, the set of tasks forming the production process of a farm would be divided between different industries, whereas ident-ical e.p.s carried out in different industrial districts would be described as parts of the same industry. This view of the productive system stresses the 'material' interdependence between commod-ities rather than the operational linkages between tasks. As a result, two or more industries would be related to one another if the output of one is an input for the other. But e.p. types related to one another in the same production process would appear to be completely unrelated, if they deliver different commodities.

The description of the productive system as a system of industries is often based on the assumption that there is a one-to-one corres-pondence between industries and commodities (see Leontief, 1941; Sraffa, 1960: pt. i). This assumption derives quite naturally from the idea that the set of e.p.s delivering the same commodity would be an industry. However, situations in which the same commodity is produced by different e.p. types, or in which the same e.p. type delivers more than one commodity, is the rule rather than the exception in economic reality. Acknowledgement of this important fact has led to the formulation of theories in which interdependence between production processes is still described in terms of input–output relationships, but the one-to-one correspondence between industries and commodities is dropped. This has been done for two complementary reasons. On the one hand, it has been recognized that the same industry may deliver different commodities at the same time (see Sraffa, 1960: pt. ii; Stone, 1961; Matuszewski, 1965; Pasinetti, 1980). On the other hand, it has been noted that in certain cases a given commodity is simultaneously delivered by two or more processes (see Sraffa, 1960, pt. ii; Stone, 1961; Quadrio-Curzio, 1967; 1975; 1980; 1986; 1990; Quadrio-Curzio, Manara, and Faliva, 1992; Quadrio-Curzio and Pellizzari, 1991). Either approach presupposes a concept of 'industry' that is considerably wider than the traditional one, for the 'industry' may no longer be defined in terms of a homogeneous output, and some degree of 'technical homogeneity' emerges as the essential element in industry description. (A concept of productive sector more comprehensive than the traditional concept of 'industry' is also adopted in models based upon the vertical integration of productive activities; see Pasinetti, 1973; 1981; 1993; and Scazzieri, 1990*a*). The above contributions suggest a possible integration with the task–process approach, in which technological interdependence is independent of the 'commodity specification' of the e.p.s. There is here a possible linkage with contributions considering the technological specificity of industries or sectors, quite independently of the commodities produced (see Kaldor, 1967; Negishi, 1985). In this connection, another possible line of research may be mentioned: the relationship between the analytical structure of multi-sectoral theory and the time-structure of production. (Important insights in this respect are due to Morishima, 1989: 249–51; 1991. Morishima's formulation is based upon the identification of distinct commodities corresponding to separate fabrication stages.) But there is another element of the 'industry approach' that cannot be reduced to the task–process view. This is the stress on material linkages between input and output flows, and on the necessary conditions for the mutual compatibility of these flows. (These are the standard 'balance' conditions expressed in the matrix of input–output coefficients.) Given the set of technical practices and the associated input–output flows, these conditions may be formulated independently of the task–process structure of productive activity. However, consideration of this structure is still essential in order to examine the dynamic processes in the course of which the input–output structure is transformed, and in order to assess the feasibility of these processes (see also Yan and Ames, 1965).

The theoretical framework of this volume is connected to important fields of research that are not directly considered in the present investigation. One is the explicit analysis of the relationship between technical and social division of labour. As pointed out above, the technical subdivision of a job into constituent tasks does not always coincide with the specialization of workers (or workers' groups) into particular tasks. As a result, a relatively complex division of labour at the social level is compatible with a primitive division of jobs into tasks (or with the lack of such a division). A case in point would be a situation in which there is a developed differentiation among activities producing finished goods, whereas there is no differentiation among the tasks required to produce each particular good. Symmetrically, a complex pattern of task-differentiation at the technical level may be compatible with a simple pattern of division of labour at the social level. An example would be an economic system in which product differentiation is limited but task-differentiation within each activity is well developed. Here, detailed investigation of the task–process network suggests the view of social division of labour as the pattern according to which a given set of labour capabilities is split into subsets characterized by relatively homogeneous classes of task-assignments. In this case, the change from one task–process network to another could lead to a considerable reshuffling of the 'pooling system' of labour capabilities, regardless even of the assignment of particular products to certain workers' groups. (For example, it may happen that spinning comes to be associated with dyeing and separated from weaving, even if the dye and the yarn continue to be separately produced.) More generally, the present theoretical framework suggests a symmetry between the social division of labour as a 'pooling system' of capabilities and the way in which the technical capabilities of machines (or other active factors) may be pooled together or separated from each other. For a change in the task–process organization of production may bring about a regrouping of 'mechanical capabilities' as well as of labour capabilities. Technical change may thus lead to an important transformation within the 'network' of labour capabilities or mechanical capabilities, and in the way in which the different groups of capabilities are related to each other.

Another theme suggested by the present analysis is connected with the theory of capital accumulation. It has traditionally been argued that, from a historical point of view, division of labour cannot be introduced to any significant degree unless a certain capital stock is previously accumulated (see Smith, 1976 [1776]: ii; see also C. Menger, 1888). The reason given for this is that, unless the individual producer is granted the availability of necessary means of subsistence, it would be impossible for him to devote most of his work to the pursuit of a specialized activity.

In this connection, the distinction between the technical division of a job and the partition of the capability space into subsets of *operationally* independent factors (such as labour, machine tools, or enzymes)[9] suggests that a change in the task–process network does not always require the transformation of existing capabilities (as is shown in certain instances of flexible productive arrangement). In other words, a particular job may be split into a greater number of specific tasks, even if there is no increase in the dimension of each capability subset (see also Scazzieri, 1992*a*; 1992*b*).

In this connection, the traditional Smithian argument may be reformulated: under certain institutional arrangements, it is indeed possible to introduce a more detailed splitting of jobs into tasks even if 'broad productive factors' (on this concept, see G. Antonelli, 1990; 1992) do not become more specialized. As a result, it is not necessary to provide for greater capital stocks to make the independent working of specialized factors possible. On the other hand, the formation of *new* semi-independent subsets of productive capabilities may require the availability of a larger capital stock, which would ultimately be a *commodity stock*, even if it takes the form of financial capital. This suggests that the accumulation of capital is relatively independent of changes that influence primarily the task–process network but not the capability structure of the economic system.

A third important field of research, connected with the present contribution but not directly taken up here, is the structural dynamics of the economic system.

The framework of this volume suggests that there may be independent sources of structural change (i.e. of change in the behavioural characteristics of the system and in the composition of the economy) due to the transformation of tasks and processes, capabilities, or materials. In fact, the possibility of detecting patterns of *relative* invariance is an essential prerequisite in the identification of determinate paths of *structural* dynamics (see Landesmann and Scazzieri, 1990: 95–8; Scazzieri, 1990*b*; Arthur, Landesmann, and Scazzieri, 1991).

The relative degree of resilience of the above three components of a production system may thus significantly influence the pattern of invariance from which new structures could emerge in the course of time.

---

[9] This means that, in principle, the factors of each group may be able to operate (i.e. to carry out a certain transformation of the material in process) independently of the factors of the other groups, even if there are factors that may be 'acted upon' by other factors of the same group (such as labour in the educational process).

References

ABRUZZI, A. (1965). 'The Production Process: Operating Characteristics', *Management Science*, 11(6) (Apr.): B98–B118.

ADDIS, W. (1983). 'A New Approach to the History of Structural Engineering', in N. Smith (ed.), *History of Technology*, 8th annual vol., London, Mansell 1–13.

ÅKERMAN, J. (1932). *Economic Progress and Economic Crises*, London, Macmillan.

—— (1936). *Ekonomisk Kausalitet*, Lund, C. W. K. Gleerup.

—— (1940). 'The Meaning of Induction in Social Science', *Theoria*, 6: 171–90.

—— (1942). 'Ekonomisk Kalkyl och Kausanalys', *Ekonomisk Tidskrift* (English translation, 'Economic Plans and Causal Analysis', *International Economic Papers*, 4 1954).

—— (1944). *Ekonomisk Teori*, i–ii, Lund, C. W. K. Gleerup (French translation of vol. ii, *Structures et cycles économiques*, Paris, PUF, 1955).

ALCHIAN, A. A. (1963). 'Reliability of Progress Curves in Airframe Production', *Econometrica*, 31 (Oct.): 679–93.

—— and DEMSETZ, H. (1972). 'Production, Information Costs, and Economic Organization', *American Economic Review*, 62(5) (Dec.): 777–95.

ALLAIS, M. (1981). *La Théorie générale des surplus*, Cahiers de l'ISMEA, ser. EM, Nos. 8–9, Paris.

—— (1986). 'The Concepts of Surplus and Loss and the Reformulation of the Theories of Stable General Equilibrium and Maximum Efficiency', in M. Baranzini and R. Scazzieri (eds.), *Foundations of Economics: Structures of Inquiry and Economic Theory*, Oxford, Basil Blackwell, 135–74.

AMENDOLA, M., and GAFFARD, J.-L. (1988). *The Innovative Choice: An Economic Analysis of the Dynamics of Technology*, Oxford, Basil Blackwell.

AMES, E., and ROSENBERG, N. (1967). 'The Progressive Division and Specialization of Industries', in *Purdue Faculty Papers in Economic History, 1956–66*, Homewood, Ill., R. D. Irwin, 345–62.

AMPÈRE, A.-M. (1834). *Essai sur la philosophie des sciences*, Paris, Bachelier.

AMSDEN, A. H. (1977). 'The Division of Labour Is Limited by the *Type* of Market: The Case of the Taiwanese Machine Tool Industry', *World Development*, 5(3): 217–33.

—— (1983) ' "De-Skilling", Skilled Commodities, and the NIC's Emerging Competitive Advantage', *American Economic Review* (May), Papers and Proceedings, 73(2): 333–7.

—— (1985). 'The Division of Labour Is Limited by the Rate of Growth of the Market: The Taiwan Machine Tool Industry in the 1970s', *Cambridge Journal of Economics*, 9: 271–84.

ANDERSON, B. L. (ed.) (1974). *Capital Accumulation in the Industrial Revolution*, London, J. M. Dent; Totowa, NJ Rowman and Littlefield.

ANTONELLI, E. (1910). 'Note sur la loi du rendement non proportionnel', *Revue d'économie politique*, 24 (July): 532–45.

ANTONELLI, G. (1990). 'Lavoro, tecnologia, ambiente nella dinamica economica strutturale', in A. Quadrio-Curzio and R. Scazzieri (eds.), *Dinamica economica strutturale*, Bologna, Il Mulino, 183–202.

—— (1992). 'Technological Change and Broad Production Factors', in G. Antonelli and N. De Liso (eds.), *Economic Analysis, Structural Change and Technical Progress*, London, Macmillan.

ARROW, K. J. (1962). 'The Economic Implications of Learning by Doing', *Review of Economic Studies*, 29 (June) 155–73.

ARTHUR, B., LANDESMANN, M., and SCAZZIERI, R. (1991). 'Dynamics and Structures', *Structural Change and Economic Dynamics*, 2(1): 1–7.

BABBAGE, C. (1835). *On the Economy of Machinery and Manufactures*, 4th ed., London, Charles Knight.

BAKSHI, M. S. and ARORA, S. R. (1969). 'The Sequencing Problem', *Management Science*, 16(4) (Dec.) B247–63.

BALDONE, S. (1989). 'Analisi interindustriale e mutamento tecnico', in S. Zamagni (ed.), *Le teorie economiche della produzione*, Bologna, Il Mulino, 93–125.

—— (1990). 'Produzione e progresso tecnico', in R. Scazzieri (ed.), *Guide bibliografiche: Economia*, with an introduction by C. D'Adda, Milan, Garzanti, 59–91.

—— (1992). 'Vertical Integration, the Temporal Structure of Production Processes, and Transition between Techniques', in M. Landesmann and R. Scazzieri (eds.), *Production and Economic Dynamics*, Cambridge.

BARANZINI, M. (1991). *A Theory of Wealth, Accumulation, and Distribution*, Oxford, Clarendon Press.

—— and SCAZZIERI, R. (1986). 'Knowledge in Economics: A Framework', in M. Baranzini and R. Scazzieri (eds.), *Foundations of Economics: Structures of Inquiry and Economic Theory*, Oxford, Basil Blackwell, 1–87.

—— (1990). 'Economic Structure: Analytical Perspectives', in Baranzini and Scazzieri (1990): 227–333.

—— (eds.) (1990). *The Economic Theory of Structure and Change*, Cambridge, Cambridge University Press.

BARBIROLI, G. (1991). *Le dinamiche della tecnologia: Misure, analisi, modelli*, Rome, Bulzoni.

BASALLA, G. (1988). *The Evolution of Technology*, Cambridge, Cambridge University Press.

BAUMOL, W. J. (1986). 'Williamson's *The Economic Institutions of Capitalism*', *Rand Journal of Economics*, 17(2) (summer): 279–86.

—— PANZAR, J. C., AND WILLIG, R. D. (1982). *Contestable Markets and the Theory of Industrial Structure*, New York, Harcourt Brace Jovanovich.

BECATTINI, G. (1962). *Il concetto d'industria e la teoria del valore*, Turin, Boringhieri.

—— (1987). 'Internal Economies', in J. Eatwell, M. Milgate, and P. Newman (eds.), *The New Palgrave: A Dictionary of Economics*, London, Macmillan, ii. 889–91.

BECCARIA, C. (1804). *Elementi di economia pubblica* (MS 1771–2), in P. Custodi (ed.), *Scrittori classici italiani di economia politica*, xi and xii, Milan, Destefanis.

BECKETT, T. M. (1977). 'Problems of size and efficiency in industry today', *Royal Society of Arts Journal*, 135(5254): 624–36.

BENVENUTI, G. (1988). 'Tecnologia, mansioni, reticoli: un contributo alla teoria dei processi produttivi', *L'Industria* (Apr.–June): 265–94.

BESSANT, J., and HAYWOOD, B. (1986). 'Flexibility in Manufacturing Systems', *Omega: The International Journal of Management Science*, 14(6): 465–73.

—— and SENKER, P. (1986). 'Societal Implications of New Manufacturing Technology', in N. Kemp *et al.*, *The Human Side of New Manufacturing Technology*, Chichester, John Wiley.

BETANCOURT, R. (1986). 'A Generalization of Modern Production Theory', *Applied Economics*, 18: 915–28.

—— and CLAGUE, C. (1981). *Capital Utilization: A Theoretical and Empirical Analysis*, Cambridge, Cambridge University Press.

BIANCHI, P. (1984). *Divisione del lavoro e ristrutturazione industriale*, Bologna, Il Mulino.

BIUCCHI, B. M. (1973). 'The Industrial Revolution in Switzerland', in C. M. Cipolla (ed.), *The Fontana Economic History of Europe*, iv: *The Emergence of Industrial Societies, pt. 2*, Glasgow, Fontana/Collins, 627–55.

BLACK, J. T. (1987). 'Cellular Manufacturing Systems' (1st edn. 1983), in C. H. Voss, *Just-in-Time Manufacture*, Bedford, IFS Publications; Berlin, Springer, 27–49.

BOISGUILLEBERT, P. DE (1707). *Factum de la France*, Paris.

BÖHM–BAWERK, E. VON (1889). *Positive Theorie des Kapitales*, Innsbruck, Wagner (translated as *The Positive Theory of Capital*, London, Macmillan, 1981).

BRITTON, K. (1951). 'Mr. Urmson on Grading', *Mind*, 60 (Oct.), pp. 526–9.

BRUCH, M. A. (1983). 'Technological Heterogeneity, Scale Efficiency, and Plant Size: Micro-estimates for the West Malaysian Manufacturing Industry', *Developing Economies*, 21(3): 267–77.

BRUNO, M., BURMEISTER, E., and SHESHINSKI, E. (1966). 'The Nature and Implications of the Reswitching of Techniques', *Quarterly Journal of Economics*, 80(4) (Nov.): 526–53.

BRYTON, B. (1954). 'Balancing of a Continuous Production Line', thesis, Northwestern University.

BÜCHER, C. (1968). *Industrial Evolution* (1st edn. 1893) (English translation from the 3rd German ed. by S. Morley Wickett first published 1901) New York, Augustus M. Kelley.

BULLOCK, C. J. (1902). 'The Variation of Productive Forces', *Quarterly Journal of Economics*, 16: 467–513.

BUZACOTT, J. A. (ed.) (1982). *Scale in Production Systems*, Oxford, Pergamon.

BYÉ, M. (1928). *Les lois des rendements non proportionnels*, Paris, Sirey.

CANNAN, E. (1929). *A Review of Economic Theory*, London, P. S. King.

CARLSON, S. (1956). *A Study on the Pure Theory of Production*, London, Kelley and Millman.

CARR, M. (1981). *Developing Small-Scale Industries in India—An Integrated Approach: The Experience of the Birla Institute of Technology's Small Industry Scheme*, London, Intermediate Technology Publications.

CARVER, T. N. (1904). *The Distribution of Wealth*, London, Macmillan.

CASTI, J. and KARLQVIST, A. (eds.) (1989). *Newton to Aristotle: Toward a Theory of Models for Living Systems*, Boston, Birkhäuser.

CASTIGLIANO, A. (1879–80). *Théorie de l'équilibre des systèmes élastiques et ses applications*, Turin, Negro.

CAZZOLA, F. (1988). 'La pluriactivité dans les campagnes italiennes: problèmes d'interprétation', in G. Garrier and R. Hubscher (eds.), *Entre faucilles et marteaux, pluriactivité et stratégies paysannes*, Lyon, Presses Universitaires de Lyon; Paris, Maison des Sciences de l'Homme, 19–31.

CHAKRAVARTY, S. (1987). *Development Planning: The Indian Experience*, Oxford, Clarendon Press.

CHANDLER, A. D., JR. (1977). *The Visible Hand: The Managerial Revolution in American Business*, Cambridge, Mass., Belknap Press.

—— (1990). *Scale and Scope*, Cambridge, Mass., Belknap Press.

CHARLTON, T. M. (1982). *A History of Theory of Structures in the Nineteenth Century*, Cambridge, Cambridge University Press.

CHAYANOV, A. V. (1966). *The Theory of Peasant Economy* (1st edn. 1925), Homewood, Ill., R. D. Irwin.

CHENERY, H. B. (1949). 'Engineering Production Functions', *Quarterly Journal of Economics*, 63: 507–31.

CHERNYSHEVSKIJ, N. G. (1886). 'Lavoro e capitale considerati come elementi della produzione', in *Biblioteca dell'Economista*, 3rd ser., Turin, Unione tipografico–editrice torinese, vol. x, tome 9, pt. ii, 814–903 (Italian translation of the article 'Trud i Kapital kak elementi proisvodstva', *Sovremennik* (St Petersburg), n.s., 82(8): (Aug.): 209–22 of the supplement).

CHILD, J. (1693). *A New Discourse of Trade*, London.

CIPOLLA, C. M. (1952). 'The Decline of Italy: The Case of a Fully Matured Economy', *Economic History Review*, 2nd ser., 5(2): 178–87.

CLARK, J. B. (1899). *The Distribution of Wealth*, New York, Macmillan.

COASE, R. H. (1937). 'The Nature of the Firm', *Economica*, n.s., 4(16) (Nov.): 386–405.

COHENDET, P., LEDOUX, M. J., and ZUSKOVITCH, E. (eds.) (1988). *New Advanced Materials: Economic Dynamics and European Strategy*, Berlin, Springer.

COLEMAN, D. C. (1959). 'Technology and Economic History, 1500–1750', *Economic History Review*, 2nd ser., 11(3), (Apr.): 506–14.

CORTES, M. (1987). *Success in Small and Medium-Scale Enterprises: The Evidence from Colombia*, New York, Oxford University Press.

CROUZET, F. (ed.) (1972). *Capital Formation in the Industrial Revolution*, London, Methuen.

CRUICKSHANKS, A. B., DRESCHER, R. D., and GRAVES, S. C. (1984). 'A Study of Production Smoothing in a Job Shop Environment', *Management Science*, 30(3) (Mar.): 368–80.

DAHMÉN, E. (1950). *Svensk Industriell Företagverksamhet: Kausanalys av den industriella utvecklingen 1919–1939*, Lund, Swedish Industrial Institute for Economic and Social Research (IUI).

—— (1955). 'Technology, Innovation and International Industrial Transformation', in L. H. Dupriez (ed.), *Economic Progress: Papers and Proceedings of a Round Table held by the International Economic Association*, Louvain, Institut de Recherches Économiques et Sociales, 293–306.

DANØ, S. (1966). *Industrial Production Models: A Theoretical Study*, Vienna, Springer.

DAVID, P. (1975). *Technical Choice, Innovation and Economic Growth: Essays on American and British Experience in the Nineteenth Century*, Cambridge, Cambridge University Press.

DEANE, P. (1967) *The First Industrial Revolution*, 2nd ed., Cambridge, Cambridge University Press.

DEBREU, G. (1959). *Theory of Value: An Axiomatic Analysis of Economic Equilibrium*, New York, John Wiley.

DELEERSNYDER, J.-L., HODGSON, T. J., MULLER, H., and O'GRADY, P. J. (1989). 'Kanban Controlled Pull Systems: An Analytic Approach', *Management Science*, 35(9) (Sep.): 1079–91.

DEMPSTER, M. A. H., FISHER, M. L., JANSEN, L., LAGEWEG, B. J., LENSTRA, J. K., and RINNOOY KAN, A. H. G. (1981). 'Analytical Evaluation of Hierarchical Planning Systems', *Operations Research*, 29(4): 707–16.

DERRY, T. K., and WILLIAMS, T. I. (1982). *A Short History of Technology: From the Earliest Times to AD 1900*, Oxford, Oxford University Press.

DI NUNZIO, G. (1988). 'Mansioni produttive e fattori fondo: un'analisi di teoria della produzione' dissertation, Faculty of Political Sciences, Bologna University.

DURBIN, P. T. (1990). *Broad and Narrow Interpretations of Philosophy of Technology*, Dordrecht, Kluwer Academic.

EDGEWORTH, F. Y. (1911). 'Contributions to the Theory of Railway Rates', s. 1, *Economic Journal*, 12 (Sep. and Dec.): 346–70, 551–71.

EILON, S. (1979). 'A Question of Size', *Omega: The International Journal of Management Science*, 7(1): 1–7.

ENCYCLOPÉDIE (1751). *Encyclopédie ou Dictionnaire raisonné des Sciences, des Arts et des Métiers*, i, Paris, Briasson.

ENOS, J. L. (1962). *Petroleum Progress and Profits: A History of Process Innovation*, Cambridge, Mass., MIT Press.

ENRIQUES, F. (1914). *Problems of Science* (1st edn. 1906) Chicago, Open Court.

ESPINAS, A. (1897). *Étude Sociologique: Les origines de la Technologie*, Paris, Félix Alcan.

EVANS, F. T. (1982). 'Wood Since the Industrial Revolution: a Strategic Retreat', in A. R. Hall and N. Smith (eds.) *History and Technology*, 7th annual vol., London, Mansell, 37–55.

FÄRE, R. (1988). *Fundamentals of Production Theory* (Lecture Notes in Economics and Mathematical Systems, No. 311), Berlin, Springer.

FALER, P. G. (1981). *Mechanics and Manufacturers in the Early Industrial Revolution: Lynn, Massachusetts, 1780–1860*, Albany, NY, State University of New York Press.

FERRARA, F. (1860). Introduction to vol. ii, 2nd ser. of *Biblioteca dell'Economista*, Turin, Unione tipografico–editrice torinese, pp. v–lxxii.

FISHER, I. (1906). *The Nature of Capital and Income*, New York, Macmillan.

FLORENCE, P. S. (1961). *The Logic of British and American Industry* (1st edn. 1953), London, Routledge and Kegan Paul.

FRANK, C. R. (1969). *Production Theory and Indivisible Commodities*, Princeton, NJ, Princeton University Press.

FRISCH, R. (1965). *Theory of Production* (trans. from Norwegian by R. I. Christophersen), Dordrecht, Riedel; Chicago, Rand McNally.

FUNTOWICZ, S. O., and RAVETZ, J. R. (1990). *Uncertainty and Quality in Science for Policy*, Dordrecht, Kluwer Academic.

GAREGNANI, P. (1966). 'Switching of Techniques', *Quarterly Journal of Economics*, 80(4) (Nov.): 554–67.

GEORGESCU-ROEGEN, N. (1969). *Process in Farming versus Process in Manufacturing: A Problem of Balanced Development*, in G. U. Papi and C. Nunn (eds.), *Economic Problems of Agriculture in Industrial Societies*, New York, St Martin's Press, 497–528.

—— (1970). 'The Economics of Production', *American Economic Review*, 60 (May): 1–9.

—— (1971). *The Entropy Law and the Economic Process*, Cambridge, Mass., Harvard University Press.

—— (1972). 'Process Analysis and the Neoclassical Theory of Production', *American Journal of Agricultural Economics*, 54 (May): 279–94.

—— (1976). 'Measure, Quality and Optimum Scale', in N. Georgescu-

Roegen, *Energy and Economic Myths. Institutional and Analytical Economic Essays*, New York, Pergamon Press, 271–96 (originally published in C. R. Rao (ed.), *Essays on Econometrics and Planning Presented to Professor P. C. Mahalanobis on his 70th Birthday*, Oxford, Pergamon Press, 1964, 231–56).

—— (1986). 'Man and Production', in M. Baranzini and R. Scazzieri (eds.), *Foundations of Economics. Structures of Inquiry and Economic Theory*, Oxford, Basil Blackwell, 247–80.

—— (1988). 'The Interplay between Institutional and Material Factors: the Problem and its Status', in J. A. Kregel, E. Matzner, and A. Roncaglia (eds.), *Barriers to Full Employment*, London, Macmillan, 297–326.

—— (1990). 'Production Process and Dynamic Economics', in M. Baranzini and R. Scazzieri (eds.), *The Economic Theory of Structure and Change*, Cambridge, Cambridge University Press, 198–226.

GIBBONS, M. (1983). 'Inside the Black Box—Technology and Economics: Book Review', *Chemistry and Industry*, 19: 751.

GILLE, B. (1966). *The Renaissance Engineers*, London, Lund Humphries.

GIMPEL, J. (1977). *The Medieval Machine: The Industrial Revolution of the Middle Ages*, Harmondsworth, Penguin.

GIOJA, M. (1815–17). *Nuovo prospetto delle scienze economiche*, Milan, G. Pirotta.

—— (1819). *Sulle manifatture nazionali e tariffe daziarie*, Milan, G. Pirotta.

GOLD, B. (1981). 'Changing Perspectives on Size, Scale and Returns: an Interpretative Survey', *Journal of Economic Literature*, 19: 5–33.

GOODSTEIN, L. P., ANDERSEN, H. B., and OLSEN, S. E. (eds.) (1988). *Tasks, Errors and Mental Models: A Festschrift to celebrate the 60th Birthday of Professor J. Rasmussen*, London, Taylor and Francis.

GOTTL-OTTLILIENFELD, O. (1923). 'Wirtschaft und Technik', in *Grundriss der Sozialökonomik*, s. ii, pt. ii, Tübingen, Mohr.

GRAZIANI, A. (1891). *Studi sulla teoria economica delle macchine*, Turin, Bocca.

GROENEWEGEN, P. (1987). 'Division of Labour', in J. Eatwell, M. Milgate, and P. Newman (eds.), *The New Palgrave: A Dictionary of Economics*, London, Macmillan, i. 901–7.

GROOVER, M. P. (1987). *Automation, Production Systems, and Computer Integrated Manufacturing*, Englewood Cliffs, NJ, Prentice-Hall.

HABAKKUK, H. J. (1962). *American and British Technology in the Nineteenth Century: The Search for Labour-Saving Inventions*, Cambridge, Cambridge University Press.

HACKMAN, S. T., and LEACHMAN, R. C. (1989). 'A General Framework for Modeling Production', *Management Science*, 35(4), (Apr.): 478–95.

HARPER, J. D. (1981). *Small Scale Foundries for Developing Countries: A Guide to Process Selection*, London, Intermediate Technology Publications.

HARRÉ, R., and SECORD, P. F. (1972). *The Explanation of Social Behaviour*, Oxford, Basil Blackwell.

HAYEK, F. A. von (1941). *The Pure Theory of Capital*, London, Routledge.

HAZLEWOOD, A. D., and LIVINGSTONE, I. (1978). *Complementarity and Competitiveness of Large and Small Scale Irrigated Farming: A Tanzanian Example*, Norwich, University of East Anglia, School of Development Studies.

HEINER, R. A. (1983). 'The Origin of Predictable Behaviour', *American Economic Review*, 83(4) (Sept.): 560–95.

HENNINGS, K. H. (1986). 'The Exchange Paradigm and the Theory of Production and Distribution', in M. Baranzini and R. Scazzieri (eds.), *Foundations of Economics: Structures of Inquiry and Economic Theory*, Oxford, Basil Blackwell, 221–43.

HERMANN, F. B. W. VON (1870), *Staatswirthschaftliche Untersuchungen* (1st edn. 1832), Munich, E. A. Fleischmann.

HICKS, J. R. (1939). *Value and Capital: An Inquiry into Some Fundamental Principles of Economic Theory*, Oxford, Clarendon Press.

—— (1959). *Essays in World Economics*, Oxford, Clarendon Press.

—— (1969). *A Theory of Economic History*, Oxford, Clarendon Press.

—— (1973). *Capital and Time: A Neo–Austrian Theory*, Oxford, Clarendon Press.

—— (1976)., 'Some Questions of Time in Economics', in A. M. Tang, F. M. Westfield, and J. S. Worley (eds.), *Evolution, Welfare and Time in Economics: Essays in Honor of Nicholas Georgescu-Roegen*, Lexington, Mass., Lexington Books, 135–51.

—— (1977). 'An Addendum to *Capital and Time*', in J. Hicks, *Economic Perspectives: Further Essays on Money and Growth*, Oxford, Clarendon Press, 190–5.

—— (1979). *Causality in Economics*, Oxford, Basil Blackwell.

—— (1989). *A Market Theory of Money*, Oxford, Clarendon Press.

HOBBES, T. (1651). *Leviathan, or the Matter, Forme, & Power of a Common–wealth, ecclesiasticall and civill*, London, A. Crooke.

HORN, J.-E. (1867). *L'Économie politique avant les Physiocrates*, Paris, Guillaumin.

HUME, D. (1752). *Political Discourses*, Edinburgh, printed by R. Fleming for A. Kincaid and A. Donaldson.

—— (1987). *Essays: Moral, Political and Literary*, ed. and with foreword, notes, and glossary by E. F. Miller, Indianapolis, Liberty Classics.

INDELLI, P. (1989). 'The Latent Choice: When It Is Worth Postponing the Decision', *Metroeconomica*, 40(1–2): 17–42.

IPPOLITO, R. A. (1977). 'The Division of Labor in the Firm', *Economic Inquiry*, 15(1) (Jan.): 469–92.

JAFFÉ, W. (1983). *Essays on Walras*, ed. D. A. Walker, Cambridge, Cambridge University Press.

JANNACCONE, P. (1904). 'Il costo di produzione', in *Biblioteca dell'Economista*, 4th ser., Turin, Unione tipografico-editrice torinese, vol. iv, pt. ii, [1]–367.

JEWKES, J. (1952). 'The Size of the Factory', *Economic Journal*, 62 (June): 237–52.

JONES, R. A., and OSTROY, J. M. (1984). 'Flexibility and Uncertainty', *Review of Economic Studies*, 51(1) (Jan.): 13–32.

KALDOR, N. (1966). *Causes of the Slow Rate of Economic Growth of the United Kingdom: An Inaugural Lecture*, Cambridge, Cambridge University Press.

—— (1967). *Strategic Factors in Economic Development*, Ithaca, NY, New York State School of Industrial and Labor Relations, Cornell University.

KALKUNTE, M. V., SARIN, G. C., and WILHELM, W. E. (1986). 'Flexible Manufacturing Systems: A Review of Modeling Approaches for Design, Justification and Operation', in A. Kusiak (ed.), *Flexible Manufacturing Systems: Methods and Studies*, Amsterdam, North-Holland, 3–25.

KAPLINSKY, R. (1981). 'Firm Size and Technical Change in a Dynamic Context', *Journal of Industrial Economics*, 32(1) (Sept.): 39–59.

KENNEDY, C. (1964). 'Induced Bias in Innovation and the Theory of Distribution', *Economic Journal*, 74 (Sept.): 541–7.

KILBRIDGE, M., and WESTER, L. (1962). 'A Review of Analytical Systems of Line Balancing', *Operations Research*, 10(5) (Sept.–Oct.): 626–38.

—— (1966). 'An Economic Model for the Division of Labour', *Management Science*, 12(6) (Feb.): B255–69.

KOCHEN, M. (1980). 'Coping with Complexity', *Omega: The International Journal of Management Science*, 8(1) 11–20.

KOHN, M. G., and SHAVELL, S. (1974). 'The Theory of Search', *Journal of Economic Theory*, 9(2) (Oct.): 93–123.

KOOPMANS, T. C. (1951). 'Analysis of Production as an Efficient Combination of Activities', in T. C. Koopmans (ed.), *Activity Analysis of Production and Allocation*, New York, Wiley, 33–97.

KOTARBIŃSKI, T. (1960). 'Concept of Action', *Journal of Philosophy*, 57: 215–22.

LANDESMANN, M. (1986). 'Conceptions of Technology and the Production Process', in M. Baranzini and R. Scazzieri (eds.), *Foundations of Economics: Structures of Inquiry and Economic Theory*, Oxford, Basil Blackwell, 281–310.

—— and SCAZZIERI, R. (1990). 'Specification of Structure and Economic Dynamics', in Baranzini and Scazzieri (1990: 95–121).

—— —— (1991*a*). *The Production Process: Description and Analysis*, Cambridge, Dept. of Applied Economics (SPES Research Memorandum).

—— —— (1991*b*). *Manufacturing Forms of Production Organization*, Cambridge, Dept. of Applied Economics (SPES Research Memorandum).

LAVINGTON, F. (1921). *The English Capital Market*, London, Methuen.

LEIJONHUFVUD, A. (1986). 'Capitalism and the Factory System', in R. N. Langlois (ed.), *Economics as a Process*, Cambridge, Cambridge University Press, 203–23.

LEONTIEF, W. (1941). *The Structure of the American Economy*, New York, Oxford University Press.

—— (1947). 'Introduction to a Theory of the Internal Structure of Functional Relationships', *Econometrica*, 15 (Oct.): 361–73.

LEPLAT, J. (1988). 'Task Complexity in Work Situations', in L. P. Goodstein, H. B. Andersen, and S. E. Olsen (eds.), *Tasks, Errors and Mental Models*, London, Taylor and Francis, 105–15.

LEROY-BEAULIEU, P. (1896). *Traité théorique et pratique d'économie politique*, Paris, Guillaumin.

LEVHARI, D., and SAMUELSON, P. A. (1966). 'The Nonswitching Theorem Is False', *Quarterly Journal of Economics*, 80(4) (Nov.): 518–19.

LILLEY, S. (1948). *Men, Machines and History: A Short History of Tools and Machines in Relation to Social Progress*, London, Cobbett Press.

LIOUKAS, S. K., and XEROKOSTAS, D. A. (1982). 'Size and Administrative Intensity in Organizational Divisions', *Management Science*, 28(8) (Aug.): 854–68.

LONGFIELD, M. (1834). *Lectures on Political Economy*, Dublin, R. Milliken and Son.

LUZZATTO, G. (1963). *Storia economica d'Italia: Il Medioevo*, Florence, Sansoni.

LÖWE, A. (1976). *The Path of Economic Growth*, Cambridge, Cambridge University Press.

MACNEIL, I. R. (1978). 'Contracts: Adjustment of Long-Term Economic Relations under Classical, Neoclassical and Relational Contract Law', *Northwestern University Law Review*, 72(6) (Jan.–Feb.): 854–905.

MALTHUS, T. R. (1815*a*). *The Grounds of an Opinion on the Policy of Restricting the Importation of Foreign Corn*, London, John Murray.

—— (1815*b*). *An Inquiry into the Nature and Progress of Rent*, London, John Murray.

MARGLIN, S. (1974). 'What Do Bosses Do? The Origins and Functions of Hierarchy in Capitalist Production', *Review of Radical Political Economics*, 6(2) (summer): 60–112.

MARRIS, R. (1964). *The Economics of Capital Utilization*, Cambridge, Cambridge University Press.

MARSCHAK, J., and NELSON, R. (1962). 'Flexibility, Uncertainty and Economic Theory', *Metroeconomica*, 14(1–3): 42–58.

—— and RADNER, R. (1972). *Economic Theory of Teams*, New Haven, Conn., Yale University Press.

MARSHALL, A. (1920). *Industry and Trade* (1st edn. 1919), London, Macmillan.

—— (1930). *The Pure Theory of Domestic Values* (printed for private circulation in 1879), in A. Marshall, *The Pure Theory of Foreign Trade: The Pure Theory of Domestic Values*, London, London School of Economics and Political Science.

—— (1961). *Principles of Economics* (1st edn. 1890; 2nd edn. 1891; 3rd edn. 1895; 6th edn. 1910), ed. C. W. Guillebaud, London, Macmillan.

—— and MARSHALL, M. (1879). *The Economics of Industry*, London, Macmillan.

MARX, K. (1983). *Capital: A Critique of Political Economy*, i: *The Process of Production of Capital* (1st edn. 1867), London, Lawrence and Wishart.

MATUSZEWSKI, T. I. (1965). *Un système rectangulaire d'échanges inter-industries à rendements non proportionnels*, paper presented at the 1st World Congress of the Econometric Society, Rome.

MAYER, H. (1925). *Produktion*, in *Handworterbuch der Staatswissenschaften*, ed. L. Elster, A. Weber, and F. Wilser, vi, Jena, Gustav Fischer, 1108–22.

MEACCI, F. (1986). 'John Hicks: A Review of Selected Works', *Atlantic Economic Journal*, 14(1) (Mar.): 127–30.

—— (1989). 'Different Divisions of Capital in Smith, Ricardo and Marx', *Atlantic Economic Journal*, 17(4) (Dec.): 13–21.

MENDELS, F. (1972). 'Protoindustrialization: The First Phase of the Indus-trialization Process', *Journal of Economic History*, 32: 241–61.

MENGER, C. (1871). *Grundsätze der Volkswirtschaftslehre*, Vienna, Braumüller.

—— (1888). 'Zur Theorie des Kapitales', *Conrads Jahrbücher für Nationalökonomie und Statistik*, 17: 1–49.

MENGER, K. (1954). 'The Logic of the Laws of Return: A Study in Metaeconomics', in O. Morgenstern (ed.), *Economic Activity Analysis*, New York, John Wiley–Chapman and Hall, 419–81.

MERMET, J. (ed.) (1981). *CAD in Medium Sized and Small Industries*, Amsterdam, North-Holland.

MILGROM. P., and ROBERTS, J. (1990). 'The Economics of Modern Manu-facturing: Technology, Strategy, and Organization', *American Economic Review*, 80(3) (June): 511–28.

MILL, J. S. (1848). *Principles of Political Economy with Some of their Application to Social Philosophy*, London, J. W. Parker; Boston, C. C. Little and J. Bourn.

—— (1965). *Principles of Political Economy, with Some of their Applications to Social Philosophy* (1st edn. 1848; 6th edn. 1865), ed. J. M. Robson, with introd. by R. F. McRae, Toronto, University of Toronto Press.

DE MONTBRIAL, T. (1974). *Essais d'économie parétienne*, Paris, Centre National de la Recherche Scientifique.

MORISHIMA, M. (1966). 'Refutation of the Nonswitching Theorem', *Quarterly Journal of Economics*, 80(4) (Nov.): 520–5.

—— (1989). *Ricardo's Economics*, Cambridge, Cambridge University Press.

—— (1991). *General Equilibrium à la Schumpeter*, mimeo (lectures given at the University of Bologna, Dept. of Economics, May 1991).

MORRONI, M. (1992). *Production Process and Technical Change: A Study of Industrial Technique and Production Unit Organization*, Cambridge, Cambridge University Press.

MUN, T. (1664). *England's Treasure by Forraign Trade*, London, printed by J. G. for Thomas Clark.

NEF, J. U. (1934). 'The Progress of Technology and the Growth of Large-Scale Industry in Great Britain, 1540–1640', *Economic History Review*, 5(1) (Oct.): 3–24.

—— (1950). *War and Human Progress: An Essay on the Rise of Industrial Civilization*, Cambridge, Mass., Harvard University Press.

—— (1964). *The Conquest of the Material World*, Chicago, University of Chicago Press.

NEGISHI, T. (1985). *Economic Theories in a Non-Walrasian Tradition*, Cambridge, Cambridge University Press.

NEUMANN, J. VON (1937). 'Über ein ökonomisches Gleichungssystem und eine Verallgemeinerung des Brouwerschen Fixpunktsatzes', *Ergebnisse eines Mathematischen Kolloquiums* (Vienna), 8: 73–83 (English translation: 'A Model of General Equilibrium', *Review of Economic Studies*, 9 (1945–6): 1–9).

NEWELL, A., and SIMON, H. (1972). *Human Problem Solving*, Englewood Cliffs, NJ, Prentice-Hall.

NORTH, D. C. (1991). *Institutions, Institutional Change and Economic Performance*, Cambridge, Cambridge University Press.

OAKEY, R., ROTHWELL, R., and COOPER, S. (1988). *The Management of Innovation in High-Technology Small Firms: Innovation and Regional Development in Britain and the United States*, London, Pinter.

O'SULLIVAN, P. (1987). *Economic Methodology and Freedom to Choose*, London, Allen and Unwin.

PAGANO, U. (1985). *Work and Welfare in Economic Theory*, Oxford, Basil Blackwell.

PANTALEONI, M. (1889). *Principii di economia pura*, Florence, Barbera.

PARETO, V. (1906). *Manuale di economia politica*, Milan, Società Editrice Libraria.

PARKER, W. N. (1971). 'Agriculture', in L. Davis *et al.*, *American Economic Growth*, New York, Harper and Row.

PASINETTI, L. L. (1966). 'Changes in the Rate of Profit and Switches of Techniques', *Quarterly Journal of Economics*, 80(4) (Nov.): 503–17.

—— (1973). 'The Notion of Vertical Integration in Economic Analysis', *Metroeconomica*, 25: 1–29.

—— (1977). *Lectures on the Theory of Production*, London, Macmillan.

—— (ed.) (1980). *Essays on the Theory of Joint Production*, London, Macmillan.

—— (1981). *Structural Change and Economic Growth: A Theoretical Essay on the Dynamics of the Wealth of Nations*, Cambridge, Cambridge University Press.

—— (1986). 'Theory of Value: a Source of Alternative Paradigms in Economic Analysis', in M. Baranzini and R. Scazzieri (eds.), *Foundations of Economics: Structures of Inquiry and Economic Theory*, Oxford, Basil Blackwell, 409–31.

—— (1988). 'Growing Subsystems, Vertically Hyper-integrated Sectors and the Labour Theory of Value', *Cambridge Journal of Economics*, 12: 125–34.

—— (1993). *Structural Economic Dynamics: A Theory of the Economic Consequences of Human Learning*, Cambridge, Cambridge University Press.

—— and SCAZZIERI, R. (1987). 'Capital Theory: Paradoxes', in J. Eatwell, M. Milgate, and P. Newman (eds.), *The New Palgrave: A Dictionary of Economics*, London, Macmillan, i. 363–8.

PENROSE, E. (1959). *The Theory of the Growth of the Firm*, Oxford, Basil Blackwell.

PERELMAN, M. (1981). 'Capital, Constant Capital and the Social Division of Labour', *Review of Radical Political Economics*, 13 (3): 43–53.

—— (1983). *Classical Political Economy: Primitive Accumulation and the Social Division of Labour*, Totowa, NJ, Rowman and Allanheld; London, Pinter.

PERRIN, J. (1990). 'The Inseparability of Technology and Work Organization', *History and Technology*, 7: 1–13.

PETTY, W. (1899). *Another essay in political arithmetick concerning the city of London* (1st edn. 1683), in H. Hull (ed.), *The Economic Writings of Sir William Petty*, ii, Cambridge, University Press, 451–78.

PHILLIPS, J. (1984). *Freedom in Machinery*, i: *Introducing Screw Theory*, Cambridge, Cambridge University Press.

POLIDORI, R., and ROMAGNOLI, A. (1987). 'Tecniche e processo produttivo: analisi a fondi e flussi della produzione nel settore agricolo', *Rivista di economia agraria*, 42(3): 335–72.

PONI, C. (1972). 'Archéologie de la fabrique: la diffusion des moulins à soie "alla bolognese" dans les États vénitiens du xvie au xviiie siécle', *Annales économies, sociétés, civilisation*, 27: 1475–96.

—— (1989). 'Norms and Disputes: The Shoemakers' Guild in Eighteenth Century Bologna', *Past and Present* (May): 80–108.

—— (1990). 'Per la storia del distretto industriale serico di Bologna (secoli xvi–xix)', *Quaderni storici*, n.s., 25(1) (Apr.): 93–167.

—— (1991). 'Local Market Rules and Practices: Three Guilds in the Same Line of Production in Early Modern Bologna', in S. Woolf (ed.),

Domestic Strategies: Work and Family in France and Italy 1600–1800, Cambridge, Cambridge University Press; Paris, Maison des Sciences de l'Homme, 69–101.

PRATTEN, C. (1991). *The Competitiveness of Small Firms*, Cambridge, Cambridge University Press.

QUADRIO-CURZIO, A. (1967). *Rendita e distribuzione in un modello economico plurisettoriale*, Milan, Giuffrè.

—— (1975). *Accumulazione del capitale e rendita*, Bologna, Il Mulino.

—— (1980). 'Rent, Income Distribution, Order of Efficiency and Rentability', in L. L. Pasinetti (ed.), *Essays on the Theory of Joint Production*, London, Macmillan, 218–40.

—— (1986). 'Technological Scarcity: An Essay on Production and Structural Change', in M. Baranzini and R. Scazzieri (eds.), *Foundations of Economics: Structures of Inquiry and Economic Theory*, Oxford, Basil Blackwell, 311–38.

—— (1987). 'Land Rent', in J. Eatwell, M. Milgate, and P. Newman (eds.), *The New Palgrave: A Dictionary of Economics*, London, Macmillan, iii. 118–21.

—— (1990). *Rent, Distribution and Economic Structure*, Milan, Istituto di Ricerca sulla Dinamica dei Sistemi Economici, Consiglio Nazionale delle Ricerche.

——, MANARA, C. F., and FALIVA, M. (1992). 'Production and Efficiency with Global Technologies', in M. Landesmann and R. Scazzieri (eds.), *Production and Economic Dynamics*, Cambridge.

—— and PELLIZZARI, F. (1991). 'Structural Rigidities and Dynamic Choice of Technologies', *Rivista internazionale di scienze economiche e commerciali*, 38(6–7) (June–July): 481–517.

QUESNAY, F. (1962*a*). Extract from 'Corn', in R. L. Meek (ed.), *The Economics of Physiocracy*, Cambridge, Mass., Harvard University Press, 72–87 (originally published in the article 'Grains' of the French *Encyclopédie*, 1757).

—— (1962*b*). Extracts from 'Taxation', in R. L. Meek (ed.), *The Economics of Physiocracy*, Cambridge, Mass., Harvard University Press, 102–7 (MS written in 1757 under the title 'Impôts'.)

RAE, J. (1834). *Statement of some New Principles on the subject of Political Economy, exposing the fallacies of the system of the free trade and of some other doctrines maintained in the Wealth of Nations*, Boston, Hilliard, Gray.

RAVETZ, J. R. (1971). *Scientific Knowledge and its Social Problems*, Oxford, Oxford University Press.

REULEAUX, F. (1875). *Theoretische Kinematik: Grundzüge einer theorie des maschinenwesens*, Braunschweig, F. Vieweg.

—— (1876). *Principi fondamentali di una teoria generale delle macchine*, Milan, Hoepli (Italian translation of *Theoretische Kinematik: Grundzüge keiner theorie des maschinenwesens*, Braunschweig, F. Vieweg, 1875).

RICARDO, D. (1815). *Essay on the Influence of a Low Price of Corn on the Profits of Stock*, London, John Murray.

—— (1817). *On the Principles of Political Economy and Taxation*, London, John Murray.

—— (1951). *The Works and Correspondence of David Ricardo*, i: *On the Principles of Political Economy and Taxation*, ed. P. Sraffa with the collaboration of M. H. Dobb, Cambridge, Cambridge University Press.

RICHARDSON, G. B. (1960). *Information and Investment*, Oxford, Oxford University Press.

ROBINSON, E. A. G. (1931). *The Structure of Competitive Industry*, London, Nisbet; Cambridge, University Press.

ROLT, L. T. C. (1986). *Tools for the Job: A History of Machine Tools to 1950*, rev. edn., London, HMSO.

ROMAGNOLI, A. (1992). 'Agricultural Forms of Production Organisation', in M. Landesmann and R. Scazzieri (eds.), *Production and Economic Dynamics*, Cambridge,

ROSENBERG, N. (1969*a*). 'The Direction of Technological Change: Inducement Mechanisms and Focusing Devices', *Economic Development and Cultural Change*, 18 (Oct.): 1–24.

—— (ed.) (1969*b*). *The American System of Manufactures*, Edinburgh, Edinburgh University Press.

—— (1972). *Technology and American Economic Growth*, New York, Harper and Row.

—— (1976). *Perspectives on Technology*, Cambridge, Cambridge University Press.

—— (1982). *Inside the Black Box: Technology and Economics*, Cambridge, Cambridge University Press.

ROTHWELL, R. (1984). 'The Role of Small Firms in the Emergence of New Technologies', *Omega: The International Journal of Management Science*, 12(1): 19–29.

—— and ZEGVELD, W. (1982). *Innovation and the Small and Medium Sized Firm*, London, Pinter.

RUSHING, W. A. (1968). 'Hardness of Material as Related to Division of Labor in Manufacturing Industry', *Administrative Science Quarterly*, 13 (Sept.): 229–45.

SABEL, C. F., and ZEITLIN, J. (1985). 'Historical Alternatives to Mass Production: Politics, Markets and Technology in Nineteenth-Century Industrialization', *Past and Present*, 108 (Aug.): 133–76.

SAHAL, D. (1981*a*). 'Alternative Conceptions of Technology', *Research Policy*, 10: 2–24.

—— (1981*b*). *Patterns of Technological Innovation*, London, Addison-Wesley.

SALTER, W. E. G. (1960). *Productivity and Technical Change*, Cambridge, University Press.

290 *References*

SAMUELSON, P. (1966). 'A Summing Up', *Quarterly Journal of Economics*, 80(4): (Nov.): 568–83.

SCAZZIERI, R. (1979). 'Scale and Efficiency in Classical and Post-Classical Theories of Production', M. Litt. thesis, University of Oxford.

—— (1981). *Efficienza produttiva e livelli di attività*, Bologna, Il Mulino.

—— (1982). 'Scale and Efficiency in Models of Production', in M. Baranzini (ed.), *Advances in Economic Theory*, Oxford, Basil Blackwell, 19–42.

—— (1983). 'The Production Process: General Characteristics and Taxonomy', *Rivista internazionale di scienze economiche e commerciali*, 30(7) (July), 597–611.

—— (1987a). 'Tasks, Processes and Technical Practices: A Contribution to the Theory of the Scale of Production', D. Phil. thesis, University of Oxford.

—— (1987b). 'Reswitching of Technique', in J. Eatwell, M. Milgate, and P. Newman (eds.), *The New Palgrave: A Dictionary of Economics*, London, Macmillan, iv. 162–4.

—— (1987c). 'Reverse Capital Deepening', in J. Eatwell, M. Milgate, and P. Newman (eds.), *The New Palgrave: A Dictionary of Economics*, London, Macmillan, iv. 172–3.

—— (1990a). 'Vertical Integration in Economic Theory', *Journal of Post-keynesian Economics*, 13(1) (fall): 20–46.

—— (1990b). 'Classical Traverse Analysis', *Dynamis* (Istituto di Ricerca sulla Dinamica dei Sistemi Economici, Consiglio Nazionale delle Ricerche (forthcoming in M. Landesmann and R. Rowthorn (eds.), *Structural Dynamics of Market Economies*, Oxford, Oxford University Press).

—— (1992a). 'Funds, Processes, and the Structure of Productive Activity', in P. O'Sullivan (ed.), *Beyond the Austrian School*, London, Macmillan.

—— (1992b). 'Actions, Processes and Economic Theory', in A. Heertje (ed.), *Making Modern Economics*, Oxford, Basil Blackwell.

—— (1992c). 'Economic Theory and Economic History: Perspectives on Hicksian Themes', in H. Hagemann and O. Hamouda (eds.), *The Legacy of Hicks*, London, Routledge.

SCHERER, F. M. (1965). 'Firm Size, Market Structure Opportunity, and the Output of Patented Inventions', *American Economic Review*, 55(5): 1097–125.

SCHNEIDER, E. (1934). *Theorie der Produktion*, Vienna, Springer.

—— (1942). *Teoria della produzione*, Milan, Ambrosiana.

SCHONBERGER, R. J. (1987). 'Just-in-Time: Replacing Complexity with Simplicity' (1st edn. 1984), in C. A. Voss (ed.), *Just-in-Time Manufacture*, Bedford, IFS Publications; Berlin, Springer, 3–13.

SCHUMACHER, E. F. (1973). *Small Is Beautiful*, London, Blond and Briggs.

SCHUMPETER, J. A. (1912). *Theorie der Wirtschaftlichen Entwicklung*, Leipzig, Duncker and Humblot (English edn., *The Theory of Economic Development: An Inquiry into Profits, Capital, Credit, Interest, and the*

Business Cycle, trans. R. Opie, Cambridge, Mass., Harvard University Press, 1934).

SCULLI, D. (1979). 'Dynamic Aspects of Line Balancing', *Omega: The International Journal of Management Science*, 7(6): 557–61.

SELLA, D. (1969). 'Industrial Production in 17th Century Italy: A Reappraisal', *Explorations in Entrepreneurial History*, 6(3): 235–53.

SEN, A. (1985). *Commodities and Capabilities*, Amsterdam, North–Holland.

SERRA, A. (1803). *Breve trattato delle cause che possono fare abbondare li regni d'oro et d'argento, dove non sono miniere* (1st edn. 1613), in P. Custodi (ed.), *Scrittori classici italiani di economia politica*, i, Milan, Destefanis, [1]–79.

SHEPHARD, R. W. (1953). *Cost and Production Functions*, Princeton, NJ, Princeton University Press.

—— (1970). 'Proof of the Law of Diminishing Returns', *Zeitschrift für Nationalökonomie*, 30(1–2): 7–34.

—— AL-AYAT, R., and LEACHMAN, R. C. (1977). 'Shipbuilding Production Function: An Example of a Dynamic Production Function', in H. Albach, E. Helmstädter, and R. Henn (eds.), *Quantitative Wirtschaftsforschung: Wilhelm Krelle zum 60. Geburtstag*, Tübingen, Mohr, 627–54.

SIDGWICK, H. (1883). *The Principles of Political Economy*, London, Macmillan.

SIMON, H. (1955). 'A Behavioural Model of Rational Choice', *Quarterly Journal of Economics*, 69(1) (Feb.): 99–118.

—— (1979). *Models of Thought*, New Haven, Conn., Yale University Press.

—— (1983). *Reason in Human Affairs*, Oxford, Basil Blackwell.

SKINNER, W. (1983) 'Operations Strategy: Past Perspectives, Seven New Initiatives and Future Strategies', *Operations Management Review* (summer): 4–10.

SKOUSEN, M. (1990). *The Structure of Production*, New York, New York University Press.

SMITH, A. (1976). *An Inquiry into the Nature and Causes of the Wealth of Nations* (1st edn. 1776), ed. R. H. Campbell, A. S. Skinner, and W. B. Todd, Oxford, Clarendon Press.

SOETE, L. (1979). 'Firm Size and Inventive Activity: The Evidence Reconsidered', *European Economic Review*, 12 (Oct.): 319–40.

SRAFFA, P. (1925). 'Sulle relazioni fra costo e quantità prodotta', *Annali di economia*, 2 (Nov.): 277–328.

—— (1926). 'The Laws of Returns under Competitive Conditions', *Economic Journal*, 36 (Dec.): 535–50.

—— (1960). *Production of Commodities by Means of Commodities*, Cambridge, Cambridge University Press.

STEUART, Sir J. (1966). *An Inquiry into the Principles of Political Economy* (1st edn. 1767), ed. and with an introd. by A. S. Skinner, Edinburgh, Oliver and Boyd.

STEWART, D. (1855/6). *Lectures on Political Economy*, vols. viii–ix of *The Collected Works of Dugald Stewart*, ed. Sir W. Hamilton, Edinburgh, T. Constable.

STIGLER, G. (1951). 'The Division of Labor is limited by the Extent of the Market', *Journal of Political Economy*, 59(3): 185–93.

STINCHCOMBE, A. L. (1959). 'Bureaucratic and Craft Administration of Production: A Comparative Study', *Administrative Science Quarterly*, 4(2) (Sept.): 168–87.

—— (1983). *Economic Sociology*, New York, Academic Press.

STONE, R. (1961). *Input–Output and National Accounts*, Paris, Organisation for Economic Co-operation and Development.

STORCH, H. (1823). *Cours d' économie politique ou exposition des principes qui déterminent la prospérité des nations* (1st edn. 1815), Paris, J. P. Aillaud, Bossange père, Rey et Gravière.

STURROCK, F. G. (1977). *Economies of Scale in Farm Mechanisation: A Study of Costs on Large and Small Farms*, Cambridge, Agricultural Economics Unit, Dept. of Land Economy, University of Cambridge.

SUVIRANTA, B. (1923). 'The Theory of the Balance of Trade in England: A Study in Mercantilism', *Annales Academiae Scientiarum Fennicae*, ser. B, vol. xvi, Helsingfors, pp. i–v, 1–171.

TALAYSUM, A. T., HASSAN, M. Z. and GOLDHAR, J. D. (1986). 'Scale Versus Scope: Considerations in the CIM/FMS Factory', in A. Kusiak (ed.), *Flexible Manufacturing Systems: Methods and Studies*, Amsterdam, North-Holland, 45–56.

TANI, P. (1986). *Analisi microeconomica della produzione*, Rome, Nuova Italia Scientifica.

—— (1988). 'Flows, Funds, and Sectorial Interdependence in the Theory of Production', *Political Economy*, 4: 3–21.

THOM, R. (1989). 'Causality and Finality in Theoretical Biology: A Possible Picture', in J. Casti and A. Karlqvist (eds.), *Newton to Aristotle: Toward a Theory of Models for Living Systems*, Boston, Birkhäuser, 39–45.

THOMPSON, J. D., and BATES, F. L. (1957). 'Technology, Organization and Administration', *Administrative Science Quarterly*, 2(3) (Dec.) 325–43.

THÜNEN, J. H. von (1826). *Der Isolierte Staat*, Hamburg, F. Perthes.

TURGOT, A. R. J. (1808). *Observations sur le mémoire de M. de Saint-Péravy en faveur de l'impôt indirect*, in *Œuvres de Turgot*, Paris, Imprimerie De Delance, iv. 312–43 (MS about 1768.)

URE, A. (1835). *The Philosophy of Manufactures*, London, C. Knight.

URMSON, J. O. (1950). 'On Grading', *Mind*, 59 (Apr.): 145–69.

USHER, A. P. (1954). *A History of Mechanical Inventions*, rev. edn., Cambridge, Mass., Harvard University Press.

VALENTI, G. (1905). 'Teoria delle proporzioni definite', *Giornale degli economisti*, 31: 507–24.

VALERIANI, L. (1817). *Discorso apologetico* . . . , Bologna, Marsigli.

VERDOORN, P. J. (1949). 'Fattori che regolano lo sviluppo della produttività del lavoro', *L'Industria*, 1: 45–53.

Voss, C. and CLUTTERBUCK, D. (1989). *Just-in-Time: A Global Status Report*, Bedford, IFS Publications; Berlin, Springer.

WAKEFIELD, E. G. (1835–43). 'Commentary' in *An Inquiry into the Nature and Causes of the Wealth of Nations* by Adam Smith, LL.D., with a commentary by the author of 'England and America', London, Charles Knight.

WALRAS, L. (1874–77). *Éléments d'économie politique pure*, Lausanne, L. Corbaz.

WARNECKE, H.-J., and STEINHILPER, R. (eds.) (1985). *Flexible Manufacturing Systems*, Bedford, IFS Publications.

WEIZSÄCKER, C. C. (1966). 'Tentative Notes on a Two-Sector Model with Induced Technical Progress', *Review of Economic Studies*, 33 (July): 245–51.

WEST, Sir E. (1815). *Essay on the Application of Capital to Land*, London, T. Underwood.

WHEWELL, W. (1860). *On the Philosophy of Discovery, Chapters Historical and Critical*, London, Parker and Son.

WICKSTEED, P. H. (1894). *An Essay on the Co-ordination of the Laws of Distribution*, London, Macmillan.

—— (1914). 'The Scope and Method of Political Economy in the Light of the Marginal Theory of Value and Distribution', *Economic Journal*, 24 (Mar.): 1–23.

—— (1933). *The Common Sense of Political Economy* (rev. and enlarged edn. of a work originally published in 1910), London, J. Routledge.

WIESER, F. von (1889). *Der Natürliche Werth*, Vienna, A. Hölder.

WILLIAMSON, O. E. (1971). 'The Vertical Integration of Production: Market Failure Considerations', *American Economic Review*, 61(2) (May), *Papers and Proceedings*, 112–23.

—— (1980). 'Emergence of the Visible Hand: Implications for Industrial Organization', in A. D. Chandler, Jr., and H. Daems (eds.), *Managerial Hierarchies: Comparative Perspectives on the Rise of the Modern Industrial Enterprise*, Cambridge, Mass., Harvard University Press, 182–202.

—— (1985). *The Economic Institutions of Capitalism*, New York, Free Press.

WINSTON, G. (1982). *The Timing of Economic Activity*, Cambridge, Cambridge University Press.

WOODWARD, J. (1982). *Industrial Organization: Theory and Practice*, Oxford, Oxford University Press.

WOODWORTH, J. V. (1905). *American Tool Making and Interchangeable Manufacturing*, London, Spon.

WRIGHT, G. H. von (1963). *Norm and Action: A Logical Enquiry*, London, Routledge and Kegan Paul.

—— (1980). *Freedom and Determination*, Helsinki, Philosophical Society of Finland.

WRIGLEY, E. A. (1962). 'The Supply of Raw Materials in the Industrial Revolution', *Economic History Review*, 15(1) (Aug.): 1–16.

—— (1988). *Continuity, Chance and Change: The Character of the Industrial Revolution in England*, Cambridge, Cambridge University Press.

YAN, C.-S., and AMES, E. (1965). 'Economic Interrelatedness', *Review of Economic Studies*, 32(4): 299–310.

YOUNG, A. (1928). 'Increasing Returns and Economic Progress', *Economic Journal*, 38 (Dec.): 527–42.

ZAMAGNI, S. (1980). 'Note sulla teoria economica della produzione agricola', in Università degli Studi di Parma, *Studi e ricerche della Facoltà di Economia e Commercio: Scritti in onore di Franco Feroldi*, Bologna, Patron, 227–45.

—— (1987). 'Economic Laws', in J. Eatwell, M. Milgate, and P. Newman (eds.), *The New Palgrave: A Dictionary of Economics*, London, Macmillan, ii. 52–4.

Name Index •

Subject Index